FRIENDSHIP

and

POLITICS

in

POST-REVOLUTIONARY FRANCE

PARIS
EN
1780

FRIENDSHIP *and* POLITICS *in* POST-REVOLUTIONARY FRANCE

SARAH HOROWITZ

THE PENNSYLVANIA STATE UNIVERSITY PRESS
UNIVERSITY PARK, PENNSYLVANIA

Library of Congress Cataloging-in-Publication Data

Horowitz, Sarah, 1978– author.
Friendship and politics in post-revolutionary France / Sarah Horowitz.
p. cm
Summary: "Explores the place of friendship in helping French society and the political system recover from the upheaval of the Revolution. Examines the interdependence of public and private in post-revolutionary France, as well as the central role of women in political reconstruction"—Provided by publisher.
Includes bibliographical references and index.
ISBN 978-0-271-06192-4 (cloth : alk. paper)
ISBN 978-0-271-06193-1 (pbk. : alk. paper)
1. Friendship—Political aspects—France—History—19th century.
2. France—Politics and government—19th century.
3. Political culture—France—History—19th century.
4. Politicians—France—Social life and customs—19th century.
5. Politicians—Social networks—France—History—19th century.
6. Women—Political activity—France—History—19th century.
I. Title.

DC252.H67 2013
306.20944'09034—dc23
2013027155

Printed in the United States of America
Published by The Pennsylvania State University Press,
University Park, PA 16802-1003

The Pennsylvania State University Press is a member of the Association of American University Presses.

It is the policy of The Pennsylvania State University Press to use acid-free paper. Publications on uncoated stock satisfy the minimum requirements of American National Standard for Information Sciences—Permanence of Paper for Printed Library Material, ANSI Z39.48–1992.

CONTENTS

List of Figures / vii

Acknowledgments / ix

Introduction: Friendship in Post-Revolutionary France / 1

1
The Sentimental Education of the Political / 21

2
The Politics of Anomie / 41

3
Friends with Benefits / 65

4
Post-Revolutionary Social Networks / 91

5
The Politics of Male Friendship / 111

6
The Bonds of Concord: Women and Politics / 133

Epilogue / 154

APPENDIX A
Béranger, Chateaubriand, Guizot, and Their Friends / 164

APPENDIX B
Detailed Social Networks in the 1820s and 1840s / 170

Notes / 175

Bibliography / 197

Index / 211

FIGURES

1 / Social networks, 1825–29
99

2 / Social networks and political affiliations, 1825–29
101

3 / Social networks, 1843–47
106

4 / Social networks and political affiliations, 1843–47
107

5 / Detailed social networks, 1825–29
170

6 / Detailed social networks and political affiliations, 1825–29
171

7 / Detailed social networks, 1843–47
172

8 / Detailed social networks and political affiliations, 1843–47
173

ACKNOWLEDGMENTS

From the beginning of this project, I have relied on the advice and guidance of mentors, teachers, colleagues, family, and friends and am grateful to have this opportunity to acknowledge the support that made this work possible. My greatest intellectual debt is to Carla Hesse, an adviser par excellence who patiently gave her time, attention, and encouragement. She believed in this project even when I did not; it was also she who first suggested looking at the circle around François Guizot, which had the effect of pulling me further into the nineteenth century than either of us could have anticipated. Thomas Laqueur was an excellent reader and lent his considerable insight to this project. Susanna Barrows was a champion and fountain of knowledge about the nineteenth century; the world is a little dimmer without her in it. Darcy Grimaldo Grigsby provided thoughtful guidance and feedback at crucial moments during my time at the University of California, Berkeley, while Randy Starn was a superb cheerleader throughout the writing process.

I am grateful to the librarians and archivists at the Archives nationales de France, the Bibliothèque nationale de France, and the Bibliothèque historique de la ville de Paris. Funding for this project came from the Institute of International Studies, the Graduate Division, and the History Department at the University of California, Berkeley, as well as the Mabelle McLeod Lewis Memorial Fund. At Washington and Lee, I benefited from research funds from the Office of the Dean of the College as well as Lenfest Grants in the summers of 2009–12. I had the good fortune to be able to attend a National Endowment for the Humanities Institute for Advanced Topics in the Digital Humanities on Networks and Network Analysis for the Humanities during the summer of 2010. The NEH and the Institute for Pure and Applied Mathematics at UCLA made two weeks of intensive math fruitful and enjoyable. I am particularly indebted to Tim Tangherlini for being the guiding spirit behind this Institute, and to Scott Weingart for his help with Sci^2. Portions of chapter 6 were originally published in *French Historical Studies* and are reprinted by permission of the publisher.

Naomi Andrews, Denise Davidson, Daniel Harkett, Penelope Ismay, Steven Kale, Tip Ragan, and Bradley Reichek read portions of this manuscript or offered valuable advice at various stages of the project. Sarah Maza provided crucial suggestions for turning the text into a workable manuscript. Sarah Hanley offered critical guidance late in the game. In France, Dominique Kalifa and Christophe Prochasson provided suggestions about the framing of this project. I would also like to thank Christophe Prochasson and Vincent Duclert for giving me the opportunity to present my work at an early stage in their seminar on democracy at the École des Hautes Études en Sciences Sociales and for the insightful critiques that they and their students offered. Catherine Coste, Aurelian Craiutu, Jérôme Grondeux, Laurence Guellec, Sheryl Kroen, and Anne Martin-Fugier were all generous with their time, knowledge, and thoughts and enriched this project in a variety of ways. I am grateful to everyone at Penn State Press for their assistance with this book, and especially to Ellie Goodman, who recognized the merits of this project and pushed me to make it better. The two anonymous readers provided thoughtful suggestions for revising the manuscript that improved it immeasurably. I would also like to thank Laura Reed-Morrisson and Nicholas Taylor for their help.

Since 2008, the History Department at Washington and Lee University has provided a welcoming home; as department heads, Ted DeLaney and David Peterson made it all the more so. Jennifer Ashworth has been an invaluable resource and resolved an infinite number of conundrums. I am also lucky to work at a place with such a dedicated library staff. I doubt that this project could have taken shape without the assistance of Elizabeth Teaff, her staff, and their ability to track down the most obscure of nineteenth-century texts for me. Brandon Bucy in Information Technology Services provided invaluable aid with producing the diagrams for chapter 4 and making them legible.

I am grateful to have the type of friends who did all the things that friends are supposed to do, and who enriched this work in a variety of ways and, more importantly, made life more fun. Christa and Nate Bowden, Mark Carey, Katie Chenoweth, Paul Gregory, Christian Jennings, Curtis Jirsa, Dan Kramer, Molly Michelmore, Debra Prager, Jon Roberts, and Rachel Schnepper have made living in this corner of Virginia more enjoyable. Dana Lamb, Emily Nacol, Nora Ng, and Vanessa van Orden reminded me that there was more to life than the early nineteenth century. Hernan Cortes, Christine Evans, Sonal Khullar, Robin Mitchell, Miriam Neirick, and Knox Peden were companions in research and writing. Friends in France, including Frédéric

Benhaim, Thibaut Clément, Nam Le Toan, Pierre Louis, and Solène Nicolas, made research trips all the more enjoyable and necessary.

Despite the fact that this is a book about the importance of friendship, I could not have completed it without the support—moral and otherwise—of my family. Ben Horowitz and Judith Liebman have been constant sources of good cheer and provided necessary distractions, particularly in the form of Aaron Horowitz. Leslie Field went above and beyond (as she always does) and is the *belle-mère* of dreams. Helen and Daniel Horowitz provided models of scholarship, but most importantly their unconditional love. Last but never ever least in my heart, I would like to thank Bradley Reichek. Without his unflagging enthusiasm and support, this book would never have seen the light of day. Ours is a relationship that cannot be mapped.

INTRODUCTION: FRIENDSHIP IN POST-REVOLUTIONARY FRANCE

In a quiet corner of Père Lachaise Cemetery stands the tomb of two men: Pierre Jean de Béranger and Jacques Antoine Manuel. Neither man is particularly well-known today but the two were famous in their time. Béranger was a songwriter who was known as "the national poet" in the early nineteenth century; he was also a hero of the left during the Restoration and July Monarchy. Manuel, his best friend, was a member of the liberal opposition during the Restoration and one of its chief orators in the Chamber of Deputies until 1823, when he was expelled from the Chamber for a speech that condoned regicide. The two men became friends in 1815 and lived together from 1824 until Manuel's death in 1827. Indeed, he died in Béranger's arms and left him a considerable legacy in his will. Although Béranger lived for another thirty years, his relationship with Manuel remained both an ideal and a central aspect to his identity. He wrote songs in which he praised Manuel's politics, ones in which he used the "tu" form, an indication of the degree to which his intimacy with his friend was crucial to his own political persona. Choosing to be buried in the same tomb as Manuel was another demonstration of his lifelong devotion. Yet this was also an era in which funerary rites and burials were intensely politicized, and their shared tomb served as a declaration of Béranger's continuing commitment to his friend's far-left politics.[1]

The intensity of these men's friendship, their devotion to each other, their acts of physical intimacy, and their shared tomb all raise the possibility that their bond may have encompassed erotic as well as platonic forms of affection. (Neither man ever married, although Béranger had female lovers.) Of course, it is impossible to reconstruct the exact nature of their feelings for each other or know what they did in the privacy of their home. But the fact that two men could be so open about their love is significant. This was an era when there was not necessarily a sharp boundary between romantic love and platonic affection and when male affection was celebrated. Thus, for instance, novels of the time, including those by Honoré de Balzac, Stendhal, and Eugène Sue, described the glories of male friendship. Conduct manuals for young men and women also reiterated the importance of this bond; without friends, one could not be happy, and friends were trusted confidantes and endlessly loyal.[2]

Aside from the issue of personal feeling, friendship had another importance for men like Béranger and Manuel, as it was intimately connected to their political identities. Béranger declared his affiliation with Manuel's radicalism by choosing to be buried with him; other political figures of the time also used testaments of friendship to serve as statements of shared political loyalty. For instance, in their wills, the politicians Prosper de Barante and Victor de Broglie left testimonials to each other and to their friendship with François Guizot; all three belonged to a political faction known as the "doctrinaires," a group that occupied a center-left position during the Restoration and a center-right one during the July Monarchy. When Barante died in 1866, he stated the following in his will about Broglie and Guizot: "I want them to know how sweet their friendship has been and I ask that they not forget me when I am gone." In turn, when Broglie died in 1870, he wrote of Guizot that "I consider our long friendship to be one of the most precious gifts that God has given me." Guizot, the last surviving member of the triad, had this last statement inscribed on a photograph of Broglie and mourned him as "my oldest, my best, and my rarest friend."[3] Like Béranger and Manuel, these men were celebrating a political partnership as well as a personal one. All three men had been friends and allies since the early years of the Restoration, when they sought to stabilize and liberalize the regime. During the July Monarchy, they came into power as men of the *parti de la résistance*, and Guizot, with the help of his friends, was the effective head of the government from 1840 until the Revolution of 1848. Yet, despite revolutions and changing political tides, these men remained loyal to one another until death.

This book takes as its subject precisely this intermingling of friendship and politics among members of the post-revolutionary political class. Ideological commitments shaped the social networks of political figures, just as friendship was central to the practice of politics during the Restoration and July Monarchy. In looking at the effect of political divisions on interpersonal ties, this work highlights how the upheaval of the Revolution affected a segment of French society and remade their personal relations. While the Revolution strained the social fabric of France and divided the nation along ideological lines, friendship helped restore trust and cohesion. It became critical to the new parliamentary regime of the era and helped the French state and the political class recover from the trauma of the Revolution. Despite the model of a strict separation between public and private that emerged in the nineteenth century, personal ties were both shaped by and crucial to the political life of the time. Likewise, although women were officially excluded from politics, in practice female friends played vital roles in parliamentary life and rebuilt the trust that allowed the political system to function. In a very real sense, then, the personal was the political in the post-revolutionary era.

This project began with the idea that studying conceptions and practices of friendship in the early nineteenth century would be an interesting way to examine how social relations were remade in an era of liberty, equality, and individualism. Historians have frequently asserted that marriage and the family were vital sources of cohesion in the nineteenth century and served as bulwarks against anomie—and that the family was the central social formation of the era.[4] While I do not deny the importance of familial ties—and while they could have a political significance—I argue that friendship was another crucial configuration.[5] Friendship was meaningful to individuals on a personal level, but also had political functions and became a way to understand how solidarity could be reconstructed in the wake of the Revolution. Indeed, as a source of cohesion, friendship had particular advantages. Friendship is a bond based on free choice, in contrast to kinship ties, and is thus an individualistic relationship; it is also typically considered a tie among equals, unlike clientage or patronage. It was thus well suited to serve as a force for cohesion among free citizens.

Beyond the question of social cohesion, the story of friendship in the early nineteenth century also highlights how the French grappled with other legacies of the Revolution: the emergence of ideological divisions and the problem of transacting politics in the post-revolutionary era. In part, this was just another manifestation of the problem of individualism, as political elites needed to practice parliamentary politics without official political parties, a strong associational life, or the structures of lineage and corporate privilege that had been central to Old Regime politics. Yet revolutionary politics also divided the nation and complicated interpersonal ties. These problems became especially acute during the Bourbon Restoration, France's first sustained period of parliamentary government, which was inaugurated by a crisis of trust. When Napoleon returned to France in 1815, many prominent citizens switched their loyalties from the monarchy to the Empire; these rapidly shifting allegiances led to a suspicion about the trustworthiness of political actors. Fears about loyalty led individuals to denounce one another and led the state to conduct extensive surveillance of its citizens. In turn, these policing and self-policing practices made individuals wary of those around them, as they learned to fear the spies and denouncers who were circulating in their midst. The intense factionalism of the era shaped the social networks of politically engaged men. Shared political views led to the formation of lifelong friendships, and men found it difficult to be friends with those with whom they did not agree. Crucially, women did not experience this difficulty to the same degree. The personal networks of elite women spanned factional divisions, and they connected different political and social groupings to one another. Factional hostilities lessened with the advent of the July Monarchy in 1830, but the social fabric of France was still regarded as strained. With the emergence of new social antagonisms, many began to fear that the pursuit of self-interest was destroying personal ties and spreading distrust. Politics was still understood to be a brutal realm where loyalty was impossible and betrayal imminent. Thus the period of parliamentary monarchy that lasted from 1815 to 1848 was a time when politics was often divisive and when social relations—and particularly those in the public realm—were regarded as profoundly troubled.

However, polities and societies need trust and cohesion in order to function effectively. Both were particularly necessary in the context of the political systems of the Restoration and the July Monarchy, given the necessity of alliances to parliamentary maneuvers and the lack of official political parties. Where, then, were trust and solidarity to be found? The answer was friendship. Because public life was seen as atomizing, political figures turned to their personal relations and to the women around them to serve as political facilitators as they had during the Old Regime. Thus politicians relied on a language of sentiment and friendship, one that had pervaded early modern political discourse, to establish norms of interpersonal behavior. This was both an adaptation and a transformation of old practices, as new ideas about gender and the emotions gave rise to the particular uses of friends in politics. Politicians relied on their male friends to serve as proxies in elections and ministerial cabinets because they understood male friendship as creating trust in the form of loyalty. Men were to act in solidarity with one another and be faithful to their commitments to their friends. Because women had special access to the emotions and interiority of the men around them and were also less factionalized than men, female friends were essential political brokers who negotiated alliances, managed political relationships, and ensured that factions remained united. Many of these tactics of political practice were not unique to France; personal ties and elite sociability were vital to the political systems of Britain and America, and in both countries women were important political facilitators.[6] However, Anglo-American political elites did not face the problem of cohesion and trust to the extent that their French counterparts did. As a result, these structures of political support were particularly crucial in the French context.

Yet while friendship helped the parliamentary system function after the Revolution, in the long run it was not particularly good at stabilizing either the Restoration or the July Monarchy. A political culture based on friendship could not force compromise among groups and so could not prevent revolutions. The centrality of personal ties to politics opened these regimes up to charges of corruption. Nevertheless, the intertwining of friendship and politics in the post-revolutionary era left a considerable legacy for French political culture. Politics have continued to be a source of social division in France, while at the same time elites have often relied on their friendship networks to transact politics.

CONTRIBUTIONS

The question of how France recovered from the Revolution has become increasingly interesting to scholars in recent decades. For many years, the Restoration and the July Monarchy were relative backwaters for historians, attracting considerably less attention than the histories of the First, Second, and Third Republics. But in the post–Cold War and post–September 11 world, questions about the transition from authoritarian regimes to representative ones have come to the fore, as have discussions about recovery from trauma. For those interested in the issue of democratization, the period from 1815 to 1848 is regarded as a laboratory in which French political thinkers and the French polity grappled with the legacy of the Revolution.[7]

Historians have thus studied how the post-revolutionary monarchies sought to legitimate themselves, as well as how questions about ideological difference, party organization, and popular participation in politics played out. Thus Pierre Rosanvallon argues that the Restoration was "the great period of apprenticeship in the ways of parliamentary government."[8] Likewise, one recent work on the Restoration has discussed how this was "the first regime to have permitted the confrontation between ideologies in a peaceful and free France, in contrast to the Revolution and the Empire."[9] *Friendship and Politics in Post-Revolutionary France* takes these two issues—the problem of ideology and the necessity of learning how to work within a parliamentary framework—as a starting point. It shows that ideological divisions hardly remained confined to the political realm, but instead shaped personal ties. It also uncovers how the politicians of the post-revolutionary era relied on old ways of transacting politics as they sorted out the new practices of parliamentary life: how to negotiate, how to organize factions, how to form alliances between political groupings, and even how to fight. And while the problems of trust, affiliation, and cooperation were particularly acute in the first half of the nineteenth century, the political figures of the Third Republic would continue to use some of the same tactics as their forebears, just as the pre-party politics of the Restoration and July Monarchy would influence late nineteenth-century party formation. As an examination of political culture, this work looks less at ideas and more at questions of practice—the customs, for instance, involved in behind-the-scenes negotiations, and the assumptions that underpinned cabinet formation. In this respect, it opens up new ways to investigate political culture by taking an almost anthropological approach to political transactions.

Alongside questions about the nature of post-revolutionary politics, historians have examined the cultural history of the early nineteenth century and how new ideas about the family, the emotions, and individual psychology helped stabilize France after the Revolution. *Friendship and Politics in Post-Revolutionary France* challenges one historiographical model that appears in many of these works: the separation between a male public sphere and a female private one. The narrative of separate spheres is a powerful one. The Revolution opened up the question of women's political rights, but because this was ultimately too destabilizing to the social and political order, women were confined to the domestic sphere, leaving men to monopolize public life. But it was not just women who were privatized. Emotions, too, were relegated to the private realm, as politics was to be an arena of rational debate among men.[10]

This work does not contest the fact that notions of a separation between public and private and the domestication of women were powerful norms in the early nineteenth century. Guizot, for instance, stated that he thought that women had no place in political life, and he frequently described the distinction between his public life as a politician and his private life with his family and loved ones.[11] Indeed, ideas about the private nature of women and the public nature of men profoundly shaped the practices of friendship, including patterns of epistolary communication. Yet the model of separate spheres was neither a sociological description of post-revolutionary France nor an accurate picture of how politics functioned, for the reality of men and women's lives was far more complicated. In practice, politicians used a language of emotion to discuss political allegiance and routinely relied on their friends, both male and female, in the political realm. Notably, women helped express and channel politically useful emotions. Guizot, for instance, never showed any hesitation about using the women to whom he was close to serve his political ends.

In this respect, *Friendship and Politics in Post-Revolutionary France* adds to the burgeoning literature on women's involvement in public life in the early nineteenth century and on the interaction between public and private. Scholars have inserted women into the public sphere of post-revolutionary France by looking at arenas such as urban culture, philanthropy, literary production, and education.[12] In addition, historians have paid attention to women's engagement with the realm of high politics. Women may not have been able to vote, speak in front of the Chambers, or hold office, but if one broadens the notion of the political to include political sociability and advocacy, it is clear that women were important political figures in the early nineteenth century. They were, for instance, crucial behind-the-scenes actors and hosted the spaces where extra-parliamentary politicking occurred.[13] Indeed, it was women's supposed privacy that made them such valuable political actors. Their access to the emotions, male interiority, and social relations—all coded as private—made them powerful political brokers uniquely positioned to build cohesion between politicians and factions. After decades of upheaval lasting from 1789 to 1815, men and women believed that no durable form of affiliation was possible in public life. Politicians resorted to private ties in order to describe and create loyalty, cooperation, and trust, an effort in which women were critical.

Friendship is thus a particularly interesting site to examine the relationship between masculine and feminine and the political and the emotional. In this respect, this book contributes to the emerging interest in this topic among historians and literary scholars. Historians have turned to friendship to investigate how personal bonds have been used to construct civil society and public life.[14] Yet it was largely scholars of homosexuality who pioneered this field as they sought to recuperate a past that included same-sex affection.[15] Like many of these works, *Friendship and Politics in Post-Revolutionary France* discusses the slipperiness between the categories of love and friendship. But it also looks at the central role of friendships between men and women, whereas most studies of friendship have concentrated on same-sex bonds.[16] Because friendship could be both public and private, it illuminates the interaction and connection between these spheres. In the context of post-revolutionary society, these two realms were mutually constitutive of each other. Politics made friendship a vital bond for elites, while public life relied on the private realm of friendship.

This work also adds a new technique to the study of friendship: social network analysis. Network analysis is a relatively new methodology that has emerged in recent decades from sociology and mathematics and has found great currency in fields as diverse as history, literature, biology, physics, and computer science.[17] Here, though, network analysis has a particular benefit, for it highlights certain structural elements of friendship—such as the difference between men and women's social ties—in ways that an analysis of novels, letters, or memoirs cannot. Thus network analysis brings an empirical methodology into the study of friendship and to cultural history more generally.

DEFINING TRUST AND FRIENDSHIP

In focusing on questions regarding friendship and trust, this work comes up against a series of difficulties concerning definitions, scope, and the limits of studying the emotional lives of long-dead individuals. First, there is the problem that neither friendship nor trust is particularly easy to define. Of the two, the latter has attracted considerable scholarly attention, especially from political scientists and philosophers. For example, the political scientist Russell Hardin defines trust as "encapsulated interest": we trust people when we think that they will take our interests into account in their interests and actions.[18] In contrast, the moral philosopher Annette Baier focuses on the issue of goodwill. We trust someone when we assume that he or she will act with goodwill toward us (and our interests).[19] In general, trust requires a positive valuation of others and that we make ourselves vulnerable. We know we could be betrayed, but we spill our secrets or loan our money anyway.[20] This work examines trust from the angles of both Hardin and Baier, for the post-revolutionary era saw considerable anxieties about how both self-interest and a lack of goodwill were tearing society apart and leading to a climate of suspicion.

Other scholars of trust have looked less at the question of definition and more at its political importance. Trust is, of course, necessary to functioning interpersonal relationships, and the political scientist Robert Putnam maintains that healthy polities require trust; citizens need to have confidence in their government and in one another. Putnam also argues for a close connection between trust and associational life, as he maintains that individuals learn habits of trust and cooperation through participation in civic organizations.[21] Problematically, the early nineteenth century was a period when civic life was at a low ebb and suffering from legal constraints; this fueled the sense of anomie in the era, as individuals faced the state and one another without the benefit of a robust civil society.[22]

Thus this work argues that private forms of solidarity were so important in the early nineteenth century because public trust was difficult. The problem with studying friendship, however, is that doing so invariably comes up against the problem of definition. Notably, are our notions of friendships fundamentally the same as those of men and women in earlier eras? To us, friendship means something quite particular—an elective, platonic bond. In this, it is different from kinship ties, as family relations are ascribed and permanent. For much of the nineteenth century, marriage was not too dissimilar from kinship. There were love matches among elites, but typically family interests weighed heavily in the selection of a spouse. Marriage may have been based on choice, but it was not necessarily the spouses who did the choosing. Since divorce was not possible, marriages were permanent as well. While relations between lovers are elective relationships like friendship, we generally make distinctions between these kinds of ties and do so largely based on sex: lovers have it, friends do not. This distinction raises all sorts of problems, not the least of which is determining the precise dimensions of the sex lives of long-dead individuals. Typically, too, we think of love relationships as being more passionate than friendships, as did the men and women of the early nineteenth century. But while we tend to draw a sharp line between erotic love and platonic friendship—and thus sometimes question whether heterosexual men and women really can be friends with each other—the elites studied here understood that the boundary between these two forms of affection was more porous. They were thus more comfortable with relations—either between men or between men and women—that included some element of erotic affinity without necessarily being sexual.

Additionally, the men and women of nineteenth-century France had a broader notion of what "ami" and "amitié" encompassed. In the 1835 *Dictionnaire de l'Académie française*, the primary definition of "amitié" is "affection that we have for someone which is typically mutual." Likewise, "ami" meant someone "with whom we are tied to by a reciprocal affection."[23] Here, affection and its return are the only requirements of this relationship. Family members, spouses, or lovers could all be considered "ami(e)s" (and indeed in contemporary French, "ami" can mean lover). Additionally, one of the secondary definitions of "ami" was "persons who are tied together by some party interest"—that is to say, political allies whose relationship may not have encompassed affection. In practice, too, lovers occasionally used this term with each other, as did siblings who were particularly close.[24] Thus "ami(e)" described those to whom one was close and whom one loved, regardless of whether that love was familial, romantic, or platonic.

Nevertheless, when they talked about "amitié" as a general concept, they referred to a bond that fits our definition of "friendship" as an affectionate, trusting relationship between relative social equals who chose to come together. Take, for instance, a passage from the epilogue of Eugène Sue's serial novel *Les Mystères de Paris*, published in 1842–43. The epilogue contains a series of letters from a German prince to his best friend, and in one the former writes, "We, the two most fervent apostles of the thrice-blessed friendship! We who are so proud to prove finally that the Carlos and Posa of our Schiller are not idealists and who, like the divine creations of the great poet, know how to enjoy the sweet delights of a tender and mutual attachment!"[25] Once again, "amitié" requires love and its return. But in this case, these two men see themselves as representatives of a particular type of affectionate relationship: one between non-kin that is loving but not sexual. They are also both young German aristocrats, suggesting similarities of age and social background. This more restricted definition of "amitié" corresponds to our notion of friendship, and it is this type of bond that this work investigates. As it does so, however, it looks at friendship from a variety of angles. It examines both how those who considered themselves friends communicated with one another as well as normative constructions of this bond. But beyond functioning as a relationship, friendship also served as a trope or a metaphor. Thus politicians invoked a language of friendship to stand in for the attributes of friendship—including trust, open communication, loyalty, and affiliation—in public life, but did so in ways that signified no emotional content.

To study friendship, this work draws on novels, conduct books, and the letters and memoirs of individuals. The first two sets of sources help us understand the cultural norms of the time, while life writings reveal how men and women described their bonds with each other, what they wanted out of their relationships, what they fought about, and how they made use of their friends. This is not to say that such sources provide transparent windows into the souls of early nineteenth-century elites. Notably, the expressions of affection in letters cannot be taken at face value, as conventions and codes of politeness bound them. For example, the salutation "mon cher ami" that male correspondents used with each other served less as a statement of feeling than as a formula. Moreover, individuals regularly deployed emotional utterances for strategic purposes; amid political negotiations, men and women used statements about their feelings to indicate their political allegiance or argue that they should be trusted. Nevertheless, correspondence was an essential element of nineteenth-century personal ties and can help us understand models of these bonds.

In particular, this book centers on three intertwined case studies, as it examines the networks and relationships of Pierre Jean de Béranger, François Guizot, and the politician and author François René de Chateaubriand. It also draws on the networks of some of the women to whom they were close, including the novelist Hortense Allart de Méritens and the *salonnières* Armande Marie Antoinette de Vignerot du Plessis de Richelieu, marquise de Montcalm-Gozon, and Albertine Ida Gustavine de Staël Holstein, duchesse de Broglie.[26] All three men occupied different places on the political spectrum: during the Restoration, Béranger was active in liberal circles, while Guizot was a journalist and activist on the center-left and Chateaubriand was one of the most prominent politicians on the right. Likewise, Allart was on the far-left, Mme de Broglie a doctrinaire like Guizot, and Montcalm in the center-right. As a result, the lives and social ties of these men and women allow us to understand the relationships between political concerns and personal ones, as well as the uses they made of friendship in politics. Although Béranger and Chateaubriand were largely retired from politics after 1830, Guizot was one of the most important politicians of the July Monarchy. Thus he provides a window into the workings of parliamentary life during this regime and to the continuities between the political culture of the Restoration and the July Monarchy.

These three men were chosen because of their level of political engagement and because they and their friends left behind enormous quantities of source material about their personal lives, including memoirs and extensive collections of correspondence.[27] In Guizot's case alone, we have around ten thousand letters that he and his intimates wrote to each other. Many of these men's friends wrote their memoirs or have published correspondence. Allart wrote her autobiography; some of her letters have been published, as have those of Mme de Broglie. Selections of Mme de Montcalm's correspondence are available, as well, as is her remarkable diary from the early years of the Restoration. The fact that these individuals and their friends had such well-documented social lives allows us to look at their friendships from a variety of angles and to examine how they communicated with their friends, how they made use of their friends in politics, and how their social networks were constructed.

There are, of course, considerable differences among these individuals. The men's politics range from conservative (Chateaubriand) to radical (Béranger), with Guizot representing a position in the middle. There is also the crucial difference of class. Chateaubriand was a member of the aristocracy, while Guizot belonged to the bourgeoisie, although he lived in the aristocratic neighborhood of the Faubourg Saint-Honoré. Both he and Chateaubriand were unquestionably part of the class of notables—the aristocrats and members of the upper bourgeoisie who ruled France between 1815 and 1848.[28] But Béranger's position in this ruling elite was much more tenuous. Descended from skilled artisans and innkeepers, he was from a humbler milieu and lived in more strained circumstances. His celebrity, though, launched him into higher strata. During the Restoration, his was the world of rich bankers like Jacques Laffitte and renegade members of the aristocracy like the marquis de Lafayette. In the 1830s and 1840s, while he lived very modestly, many of his friends were decidedly among the elite; he was particularly close to Alphonse de Lamartine, the abbé de Lamennais, and Chateaubriand. It is unlikely that he ever met the property qualifications that would have allowed him to vote, but he was deeply engaged in political causes and a central figure in left-leaning circles during both the Restoration and the July Monarchy. As a result, he gives us access to a world of radical journalists, activists, and politicians in both of these regimes. Broadly speaking, then, these three men's networks can help us understand the nature of social ties among the Parisian political classes.

Beyond these social differences, these three men had varying personalities and approaches to friendship. Béranger was known for his unmatched sociability; indeed, one of his landlords complained that the great quantity of visitors who came to see him was destroying the staircase to his quarters.[29] Because he never married and was not particularly close to any of his family members during his adulthood, friendship was the primary relationship in his life. He relied on his friends for financial support and wrote songs about this bond, ones sung in groups of carousing men.[30] For his part, Guizot was deeply attached to his family, but nevertheless retained a need for the company of friends. He was proud of his relationships that lasted for decades and was a remarkable correspondent, especially with women. While he could be a loyal friend, he could also be a difficult one and his public persona was cold and austere. Yet both men, despite their dissimilarities, put great stock in their friendships. Chateaubriand, however, presents a different case. Immensely proud and immensely prickly, he valued solitude. In the words of one biographer, he was a "skeptic about friendship."[31] Some of his relationships were long lasting and relatively uncomplicated, such as that with Jean Guillaume Hyde de Neuville, a longtime ally, or his surprising bond with Béranger that developed in the July Monarchy. Other friendships were far more troubled, and he disappointed some of his female friends with his lack of loyalty and affection.

While recognizing these differences, this study concentrates primarily on the similarities among these men, their milieus, and their relationships. All three of them, for instance, relied on women to serve as confidantes. Guizot and Chateaubriand used male friends in exactly the same way in negotiations over the composition of ministries. They also all struggled with the question of whether personal loyalties could override political commitments, although at times they came up with different answers. For these reasons and to illustrate the general workings of friendship, the social lives and political dealings of these men and their friends are discussed side-by-side and not on a case-by-case basis. In addition, much of this work is not organized chronologically. For instance, discussions of the practices of post-revolutionary politics do not necessarily progress from the Restoration to the July Monarchy. Although the political cultures of these two regimes were not the same, the politicians of the July Monarchy confronted many of the same problems as those of the Restoration and relied on the same ways of transacting politics.

Like any series of case studies, this one has limitations. First, there is the problem of how representative these men and women are. I make no claim that they were typical. After all, few ultras had Chateaubriand's literary genius. Nor was he a particularly good conservative; during the second half of the 1820s, he often collaborated with those on the left. For his part, Béranger was the most famous songwriter in an era when songs were an essential element of political protest, but he never ran for office, despite the constant urging of his friends.[32] His participation in politics was always indirect, except in 1848 when he briefly and reluctantly was a member of the Constituent Assembly. Neither man remained active in politics after 1830, with the exception of Chateaubriand's involvement in the duchesse de Berry affair and Béranger's service in the Constituent Assembly. Guizot's political engagement spanned the entire period between 1815 and 1848, and indeed he has been seen as representative of the age.[33] Again, though, he was hardly "typical" of his time or of the men of the juste milieu, given his Protestantism. Nevertheless, all three were well integrated into different political circles during the Restoration. Indeed, Béranger and Chateaubriand's lack of political involvement in the July Monarchy can even show how their distance from politics shaped their personal networks. Significantly, too, it was not just they who used friendship in particular ways, but also their friends, allies, and rivals who did as well, indicating that some of their assumptions about the interworking of friendship and politics were widely shared.

Another limitation is inherent in the source material. While there are some letters between women in these circles, such as those between Mme de Broglie and her female friends, or Mme de Montcalm and some of hers, correspondence between women was less likely to have been saved and made available to the public. Because of this and because the ways of friendships between women—which were often passionate, intense, and turbulent—is its own topic that deserves a fuller explanation than can be offered here, this work concentrates primarily, although not exclusively, on relations between men or those between men and women.

Even if we had all the letters these men and their friends wrote and received, there remains the problem of writing about the emotional lives of long-dead individuals. In looking at what individuals wanted in their friendships, what disappointed them, or how they behaved in moments of grief, I presuppose that these men and women had feelings and that we can study their sentimental lives. Historians of the emotions maintain that emotions are not entirely rooted in biology, but are culturally and historically mediated. In particular, William Reddy has suggested that the history of the emotions can be understood in terms of "emotional regimes," or the emotional states and norms of restraint and communication that underpin political regimes.[34] This work examines some of the emotional codes of the post-revolutionary era, looking, for instance, at how friends expressed their affection for each other and at the central role that love between friends played in the political culture of the time. Thus my primary interest is in the cultural work accomplished by these expressions of sentiment. When, for instance, I discuss the role of women in communicating emotions between politicians, for the most part the questions are how and why these women did so, and not whether their statements were verifiably true in some sense. This is to say that I am primarily interested in the performance of emotions—and what role these performances played in the social and political order of the time. In certain cases, it is clear that the expressions of emotion were to be understood as empty of any real sentiment, while in other instances, emotions were consciously deployed and manipulated in order to convince others to act in particular ways. Hence, even if we are not talking about "real" emotions, words of affection had clear uses.

However, there are other cases when I examine the specific emotional states of some of the individuals discussed here, such as, for instance, the degree to which two men actually had affection for each other, or the sense of bitterness and hostility that was unleashed into French society in 1815. Discussing actual emotions is inherently more problematic than focusing on a culture's emotional style or its views about the role of emotion. After all, the sources about these men and women's sentimental lives—whether letters, memoirs, or diaries—are not necessarily to be trusted, especially since the men and women featured in this study could be cynical about their claims to love one another. Alternately, some forms of emotional expression can be pure convention; when we use "dear" as a form of address in a letter, this does not necessarily mean that the addressee is, in fact, dear to us. Nonetheless, I assert that it remains possible to discuss aspects of the emotional lives of the men and women who lived two centuries ago. When numerous works from authors across the political spectrum state that a series of political events gave birth to a sense of estrangement and suspicion, and when individuals had very good reasons to distrust one another, I think it is fair to say that we can talk about the difficulties of this particular period. Alternately, when a preponderance of evidence—taken from letters, memoirs, and biographies—states that two individuals valued their friendship, I think this allows us to conclude that they probably did.

A related problem in discussing the personal relationships of the men and women studied here is the issue of whether they actually had friends in any meaningful sense of the term. After all, there were a number of opportunistic reasons for them to claim that their friendships were important. Friendship was a crucial cultural value in the early nineteenth century. Having friends spoke well of one's morality, as it suggested that one was generous and open to others. Friends could also provide considerable benefits, whether in the form of financial assistance or access to patronage networks. Moreover, politicians are a class of individuals hardly known for their loyalty or the durability of their personal ties. For instance, even if we know that two particular men socialized frequently with each other, corresponded on a regular basis, and discussed their feelings, this would only indicate that these men wanted to be considered friends, and not that they actually bore affection toward each other.

Thus the question remains: did the ties discussed in this work actually contain some level of affection, loyalty, and trust, or did they merely reflect either the emotional conventions of the day or a desire to pursue the benefits of friendship? Although the innermost feelings and motives of others will always remain somewhat of a mystery, it is possible to make some judgments. Some relationships that these men and women pursued were for their political gain or to advance their social standing. In a few cases, the parties did not seem to like each other all that much.[35] Yet even these cases are revealing, for these relationships followed what could be considered a cultural script of friendship, as when the individuals wrote each other on a regular basis, used forms of address that were markers of friendship, and expressed concern for each other. As a result, these exchanges can illustrate the patterns of friendship and highlight some of the uses of friendship in the early nineteenth century. Because in many cases this work is concerned with the outward signs of friendship, such emotional performances say a great deal about the conventions and norms of post-revolutionary bonds.

If instances of the opportunistic use of friendship did exist, they do not rule out other possibilities, as I maintain that the men and women studied here had significant friendships in the fullest sense of the term. They had *some* relationships that went beyond concerns about interest, patronage, and politics, even if not *all* of their relationships did. After all, saying that emotions and their expression are culturally mediated is not the same thing as saying that basic emotions like affection did not exist in the past. In a curious way, evidence of true friendship comes from worry about its opposite. The individuals in this book were themselves deeply concerned with the question of authenticity. For example, Charles de Rémusat, one of Guizot's friends, returned repeatedly in his memoirs to the question of whether Guizot actually loved him. After the two split over political differences in 1840, Rémusat was left wondering if Guizot had in fact truly cared about him. To put it in twenty-first-century terms, he wanted to know whether Guizot was performing friendship, or whether Guizot felt some authentic connection with him.[36] Likewise, in the wake of the events of 1815, Mme de Montcalm found herself estranged from many of those she had previously regarded as her friends, including Chateaubriand. In her diary, she flirted with the question of whether friendship was an illusion: she stated that while she wanted to have friends, she was not sure this was possible.[37] The fact that both Rémusat and Montcalm questioned the ability of those around them to be friends shows that affection and friendship were important categories for them, ones that they thought should exist, even if they were concerned that love and devotion were impossible at particular moments or absent from specific relationships. If professions of friendship were only mere performances to them, Rémusat and Montcalm would hardly have been concerned with such questions of authenticity.

In addition, the idea that these men and women thought only in terms of their own interests does not fit their actions. It does not explain why they trusted their friends or why they were so often generous with one another. Béranger, for instance, frequently relied on his friends for financial assistance and aided them whenever he could. At various times Chateaubriand's intimates, including Hyde de Neuville and Béranger himself, offered to help support their friend. It is possible to see motives other than pure generosity behind these acts; Hyde de Neuville might have wanted the fame of being able to say that he had secured Chateaubriand's financial stability. Alternately, Béranger might have thought that if he were generous with those around him, they would reciprocate when the time came. Friends also revealed secrets to each other. During the 1830s, for instance, Guizot described his disappointment with his son Guillaume to Mme de Broglie; if this information had gotten out, it could have caused him some amount of grief or at the very least embarrassment. Of course, he may have told her because she was a prominent *salonnière*, and engaging in such self-revelation may have been a way to win her over to his side. But it also speaks to his trust in her. This is not to say that interest did not enter into these relationships. Rather, this is to suggest that it is easier to maintain that at least some of the ties discussed in this work contained genuine affection than to hold that they did not. Thus friendship was both an ideal and a lived reality for these men and women. If the signs of friendship were sometimes performative gestures, they were related to these individuals' emotional lives in other instances. In all cases, though, they were meaningful and revealing about aspects of early nineteenth-century French society.

OUTLINE

The intertwining of the personal and the political arose out of both long-standing political practices and the legacy of the Revolution; chapter 1 examines these questions. In early modern France, social ties were vital political resources and love was the glue of the political system. Affection remained crucial to the reconceptualization of society and the polity that occurred in the eighteenth century, as thinkers used sentiment to imagine the possibility of a more individualistic social order. In turn, revolutionaries understood love to be a force for national unity. In practice, bonds of friendship facilitated revolutionary politics, and the Revolution unleashed both positive emotions (especially in its early years) and negative ones (particularly after 1792). Indeed, the Terror divided citizens along ideological lines and spread suspicion throughout society. In this atmosphere, any dreams of nationalized, universal love became impossible. Napoleon attempted to heal the divisions among elites and impose a dirigiste model of society, but the heavy hand of Napoleonic policing gave men and women even more reasons to be suspicious of one another. Thus one legacy of the revolutionary and Napoleonic eras was a sense of atomization, and this chapter ends with a discussion of the discourse of individualism in nineteenth-century France.

Chapter 2 takes up the problem of social relations in the Bourbon Restoration and July Monarchy and locates the fears about individualism in the particular political contexts of these two regimes. Associational life was particularly weak in the early nineteenth century and subject to the state's strict supervision. The opening years of the Restoration saw the reemergence of the ideological divisions of the Revolution, and the political hostilities of the era led to a sense that the nation was split into two antagonistic camps. Factionalism led citizens to denounce one another and the state relied on police surveillance in order to assuage its fears about the loyalty of the citizenry. The policing and self-policing among citizens were regarded as destroying personal relations and spreading suspicion within society. After 1830, although ideological tensions abated, many authors became increasingly concerned about the corrosive nature of self-interest. Further, politics was still seen as brutal and competitive, an arena in which loyalty was impossible. This chapter ends with an analysis of Honoré de Balzac's 1839 novel *Lost Illusions*. Set in the Restoration, this work highlights the fears about the destructive effects of factionalism and self-interest. Yet Balzac uses friendship to imagine loyalty, trust, and social cohesion, if only in a private and limited form.

Chapter 3 examines how ties of friendship were understood by looking at this bond as a unique space of trust and cohesion, one that was regarded as removed from the wider world. Friends described themselves as psychically part of one another and celebrated a special connection between friendship and open communication. Yet the particular workings of friendship were highly gendered. Bonds between men revolved around the ideas of similarity, union, loyalty, and generosity, and these friendships could activate ties of obligation. In contrast, in their relationships with women, men sought out confidantes as well as the opportunity to give and receive affection. Female friends also connected men to their social worlds and maintained male social networks by communicating affection between men. Thus male friends were regarded as trusted companions in action, while male/female ties allowed men to engage in personal and emotional revelation.

In order to explore how the ideological tensions of the post-revolutionary era shaped personal ties, chapter 4 looks at the friendship networks of Béranger, Guizot, and Chateaubriand, as well as those of some of the women to whom they were close. During the Restoration, politics sharply divided male social networks, as few men were able to maintain social ties across factional divisions. In the July Monarchy, ideological tensions were less crucial in shaping male networks, although politics was still a force for division among men. Guizot in particular—the only one of the three who remained active in politics—found it impossible to maintain friendships with men who did not share his political commitments. Yet throughout both regimes, politics did not determine women's networks and women connected different social groups and factions to one another.

The next two chapters turn to the problems of trust and cohesion in political life and the uses of friendship in political negotiations. Chapter 5 discusses how the politicians of the Restoration and the July Monarchy relied on their personal ties and a language of affiliation from the private realm to transact parliamentary politics. During moments of disagreement, politicians who were not friends often negotiated with each other using a rhetoric of friendship and affection to discuss allegiance. And because male friendship was based around notions of similarity and loyalty, male friends were often used as proxies in cabinets and during elections.

Chapter 6 highlights the role female friends played in parliamentary life. Although women were denied any official political role, they were crucial political actors. Indeed, in large measure, they were so useful because of their official exclusion from the public realm. As relatively neutral actors who had little stake in the triumph of one particular faction, they could create trust and work between different politicians and groupings. Thus women ensured factional cohesion, managed relationships between prominent politicians, and formed alliances between factions. These roles for women called on their ability to maintain ties across factional divides and their facility with emotions and social relations. Ultimately, women were responsible for building the trust that allowed the parliamentary system to function. In some cases, too, these roles for women allowed them to wield considerable political influence.

The epilogue serves as a conclusion and then discusses why, in the long run, a political culture based on friendship could not stabilize the parliamentary system and why it could not prevent the Revolutions of 1830 or 1848. The legacy of the early nineteenth century remained a powerful force, however. Politicians frequently relied on their friends for support in the Third Republic, for instance, and official political parties crystallized around social networks. In these respects, the Restoration and July Monarchy shaped the political culture of modern France, and their impact has continued to be felt for many generations. Even as France moved into a more democratic era and one with official political parties, politics have remained an intensely personal affair that was capable of unleashing bitter divisions into French society.

1

THE SENTIMENTAL EDUCATION OF THE POLITICAL

The uses of affection and mobilization of personal ties to practice politics emerged in part from long-standing traditions that dated back to at least the sixteenth century. Throughout the Old Regime, ruling elites relied on social relationships to access power. Love also had a public role as the bond of the hierarchical corporate order and as an element in the language of politics. In practice, however, the nature of politics during the Old Regime imposed considerable emotional constraints. In the eighteenth century, the culture of sentimentalism came to challenge this emotional regime. Sentimentalists maintained that love was an essential element of the social order, but they saw love as operating horizontally, not vertically. Affection was an equalizing force and a tie between individuals, as opposed to the bond between hierarchically disposed members of a corporate social order. This new vision of society would intersect with an increased emphasis on friendship as a freely chosen bond among individuals, and with the flourishing of an associational life that allowed men and women to interact with one another based on shared interests as opposed to corporate identities.

The revolutionaries were the heirs to this culture of sentimentalism, just as they drew on the legacy of how men and women practiced politics in the Old Regime. Historians have also come to see the Revolution as a particularly emotional experience, as politicians cycled rapidly from joy to fear. Until the end of the Terror, many revolutionaries hoped that love would tie the newly regenerated nation together. In practice, however, ideological positions redrew the lines of personal networks and the course of revolutionary politics complicated interpersonal relations. The ideological divisions and negative emotions that came to the fore during the Terror led individuals to distrust one another and even the meaning of emotional expressions. Hence, in the aftermath of the Terror, affection could no longer be understood as an element of the social order, as it had been for centuries.

Napoleon attempted to heal the ideological cleavages within French society and create a new unified elite. While he largely abandoned any notions of marshaling sentiment to solidify his regime, he placed high society under his control through both the annexing of elite sociability and the extensive use of police surveillance. In turn, this police state sowed increasing distrust among elites. As a result, the men and women of the post-revolutionary era had to contend with this legacy of distrust and division, as well as the successive collapse of two social orders, one based on authority and one based on egalitarian love. And thus, from the Thermidorian period until the mid-nineteenth century, authors and political figures spoke of the Revolution as an atomizing force, one that left nothing but a society of individuals.

While this chapter discusses pre-revolutionary and revolutionary models and uses of friendship, it concentrates on questions about personal ties and the emotions more generally. It also focuses on the issues that would become prominent in the period after 1815: the reliance on personal networks to practice politics, the role of the rhetoric of friendship in political negotiations, the ability of ideological divisions to reshape social bonds, and the gendering (or lack thereof) of political functions. Thus one aim of this chapter is to show how the men and women of the post-revolutionary era both drew on and transformed old habits and practices. At the same time, it also illuminates some of the origins of the problems the political elites of the early nineteenth century faced as they coped with a society that had been pulled apart by distrust and ideological tensions.

POLITICS IN THE OLD REGIME

The idea that politics was a deeply personal business would have been familiar to the elites of early modern France. The patronage-based politics of the sixteenth and seventeenth centuries required the cultivation of personal networks; men and women also used emotional rhetoric to describe their allegiances. At the court of Versailles, factions formed around ties of kinship and friendship. And while there were significant differences between the political systems of the sixteenth and early seventeenth centuries and that of the late seventeenth and eighteenth centuries, both forms of governance required the mastery or deployment of emotions for strategic gain. In both periods, too, social ties facilitated politics within the confines of a hierarchical, corporate social order.

In early modern France, a period when the French state was not yet centralized or bureaucratized, all politics were personal. In the words of Jay Smith, "In the sixteenth and early seventeenth centuries, all who exercised power still took it for granted that relationships of one individual to another formed the basis of order in every community."[1] Political theorists maintained that love was fundamental to the social order, as it bound individuals and corporate groups together in vertical chains.[2] Correspondingly, the language of politics was one of affection, and patron/client ties were suffused with a rhetoric of emotional devotion. For instance, in 1648, Charles de Grimaldi, the marquis de Régusse, sought the patronage of cardinal Mazarin and so wrote Mazarin a letter in which he stated, "Of all Your creatures, there will never be one more submissive or attached than I. . . . I shall seek every day an occasion to show you the growing esteem and friendship which makes me affectively inclined to render you service."[3] This was a vision of friendship as a tie of dependence, hence Régusse's use of words like "submissive" and "creature." He was not offering to be the companion of Mazarin's days, but to be a faithful servant through such words of affection. Nor were Régusse's words meant to serve as a reflection of his actual feelings. Rather, emotional expression was a tool for political advancement.[4]

Likewise, social ties were vital resources in the patronage economy of the sixteenth and seventeenth centuries. Patronage networks typically included family members, domestic officers, and those who worked on a noble's estates.[5] An individual's first recourse was usually to members of his or her lineage.[6] For instance, Jean Baptiste Colbert got his start in government service through a cousin, Michel Le Tellier's brother-in-law. When Le Tellier became secretary of state for war, he rewarded both Colbert and Colbert's cousin with positions.[7] Bonds with non-kin also helped individuals find advancement; Le Tellier, for instance, owed his post to his friend Mazarin.[8] Corporate ties opened up doors to potential patrons and clients as well. Thus Anne de Montmorency, who wielded great power under François I and Henri II, aided the men who belonged to the company he captained.[9]

In this system, noblewomen served as both patrons and clients. Royal women had the most direct access to political power; for instance, François I invested his sister Marguerite de Navarre with considerable authority. He gave her the duchy of Berry, and her marriage contract stipulated that she—and not her husband—controlled her lands. Marguerite was thus François's client and an individual who dispensed considerable patronage on her own. She was also an important broker who served as the link between her own clientele and that of the king, and connected the families of her birth and her marriage. This last function was a gendered one; women, unlike men, belonged to multiple families. Yet many of the other roles that women played were not gendered. Women as well as men served as brokers, and prominent noblemen acted as bridging figures between regional and royal patronage networks.[10]

While patronage power shifted from the hands of the nobility to the monarchy during the reign of Louis XIV, personal ties remained crucial to political activity. For instance, Emmanuel Le Roy Ladurie notes that kinship and friendships held together the three different political groupings prominent at Versailles in 1709. The first, organized around Mme de Maintenon, was the most conservative and oriented toward the military; another centered on the dauphin; while the third—the most reformist—looked toward the dauphin's son, the duc de Bourgogne. These factions were organized around personal networks. Maintenon's cabal included members of the Le Tellier clan as well as Marshal Harcourt, who had been friends with the late Michel Le Tellier. Among the members of the second groups were the dauphin's half sister Madame la Duchesse and another one of her half brothers; members of the Colbert family clustered around the duc de Bourgogne. There were also ties between cabals; since Louis XIV was aging, the men of the first cabal—the one most closely aligned with the king—realized full well that they needed to be on good terms with the dauphin. Women also served as intermediaries between these groupings and maintained connections between camps. The duchesse de Bourgogne was married to the leader of the third cabal and friends with Mme de Maintenon.[11] Thus, while once again women had important roles as go-betweens, this was not exclusively a role that belonged to them, as men retained good relations among factions. Women, too, could be just as invested in the success of their particular cabal as men were; after all, Mme de Maintenon was the leader of one of these groupings.

During the reigns of Louis XV and Louis XVI, the nobility no longer conceived of politics as being an entirely personal affair. Military officers, for instance, ceased to understand that they acted out of personal loyalty to the king. Instead, they saw themselves as servants to the state or the public.[12] Yet the same importance of social ties to the political system is also apparent in the court politics of Louis XV and Louis XVI. Under these two kings, ministers sought to win over those close to the king—and wives and mistresses most notably. In part, this was because of the necessity of intermediaries within the courtly politics of Versailles. In a system with a vast number of supplicants asking for favors, individuals had to appeal to the king through those close to him to get his attention. Alternately, for ministers advocating for their position, obtaining the support of the king's mistress (in the case of Louis XV) or the king's wife (in Louis XVI's case) ensured that they would have an advocate in the king's inner circle, one whose access to him was unreserved. And in this climate where social relations determined one's success (or failure), all interpersonal contact was a matter of self-interest and scrutiny, just as emotional expressions had to be controlled in order to master the game of court life. Thus the goal of every personal interaction was not the expression of one's true feelings, but obtaining some advantage and advancing within the hierarchical confines of Versailles. For this reason, courtiers had to master their emotions; expressing what one truly felt would reveal too much about one's intentions. Failure to control one's affects was thus a sign that one did not have the fortitude to survive at court.[13]

Hence, in certain structural respects, the politics of the court of Versailles were similar to the early modern patronage-based system. These were both hierarchical political cultures in which success was a matter of finding favor and attention from one's superiors, whether a great noble or the king. And to master the game within these vertically oriented systems, individuals needed to marshal their emotions and their personal relations. Because power was often informal and based on personal connections, women served as brokers and backers, although men also functioned as intermediaries, patrons, and leaders of political groupings.

THE SENTIMENTAL SOCIAL ORDER OF THE EIGHTEENTH CENTURY

The eighteenth century saw the rise of a new conception of society and the self that challenged the hierarchical corporate social order. The cultural movement known as sentimentalism offered a new model for personal relations based on open expressions of sentiment. Sentimentalism also stressed individualism and choice and contained an egalitarian strain within it. Friendship—an elective bond based on affection—fit with this new desire to imagine a society based on horizontal affection and not vertical authority.

Correspondingly, new spaces of sociability opened up and the eighteenth century saw a burgeoning associational life in which men and women came together based on personal inclination.

In contrast to the norms of emotional control at Versailles, sentimentalism placed the examination and expression of feelings front and center. Novels—perhaps most famously Jean Jacques Rousseau's *Julie; ou, La Nouvelle Héloïse*—were replete with profusions of emotion, as characters poured their hearts out to each other and cataloged the nature of their affections in exacting detail. Sentimentalism had philosophical dimensions as well. Denis Diderot, Adam Smith, and David Hume all described the importance of emotions for the self and society. For instance, in *The Theory of Moral Sentiments*, Adam Smith states that feeling was the basis for morality. In turn, sentimentalists regarded emotionality as an indication of sincerity, openness, and virtue.[14] In these respects, sentimentalism was an oppositional movement that challenged the social and political structure of the Old Regime. After all, if morality arose from sentiment, then individuals just needed to cultivate their innate capacity for feeling to be moral creatures, and they therefore did not need the strictures of the Church or the state. Crucially, too, sentimentalism contained a democratic current within it; sentimentalist novels, for instance, allowed readers to imagine a society that was individualistic and egalitarian and not hierarchical and corporate. In the words of Lynn Hunt, "Novels made the middle-class Julie and even servants like Pamela, the heroine of Samuel Richardson's novel by that name, the equal and even the better of rich men such as Mr. B, Pamela's employer and would-be seducer. Novels made the point that all people are fundamentally similar because of their inner feelings, and many novels showcased in particular the desire for autonomy."[15]

Sentimentalism was a significant reworking of earlier notions regarding the operations of love in both political and familial contexts. It challenged—rather than upheld—established hierarchies precisely because sentimentalist affection worked horizontally, not vertically. For instance, if love and not paternal power was the bond between family members, fathers could no longer serve as distant rulers of their children. Similarly, the idea that marriages should be founded on love, not economic consideration, meant that the spouses should choose their partners.[16] Likewise, the royal politics of sentiment in the eighteenth century acquired a new cast. During the reign of Louis XV, royal apologists spoke of the king as "le Bien-Aimé" ("the well loved"). If Louis XV was noted for being beloved, this meant that he was beholden to his subjects, not just vice versa. The love between the king and his people was also "notable for its narrowing of the social and political distance between subject and sovereign."[17]

The eighteenth century also saw the flourishing of associational life in the form of provincial academies, clubs, and Masonic lodges and the growth of opportunities for socializing in salons and cafés. These institutions and spaces expanded the horizons of the men and women who frequented them; the ties of family, religion, and corporate order no longer defined an individual's social orbit. Freemasonry is paradigmatic of this shift. Masonic lodges allowed aristocrats and members of the Third Estate to come together, and in theory one ascended the Masonic hierarchy based on merit and not status. Participation was also voluntary; one chose to be a Mason, while in contrast, one did not necessarily chose one's corporate status in the Old Regime. Thus Ran Halévi argues that Masonry was fundamental to the emergence of a "democratic sociability" in the eighteenth century.[18] Alternately, Richard Sennett describes how the associational life of the eighteenth century taught individuals how to enjoy public, impersonal forms of sociability.[19] Clubs and salons thus allowed for the construction of new identities and forms of cooperation and trust among the elites who participated in them.

Ties of friendship were also part of sentimentalism and the emergence of new forms of sociability. For instance, terms of friendship permeated Masonry, as Masons called one another "friends" and lodges were named "Les Vrais Amis" or "La Réunion des Amis Intimes."[20] Many salonnières also idolized friendship as the cement of their gatherings, while sentimentalist authors praised friendship as a perfect human relationship.[21] In Rousseau's *Julie*, for example, friendship is a site of transparency and idealized affection. In one letter to his friend Milord Édouard, Saint-Preux describes the joys of mornings with Julie and her family by stating, "Breakfast is the meal of friends; the house staff are excluded, the unwanted do not intrude; we say everything we think, we reveal all our secrets, we constrain none of our sentiments; there we can give in without imprudence to the satisfactions of confidence and intimacy."[22] As an epistolary novel, this work relies on the free communication between correspondents to enable readers to grasp the feelings and intentions of the characters. We know of the sincerity and depth of Julie and Saint-Preux's passions both because of their letters to each other and because of their correspondence with their friends.[23]

In the eighteenth century, then, affection had a clear public significance as the cement of a new civic order. And in contrast to earlier understandings of the political role of love, affection was horizontal and not vertical in its orientation. This more egalitarian vision of society was also more individualistic, for men and women could find affiliations outside of kinship networks and corporate ties. These new understandings of personal relations were thus less a support for the existing political and social order than a challenge to its very nature.

THE PASSIONS OF THE REVOLUTION

This ideal of universal, egalitarian, and individualistic affection held a powerful appeal during the Revolution. With the destruction of the hierarchical, corporate social order of the Old Regime, revolutionaries were left with the task of understanding what could unite the citizens of a regenerated nation. An all-embracing love in the form of *fraternité* became one source of connection between the men and women of the new France. In practice, too, revolutionary politics created new bonds of solidarity as political groupings crystallized around personal networks. But positive, unifying emotions were not the only feelings brought to the fore. After 1792 fear, distrust, and anxiety became more prominent among both revolutionaries and their opponents. Revolutionary politics also divided citizens along ideological lines and made having the wrong friends deadly. Hence, while politicians continued to operate in a sentimental mode even during the Terror, the actions of revolutionaries revealed both the impossibility of understanding sentiment as a force for national unity and the danger of relying on public emotions.[24]

Although both positive and negative emotions were close at hand from the beginning of the Revolution, historians see expressions of affection and hopes for reconciliation as dominating its early years.[25] Thus the opening of the Estates General was an emotional affair; one deputy wrote in his diary that "it was impossible to hold back tears" and that "all deputies blessed with a little sensibility must have regarded this day as the most beautiful and the most glorious of their lives."[26] Such transports of happiness also accompanied the arrival of members of the First and Second Estate into the National Assembly. As Jean François Gaultier de Biauzat described it, "We openly wept with indescribable joy, like people whose hearts are so unaccustomed to happiness that they cannot hold up under the emotion caused by such a strange new order of things."[27] Gaultier's reference to the "strange new order of things" indicates how the political ferment of the moment liberated positive affects. Indeed, even those who were not directly involved in the Revolution could find themselves swept away by its emotional tide. Writing of the relationships among radicals in 1790s Britain, Lynn Hunt and Margaret Jacob claim that the Revolution "generated a new affective intensity among men" and opened up a space for social, sexual, and emotional experimentation. Indeed in a letter to Samuel Taylor Coleridge, the poet Robert Southey wrote of the "orgasm of the Revolution."[28]

The summer of 1789 also saw darker emotions among revolutionaries—most notably fear. Popular violence was one source of anxiety, particularly around the fall of the Bastille. Deputies feared for their own personal safety and an attack from the king's forces.[29] One deputy stated that he and his colleagues were "continually alternating between fear and hope" due to the course of events.[30] It was also the essence of revolutionary politics that led to this emotional instability. As Timothy Tackett writes, "Fluctuations of this kind could be attributed in part to the nature of the situation in which the deputies now found themselves: a kind of liminal state between the old and the new, in which much of the world they had previously known was collapsing or being torn down around them."[31]

The momentous events of August 4 are representative of how emotions—both positive and negative—shaped revolutionary politics. Fears of rural unrest drove the deputies to abolish feudal privileges at the same time as love and a desire for reconciliation led them to begin the process of destroying the corporate order. In their letters and memoirs, deputies recalled the emotional intensity of this night. One exclaimed, "We wept, we hugged one another. What a nation! What glory! What an honor to be French!" while another stated, "We wept with joy and emotion. Deputies, without distinction, treated one another with fraternal friendship."[32] August 4 was a sentimentalist's dream come true: love was remaking the nation around the principles of individualism and equality.

At the same time, political ferment reshaped friendship networks, elite sociability, and associational life. More than one thousand political clubs opened up in the first three years of the Revolution, while Parisian salons became increasingly politicized. Some salons served as meeting places for like-minded politicians, while others were more ideologically heterogeneous and allowed political figures to reach out to potential allies.[33] Ideological positions also drove politicians apart and brought them together. By 1790, men of different factions found that they could no longer be friends with one another. One deputy named Périsse felt he had to cut his ties to the comte de Virieu, who was to his right. He wrote, "The division within the Assembly is so extreme, that I would be suspected by the Friends of the Constitution if I were seen having relations with any of them."[34] Shared politics was also a force for cohesion. In the words of one Jacobin deputy, "There are two or three hundred of us [i.e., Jacobins] here bound together forever. Without even knowing one another's names, we are such good friends, and so strongly linked, that hereafter, it will be impossible to travel in the kingdom, without encountering colleagues and friends."[35] As a vision of friendship, this was a remarkably impersonal one; all that was required was a shared political affiliation and not actual knowledge of another.

This description of friendship bears striking similarities to the notion of fraternity, the last element of the revolutionary triad and the one that dealt most specifically with how the citizens of France should relate to one another. Fraternity was another adaptation of the sentimentalist social order, for it proposed that love was the bond of society. In the early years of the Revolution, fraternity was a way to imagine national unity and to understand how the men and women of France could overcome social divisions. This initial impulse toward fraternal desire came not from the central government, but largely from the ground up and from the members of the National Guard, who swore oaths to fraternity. If fraternity was a disposition to one's fellow citizens, it could also be a guiding principle of behavior toward all peoples. For instance, revolutionary legislators abolished the *droit d'aubaine* (a rule by which all the property of a deceased foreigner was confiscated to the use of the state) on the grounds that it was "against the principles of fraternity which should tie all men, whatever their country and their government."[36]

It was this universalism and the very public nature of fraternity that made it distinct from friendship. The latter bond was particularized; one was friends with a select few. Fraternity, however, did not depend on choice and had nothing to do with recognizing the special qualities of those to whom it was extended. It was instead the reflexive way one treated others. Fraternity was thus transparent and public, whereas friendship was a private passion. Friendship implies notions of preference, too, while fraternity did not recognize personal inclination. This is not to say that friendship and fraternity were seen as conflicting passions; instead, they could be regarded as different forms of the same love for humankind, one of which was more intimate and the other of which was universal.[37]

As the Revolution radicalized, both the workings of fraternity and the more general emotional tone of the revolutionaries shifted, and historians argue that darker feelings—and fear in particular—predominated after 1792.

The flight of the king to Varennes in June 1791 left revolutionary politicians feeling betrayed, and fueled fears about counterrevolutionary conspiracies. Such intense suspicion drove the violence of the more radical stages of the Revolution.[38] In the words of Patrice Higonnet, "For the men—and women—of 1791–2, the decomposition of the Jacobins' universalizing purpose and the ruin of their Enlightened hopes brought into question their newly acquired and constructed sense of self, their social purpose and their understanding of world history." In turn, the revolutionaries reacted to the failure of their dreams through "private rage and then discouragement and fright"; it was this fear—or trauma, in his terms—that would give birth to the Terror.[39]

Despite the swirl of negative emotions, the revolutionaries continued to cling to their sentimentalist vision of society, although they turned to a more *étatiste* model of universal affection. For one, in contrast to the early years of the Revolution—which saw a flourishing of clubs and organized political sociability—the government became increasingly opposed to associational life. As Christine Adams states, "Because the National Convention—the state—represented the general will, which was sovereign, it had to destroy all individual initiatives . . . that might impede its reach. Accordingly, the Convention abolished all educational, literary, scientific, and charitable societies."[40] The state—and not its citizens—would direct civil society. Pierre Rosanvallon calls this formation "utopian generality," as revolutionaries felt that intermediary bodies prevented social and political unity.[41] This was a vision of individualism in which nothing was to obstruct the relationship between state and citizen.

The period after 1792 also saw the centralization of political love. The Jacobins, for instance, maintained that fraternity was a duty.[42] Saint-Just was particularly preoccupied with friendship. In his "Institutions républicaines," he describes that anyone without friends was immoral and therefore should be banished from his ideal state.[43] Yet fraternity was no longer understood to be universal and was not necessarily extended to the Revolution's enemies. In the words of Bertrand Barère, "During revolution patriots should concentrate their fraternity on each other as they are united by a common interest. Aristocrats have no home here and our enemies cannot be our brothers."[44] Likewise, the Montagnards began to see fraternity as a sentiment that had to be imposed (or at the very least cultivated), and relied on revolutionary festivals to do so.[45] This same marshaling of the affections is apparent in legislation, as laws mandated emotional dispositions. Notably, the Law of Suspects decreed the arrest of "those who, either by their conduct or by their relations, by their words or writings, have shown themselves to be partisans of tyranny . . . or enemies of liberty," while relatives of émigrés needed to have "constantly shown their attachment to the Revolution" if they wanted to avoid detainment.[46]

Affection was also to have a role in overcoming the divisions within the nation—and factional ones in particular. Most famously, there was the kiss of Lamourette; on July 7, 1792, Antoine Adrien Lamourette, a deputy to the Legislative Assembly, convinced his colleagues that the problems facing France—a war that was going badly, a monarchy conspiring against the Revolution, and a government fracturing under the weight of political divisions—could be solved if the deputies loved one another more. Responding to Lamourette's speech, the members of the Assembly embraced one another and vowed their undying affection for one another.[47] Alternately, consider an August 1793 letter from Joseph Fouché, then *député en mission*, in which he describes the events in a small town in the Nièvre. He writes, "The hellish demon who is tearing into one part of the Republic had managed to divide citizens, friends, brothers, spouses and their unfortunate children." But through Fouché's work, "all the citizens came together and embraced each other. Light-hearted songs, dances, patriotic sounds of a warlike music, artillery salvos, prolonged cries of 'Long live the Mountain! Long live the Constitution!' announced to all the neighboring communes the happy festival of a general and fraternal reunion around the tree of liberty."[48] Love conquered all as factional fighting gave way to union and joy.

Personal ties remained central to radical politics as political coteries continued to function as friendship networks. This was especially true for the Girondins. Many Girondins had been friends with one another since before the Revolution, as was the case with Jean Marie Roland and Jacques Pierre Brissot, two of the most prominent members of this faction. Some of the Montagnards were friends as well. Robespierre was close to both Saint-Just and Georges Couthon, two of his chief collaborators, and he relied on friends to recommend individuals for governmental positions.[49] Sociability also helped politicians coordinate their actions. Mme Roland stated that at her salon her guests "kept up the kind of liaison that is needful among men devoted to public affairs . . . who must be well informed, the better to serve the public."[50]

Yet such personal ties between politicians could also be very dangerous. Some Jacobin thinkers, for instance, perceived that friendship was too exclusive. As a private passion, it detracted from the universal commitment to others that the Republic required. Transacting politics through friendship was seen as highly problematic because it was a form of politics that lacked transparency, and in some cases ties of friendship offered proof of conspiracy. Thus, when twenty-one Girondins were tried in October 1793, their personal connections to one another were regarded as a sign of how suspect they were. In the absence of any evidence that the Girondins were actually conspiring together, the Montagnards used proof of the close ties between these men to suggest that they were working against the revolutionary government. Others, too, found that there were perils to being friends with the wrong person. Camille Desmoulins, for instance, attributed his death sentence to his friendship with Georges Danton.[51] This notion that one's personal connections were a sign of counterrevolutionary beliefs or activity was enshrined into law, as the Law of Suspects proposed that individuals could be detained if they had social ties with counterrevolutionaries.

The Terror also spread distrust into society and divided the nation along ideological lines. Indeed, suspicion was inherent in revolutionary politics—what, after all, is the obsession with conspiracies if not a profound distrust of the motives and methods of others? Again, the necessity of suspicion became a legal matter. Under the Law of 22 Prairial, citizens had a duty to turn in any counterrevolutionaries they encountered. Hence, good revolutionaries had to be on the watch for suspicious activity and to distrust those around them. Nor could one count on personal loyalty during the Terror. Perhaps most famously, Desmoulins was a childhood friend of Robespierre, but Robespierre nonetheless signed his death warrant in March 1794.[52] Their relationship is but one example of how ideological differences destroyed personal ties. The two had been allies for years, but their friendship ended—with deadly consequences—when Desmoulins came to oppose Robespierre and other Montagnards in winter 1793–94. Personal betrayal was even a task for all good citizens as denunciation became a patriotic duty during the radical stages of the Revolution. Denunciation both arises out of distrust and is a betrayal of trust, for it can occur when an individual confides in a friend or family member who discloses sensitive information to the government. Good citizens were to betray their intimates; anyone with anything to hide had to be fearful of friends and family members.[53]

Lastly, the Terror showed the limits of basing a political order around sentimentalism. For one, it became clear that the dream of reconciliation through love was impossible. Despite Lamourette's kiss, factionalism plagued revolutionary politics. In creating ideology—including the notions of "left" and "right"—the Revolution engendered divisions that were too powerful to overcome through outpourings of affection.[54] Alternately, consider a February 1793 letter from Robespierre to Danton. After the latter's wife died, the former wrote, "I love you more than ever, and unto death."[55] Robespierre's claim may very well have been sincere, but the state of Robespierre's feelings in early 1793 did not prevent him from helping usher Danton to that death over a year later. If one problem with the revolutionary politics of sentimentalism was that the emotions were too unstable, another was the issue of hypocrisy. In a political culture in which individuals were to marshal and display their emotions, how could anyone trust that others were actually feeling what they said they were feeling? Could one even trust oneself to be overcome by the appropriate emotions at the appropriate time?[56]

The fall of Robespierre and the liquidation of the Terror saw a retreat from sentimentalist politics. Historians have spoken of the emotional tone of the Thermidorian period and the Directory as being one of cynicism, disillusionment, and bitterness, a climate in which revolutionaries could no longer promote ideals of universal love. Instead, self-interest became the foundation of the social order. Philosophers asserted that interest, not emotion, was the basis for morality, while the Constitution of the Year III, in which voting rights were based on ownership of property, established that interest was the guarantee of order.[57]

The Thermidorian period also saw the articulation of anxieties about social dissolution, ones that would resonate into the nineteenth century. When they spoke of the effects of the Terror, revolutionary politicians focused on the anomie of French society. Thus, for instance, the Conventionnel Jean Lambert Tallien gave a speech in September 1794 in which he stated, "The Terror breaks all bonds, extinguishes all affections; it defraternizes, desocializes, demoralizes."[58] He also described how the Terror spread fear and distrust throughout society by "setting a trap under each step, placing a spy in every home, a traitor in every family."[59] To be sure, Tallien's speech allowed him to distance himself from his own participation in the Terror and paint himself as its victim.[60] Yet others spoke of a perceived lack of cohesion within French society and the problems of a heightened sense of suspicion. Many ordinary citizens stated that revolutionary family legislation had sewn discord into families, while medical professionals became interested in the operations of fear in the wake of the Terror.[61] Certainly it is understandable how the events of 1793–94—the escalating levels of violence, the prevalence of denunciation, and the laws requiring suspicion—led individuals to feel estranged from one another. The limitations on associational life cannot have helped either, as the state attempted to overtake civil society. Further, citizens had to contend with the successive collapse of two models of social organization—the hierarchical one and the sentimental one. For centuries, love, either vertical and corporate or horizontal and individualistic, had been the bond of society. But if the polity was founded on interest, citizens had no tie that connected them to one another. The sentimentalist individualism of the earlier stages of the Revolution gave way to an individualism evacuated of sentiment.

The years between 1789 and 1794 saw the rise, transformation, and liquidation of a sentimentalist politics. The events of the Revolution unleashed emotions—from love to fear—and attempted to inculcate them in the citizens of a regenerated France. But in the end, basing politics on the emotions was impossible. Love could not overcome the ideological divisions that the Revolution unleashed, and the vision of a sentimentalist polity opened the door to too much instability. The course of revolutionary politics destroyed trust and made connecting with others a dangerous and difficult prospect. The men and women of the post-revolutionary era would struggle with this legacy of suspicion, the problems of factionalism and denunciation, and the question of how to imagine social cohesion in a world of liberty and equality but not fraternity.

THE NAPOLEONIC ERA AND THE SEARCH FOR AN *ÉTATISTE* ORDER

Like the men of Thermidor, Napoleon confronted the problem of social atomization as he attempted to solidify his rule. He worked to ease ideological tensions and placed high society under his direction by creating a new elite, annexing associational life and salon culture, and heavily policing sociability. Yet this last effort compounded the problem of distrust and complicated the project of social reconstruction. In the end, what Napoleon offered was an *étatiste* model of social organization and post-revolutionary reconstruction, one where the state directed high society and social relations for its own benefit.

In his memoirs, Guizot described how "social pacification" marked the period between 1799 and 1815. If he had little praise for Napoleon, he spoke with no small amount of nostalgia for the relative tranquility of this era.[62] Indeed, historians generally agree that ideological passions cooled (but did not disappear) during this regime. For example, Napoleon dismantled the republican political apparatus, and most republicans either supported his regime or did not openly oppose it. He was less successful with those on the right, as many aristocrats were estranged from his regime. If ideological divisions and opposition remained, they were not at the forefront in the way they had been during the Revolution and became again during the Restoration.[63] The relative lack of discord was even apparent among Napoleon's closest collaborators. In the words of Isser Woloch, "In the years of the Consulate, at least, the forced depoliticization created a climate where men of talent and experience but of differing opinions could work together, listen to each other, debate in good faith, and marshal their eloquence and expertise to reach consensus with the first consul over the thorniest of issues."[64] Other organs of government saw an even more definitive silencing of political passions as Napoleon banned debate in the Corps législatif in order to avoid an airing of ideological divides.[65]

Napoleon also wanted to create a new social order, and in a speech to the Conseil d'État, he spoke of the work of the Revolution and the needs of a new France: "There is a government, there are powers; but what is the rest of the nation? Grains of sand. . . . We are scattered, without any system, without union, without contact." He stated that he wanted to sow "blocks of granite in the soil of France."[66] Napoleon's terms bore a strong resemblance to the words Tallien used to describe the effects of the Terror and are strikingly similar to the discourse of individualism that became prominent during the Restoration and July Monarchy. In all these cases, the Revolution spread anomie into society and left citizens fundamentally estranged from one another. Napoleon's solution, though, was characteristically dirigiste as he proposed to bring French society together through new government institutions, including lycées and a strengthened administration.

Central to this effort to reestablish French society was the creation of a new elite based around the model of state service and an elite sociability that was to be "an instrument of a social policy designed to bolster the stability and legitimacy of his regime."[67] The Légion d'honneur and the imperial nobility were designed to fuse the elite of the Old Regime with that of the revolutionary and Napoleonic eras. Associational life served this same purpose of bridging the divide between the old and the new France. Freemasonry had a particular importance during the Napoleonic regime. It received official recognition from the state, and many of those close to Napoleon held high positions as Masons, including two of his brothers. But Napoleon also placed civic organizations under close surveillance, and article 291 of the Penal Code stated that the state had to authorize all organizations with more than twenty members.[68] If the regime was more permissive toward associations than that of the radical Revolution, civil society was to serve the ends of the state.

The Napoleonic era also saw the revival of court life and an attempt to appropriate salon culture, efforts that gave some women political roles. Claire de Rémusat, Charles de Rémusat's mother, was a salonnière whose task was to bring the old and new elites together. Related to the comte de Vergennes, she married a member of the Provençal nobility; both she and her husband were attached to the imperial court. With Napoleon's backing and financial support, she maintained a salon for writers and artists, including Chateaubriand.[69] Napoleon also credited Josephine in his efforts at elite fusion. In his memoirs, he stated that she helped him reach out to aristocrats of the Old Regime: "Without my wife, I never would have been able to have any natural connection to this party."[70] Napoleon, though known for his aversion to women's political engagement, recognized that women could build support for his regime. In certain respects, Josephine's functions were similar to those of the women at the court of Versailles, as she was an intermediary between the monarch and noble factions. Yet, whereas the women of the Old Regime helped aristocrats find favor with the king, Josephine did the opposite—she helped her husband facilitate contact with and find support among those otherwise distant from his rule.

Some of the regime's attempts to control elite sociability complicated interpersonal relations. The imperial court imposed constraints that were similar to those at Versailles. Jean Jacques Régis de Cambacérès, one of Napoleon's chief collaborators, stated that imperial courtiers lived with "the naive fear . . . that if we were lacking in the slightest thing we would receive a reproach"; consequently, the court was characterized by a "silence that we kept about everything."[71] Once again, the monarch's watchful gaze created an atmosphere of fear and prevented individuals from connecting in any meaningful way with one another. Observers also credited Napoleon's efforts to monitor high society with creating a sense of estrangement among elites. The regime oversaw the considerable expansion of state surveillance, although for centuries the government had spied on its citizens.[72] Napoleon and Fouché, his most prominent spymaster, established the administrative structure of the modern police state, one inherited by the Restoration and July Monarchy.[73] Under Napoleon, spies went to theaters, cafés, secret societies, salons, and events such as balls and the races at Longchamps. He also had informers who circulated in high society, including Madame de Genlis and Joseph Fiévée.[74] As a result, speaking freely at a social event was a risky proposition. Salon-goers lived in fear as they attempted to determine who among them was a police agent and whether what they said was being relayed to the government. The idea that the over-policing of society was troubling social relations became part of the black legend of Napoleon. Thus the anti-Napoleonic propagandist Jean Baptiste Couchery wrote in his *Le Moniteur secret; ou, Tableau de la cour de Napoleon, de son caractère, et de celui de ses agens* that the term "tyrant" was "a word that one hardly dared speak in the silence of a retreat or in the confidence of friendship because one is so surrounded by spies and denouncers."[75] As at the court, elites resorted to silence to evade the gaze of the state. Couchery's opposition to the regime undoubtedly motivated his discussion of the deleterious effects of state surveillance. Yet even Fouché spoke in much the same way about his handiwork. He said that police spying resulted in "no more communication, no more expansion, no more trust between citizens. It was only inside families and in the bosom of friendship that public unhappiness dared to express itself with smothered voices."[76] Here, only the closest of personal ties could withstand the pressure of an intrusive state.

There was one realm in which the regime relied on love as a force for public cohesion: the military. For Napoleon, his generals, and his soldiers, love united the army. Military thinkers understood that close ties between soldiers promoted unity within the ranks and led men to become better fighters. Indeed, intense sentiment tied Napoleon to some of his chief subordinates, including Marshal Lannes, Marshal Duroc, and General Junot, while rank-and-file members of the army often spoke of the mutual fondness between themselves and the emperor. For these men, too, friendship was a crucial survival strategy. During the disastrous Russian campaign, having a friend was sometimes the difference between life and death. Friends shared food with each other, cared for each other when wounded, and provided crucial forms of emotional support.[77]

In many ways, then, the regime's attitude toward high society was an attempt to solve the problems the Revolution had posed. It tried to heal—or at the very least silence—the ideological divisions engendered during the previous decade, to create an elite that would reconcile the old and the new France and end the perceived atomization of French society. Unity and order came from the state and not from the emotions (with the significant exception of the army), and the regime generally saw a retreat from the use of sentiment as a force for public cohesion.

POST-REVOLUTIONARY SOCIETY AND THE PROBLEM OF INDIVIDUALISM

In the aftermath of the revolutionary and Napoleonic eras, French thinkers were preoccupied with the question of how the Revolution had changed France. Among those who set out to investigate the nature of this society, a chorus of authors repeated the same set of ideas: the Revolution had destroyed French society. Now France was nothing but a collection of individuals.[78]

The first writers to discuss individualism as a problem were conservatives and Catholics during the Restoration. They decried the state of a nation that had turned its back on hierarchy, tradition, and order in favor of individual rights and liberties. For them, the twin evils of democracy and irreligion, as embodied in the Revolution, had destroyed all social bonds. Thus an 1825 article in *Le Mémorial catholique* stated that "individualism is a sore on the social body and one of the consequences of revolutions," and that the Revolution had "divided all interests and broken all ties of religion, the state, and the family."[79] As a result, the citizens of France were now entirely preoccupied with their own selves.[80] Other thinkers and politicians on the far-right, including Chateaubriand and Joseph de Maistre, expressed a concern about an isolating self-absorption that seemed to be so characteristic of their day. Indeed, de Maistre has been credited with coining the term "individualism."[81] In his mind, this word had wholly negative connotations, for it suggested a world of too much freedom, one in which division and anomie reigned.

In this respect at least, de Maistre was within the mainstream of early nineteenth-century thought. Indeed, in this period the word "individualism" was not associated so much with freedom or self-development but atomization. Its closest synonym was "egoism."[82] During the Restoration and July Monarchy, liberals also spoke of the pervasive anomie of the day. The doctrinaire theorist and politician Pierre Paul Royer-Collard stated that France was a "society reduced to dust" as a result of the Revolution.[83] This was also a theme of Alexis de Tocqueville's work. In *Democracy in America*, he maintained that democratic societies (which France was inevitably becoming) lacked a bond to connect free and equal citizens. In his mind, the danger was that individuals would retreat to the private sphere and disengage from the wider social and civic order.[84] Socialists of the July Monarchy also took up this discourse of social dissolution to demonstrate the need to build a new, more communitarian society. For these authors, the problem was that the Revolution had created a socioeconomic order based on competition, not cooperation. Thus, in 1831, the Saint-Simonist philosopher Pierre Leroux echoed

Royer-Collard by stating, "Society has been reduced to dust because men are no longer connected to one another, because nothing unites them, because man is stranger to man."[85]

In large measure, the problem of individualism was a French problem. German, American, and British authors wrote about individualism as well, but they often (although not always) saw it in positive terms instead of the far more pessimistic French vision. German thinkers typically associated this concept with self-expression and self-development, while American ones thought in terms of free markets and democracy. In turn, British uses of the term often referred to religious nonconformity.[86] Such positive connotations were undoubtedly due to the strength of specific traditions, whether Romanticism in Germany or the history of religious dissent in Britain.

In contrast, in France, individualism was seen as the work of the Revolution. It was thus regarded as fundamentally new, and the product of political turmoil and even violence. French thinkers also perceived that individualism was about a lack and tied it to the weakness of civil society in the early nineteenth century.[87] The specifically French anxiety about individualism and social dissolution also arose out of the successive failed efforts to imagine a new social order. From the eighteenth century to the early nineteenth, French citizens saw three distinct models of social organization: the corporate and hierarchical, the sentimental, and the Napoleonic vision of a society under the government's tutelage. Going back to the first was impracticable; corporate groups and legal privilege no longer existed. The sentimental model had proved to be both dangerous and impossible during the Terror, while the Napoleonic one had little appeal. The post-Napoleonic regimes also evinced less desire to direct social relations and reconstruct society around the state. The Revolution thus left individuals as the only actors on the scene while making it difficult to imagine that there was any bond between citizens. Ultimately, this gets to the heart of the problem of post-revolutionary individualism and the legacy of the Revolution for the French social order. Men and women had friends and family members; elites circulated in the dense world of high society. Following Tocqueville's line of thought, though, what was lacking was any sense of public cohesion—and it is to this problem that the next chapter turns.

2

THE POLITICS OF ANOMIE

When Joseph de Maistre coined the term "individualism" in 1820, he described the problem as being political in nature. He stated that the ideological tensions in France had led to "the profound and terrifying division of souls, this infinite division of doctrines, this political Protestantism which is pushed to the most absolute individualism."[1] Here, de Maistre managed to get in a dig at Protestantism, with its stress on an individual's relationship with God and the necessity of reading the Bible for oneself. Only Catholicism could hold society together. But the major problem for him was the clash of ideologies. The overwhelming variety of political beliefs possible in the post-revolutionary era made concord impossible because no one shared the same ideological position. De Maistre was not alone in his conclusion; many understood that social relations were so strained during the period between 1815 and 1848 due to the nature of post-revolutionary politics. In the early nineteenth century, trust and cohesion were difficult to find, and particularly so in the public realm. Associational life was weak and both politics and the marketplace were understood to be arenas where no permanent forms of attachment were possible. The deep factional divides of the Restoration also led to an outpouring of negative emotions and made politics especially divisive. Indeed, elites of the Restoration had good reason to feel isolated from and distrustful of one another, given the political upheaval of 1815 and the prevalence of spying and denunciation in this era. During the July Monarchy, ideological divisions quieted down, but many came to see the social and political order as being based on isolating self-interest. Thus, although the sources of distrust were somewhat different, social relations in both regimes were regarded as deeply troubled.

Yet trust and connection were still possible to imagine, if only in private life. This chapter ends with a discussion of Honoré de Balzac's *Illusions perdues*, a work written during the July Monarchy but set in the Restoration, which centers on the corrosive effects of factionalism and self-interest. Here, though, Balzac imagines a solution to these sources of division and to the problem of individualism: the utopian space of friendship. In this novel, ideal friendship leads men to act with generosity and cease their ideological hostilities. Yet if friendship could serve as a source of connection, it could only do so in a partial fashion and among chosen intimates, as love was private and no longer public.

DISTRUST AND DIVISION IN THE RESTORATION

The notion that after the Revolution, ideology divided the nation is a standard trope of histories of the early nineteenth century and was a commonplace among authors of the time.[2] On one side lay those who had made gains since the Revolution, including individuals who bought land that had been nationalized during the Revolution, or Protestants and members of the bourgeoisie who benefited from the new forms of legal equality. On the other side, there were émigrés whose lands had been nationalized, or those whose status had been harmed by the Revolution, including aristocrats and Catholics. This notion of division and of the "two Frances" is regarded as a constant feature of modern French society and was particularly prominent in the Restoration because of the deep factional divides that came to the surface and crystallized after 1815. These ideological divisions were seen as unleashing a torrent of hostility into French society and led citizens to denounce one another, a phenomenon that many felt further poisoned social relations. And because the government felt itself to be on such shaky ground and had so much distrust for the citizenry, it doggedly policed elites; the practices of surveillance were also held responsible for a heightened sense of suspicion within society. In this environment, trusting others could be a dangerous prospect.

Napoleon's internal peacemaking fell apart in a dramatic fashion in 1815, a year that reignited factional violence, and one when many men and women learned to distrust one another and even themselves. In particular, Napoleon's return during the Hundred Days reopened the ideological divisions of the Revolution. When he landed in France in March 1815, every citizen had to make a choice between an allegiance to him or to the Bourbon monarchy.

In contrast to the situation in 1814, when few looked forward to the prospect of continued imperial rule, the Napoleon of 1815 had considerably more appeal. In their short time on the throne, the Bourbons had not proved very popular. But Napoleon returned from Elba promising liberalization. He gave assurances of freedom of the press and a broader franchise than the one that the Bourbons had offered, and he successfully attracted prominent liberals to his cause. Most notably, Benjamin Constant wrote the *Acte additionnel*, the new constitution of the Hundred Days. This was despite the fact that he had attacked Napoleon in an 1814 pamphlet titled "De l'Esprit de conquête et de l'usurpation" and had previously supported the return of the Bourbons as the best hope for liberty. The most famous case of such shifting loyalties, however, was that of Marshal Ney, a Napoleonic officer who had encouraged Napoleon to abdicate in 1814. At the beginning of the Hundred Days, Ney swore to Louis XVIII that he would bring Napoleon back in an iron cage—but he quickly went over to the emperor's side and urged others to do so as well. Even the king went back on his word; he had vowed that he would stay and fight Napoleon—but then fled to Ghent. On a less spectacular level, many officeholders switched their allegiance from Napoleon to the Bourbon monarchy and then back again to the Empire. These men who seemingly so easily changed their loyalties from one regime to another were called "girouettes" or weather vanes. After the Hundred Days, there was a spate of books that listed these men, their variable allegiances, and the positions they had held under different regimes.[3]

All this tacking back and forth from regime to regime led to a sense that no one's promises could be trusted. In the words of Chateaubriand, "This era, when no one was honest, shook the soul: everyone took oaths as if they were footbridges thrown down to cross the problems of the day; then once the obstacle was cleared, they changed direction." Because of "this disagreement between words and actions, one felt seized by disgust for the human race."[4] The events of 1815 had shown that professions of loyalty were meaningless, a mere tactic to be used to advance one's career. The fact that each successive regime required those who served it to take an oath of loyalty magnified this problem of distrust. The men who switched their allegiance from regime to regime went back on their word, a violation of the male honor code.[5] Yet the problem of trust went beyond an inability to have faith in others. After the Hundred Days, many individuals came to feel that they could not trust themselves. While they might intend to be loyal to one regime, when push came to shove they might quickly go back on their promises. Hence, the instability of

1814–15 convinced many that public life was an unpleasant realm of constant betrayals.[6]

After the Hundred Days, those on the right—those who would become ultras—came to feel that Napoleon's return had revealed the true duplicity in the hearts of men. This belief profoundly shaped the conservatism of the Restoration. Although Chateaubriand stated that 1815 spoke badly about everyone, many of his fellow conservatives had a slightly different response. In their minds, only those who had protested the emperor's return by resigning or following Louis XVIII into exile could be trusted. As one ultra deputy stated, the Hundred Days "traced a dividing line between good and bad citizens."[7] Thus, when many hard-core royalists looked out on to France, what they saw was a dispiriting sight, as the vast majority of citizens were immoral and untrustworthy. As a result, the ultras began this new era of parliamentary monarchy with a sense of estrangement from all those who did not follow their particular—and strict—path.

For those who were not hard-core royalists, the response to the perceived betrayals of the Hundred Days provided plenty of reasons to be suspicious of conservatives. After Waterloo, both the state and ardent royalists launched a wave of reprisals in the form of the White Terror. Although the first Restoration had been relatively pacific, the return of the Bourbons in 1815 unleashed a series of trials, executions, and extralegal violence against those who had declared their loyalty to the emperor. In some cases, those who had benefited from the Revolution, such as individuals who bought nationalized Church land or priests who had married, were targeted. The most horrific violence was in the South, where confessional divisions overlapped with political allegiances and where mobs of citizens out for revenge killed approximately three hundred persons. For instance, Marshal Brune, a Napoleonic officer, was brutally murdered in Avignon; after he died, his body was thrown into the Rhône. Alternately, in Toulouse, General Ramel was assassinated in August for his loyalty to the emperor. In a less spectacular fashion, the government tried and executed four Napoleonic officers, imprisoned thousands more, and purged between fifty thousand and eighty thousand *fonctionnaires* from its ranks.[8]

Even those who were not directly affected had reason to fear that they might be. The ultra politician François Régis de La Bourdonnaye proposed that anyone who had occupied a post in the upper administration or military command during the Hundred Days should be executed, while any regicides who had shown loyalty to the emperor should be exiled. If he had had his way, 1,200 people would have been affected.[9] La Bourdonnaye was also famous for a speech in which he proclaimed that those responsible for the Hundred Days should be subject to "irons, execution, [and] torture."[10] Thus, just as the Hundred Days gave those on the right a sense that all others were dishonorable traitors, those on the left had good reasons to distrust conservatives. Ultras, some of whom were thought to be involved in the extralegal violence, had shown themselves capable of brutality. They had turned on their adversaries with great savagery: what was to stop them from doing so again?

Those on the left also leveled charges of disloyalty at ardent monarchists. Liberals saw the supporters of the Bourbons as bad citizens who had betrayed their country. Many émigrés had served in the Allied armies during the Revolution and thus had fought against French troops. Additionally, because an Allied military occupation accompanied the second Restoration, many conservatives welcomed the success of the invading armies and the losses of the French military. In his autobiography, Béranger writes of seeing foreign troops lead a group of wounded and captured French soldiers through the streets of Paris. The good workers of Paris were concerned about their injured compatriots, but royalists in better-off neighborhoods cheered the foreign soldiers. This, he said, was not only unpatriotic but betrayed "a lack of humanity," as the wealthy had no pity for the wounded.[11] Throughout the Restoration, politicians on the left continued to maintain that they were the true patriots and that their conservative opponents were bad citizens who were indebted to foreign powers.[12] Once again, those on the opposing side were cast as having character defects, as the France that had supported Napoleon during the Hundred Days felt estranged from the France that was loyal to the Bourbons.

Of course, such mutual charges of immorality and betrayal are a perfect illustration of the idea that the inability to imagine a loyal opposition is characteristic of French political culture.[13] Ultras were unable to conceive why anyone would not be entirely devoted to the Bourbon monarchy, while men such as Béranger found it hard to understand the appeal of an Allied occupation. Yet in 1815, the problem of the loyal opposition was not just one of the political imaginary. Both sides felt they had incontrovertible proof that their political opponents were not to be trusted.

The Hundred Days and the White Terror had a profound effect on the politics of the Restoration. At the most basic level, the events of 1815 formed the two most important political factions of the Restoration: the ultras and the liberal opposition. The ultras were those who wanted to return to the Old

Regime and the days of absolute monarchy (at least in theory, for they did not always agree with the relatively moderate Louis XVIII). Although there were those who had been opposed to any reform of the monarchy since the very beginning of the Revolution, the ultras' sense of the urgency of their mission was largely a product of 1815.[14] The ultras were also defined by their tone. What René Rémond calls their "immoderate excesses and verbal violence" can best be understood as part of their response to the Hundred Days.[15] Moreover, Napoleon's efforts to liberalize the Empire were the crucible in which the liberal opposition was forged. Unlike the ultras, this faction had little ideological coherence to it. It included adherents of liberalism, such as Constant, as well as republicans and Bonapartists. What united these men was largely the Hundred Days, for Napoleon's overtures to liberals fused liberalism and Bonapartism, two ideological currents that had been opposed to each other before 1815.[16]

Historians have argued that these early days of the Restoration ultimately weakened the regime by polarizing opinion between left and right and by making any reconciliation impossible.[17] With or without the events of 1815, it was inevitable that a sharp division between left and right would emerge in the new parliamentary system. After all, even if Napoleon had not returned from Elba, and even if liberals had shown a more consistent attachment to the Bourbons, the monarchy that men like Constant wanted was not the same as the one that ardent ultras desired. Yet the effects of the Hundred Days made these political divisions particularly apparent and rancorous.

Observers of the time also described how all this political upheaval unleashed a torrent of negative emotions into French society. For example, in his 1819 *Vues politiques*, the moderate liberal Narcisse Achille de Salvandy stated that after 1815, France had been split into "two opposing camps" marked by "their mutual hatred." In his mind, this enmity challenged the sociable spirit of the French. Instead of courtesy and refinement, there was now only hostility and bitterness. He writes, "With its violent irritations, I no longer recognize this society which used to be so gracious and polite, where civil war finds a refuge in comments, where those of different opinions despise each other."[18] Mme de Montcalm provided another similar—and more personal—view in her diary. She was an on-again/off-again friend of Chateaubriand and the sister of the duc de Richelieu, leader of the government during the early years of the Restoration. Like her brother, she was a moderate, but as a salonnière in the aristocratic and conservative Faubourg Saint-Germain, she was surrounded by ultras. In her journal, she repeatedly wrote of the hostility of the society in which she circulated. In one entry from July 1815, she stated, "Bitterness quickly establishes itself between those who do not have exactly the same opinions. One ends up being unhappy with oneself and others and a fatal sadness, an absolute disgust enters into one's soul; yet one still feels a desire for different emotions."[19] As in Salvandy's and de Maistre's accounts, the political climate made it impossible for those who had even minor differences of opinion to get along. And likewise, the political upheaval of the time had the effect of releasing a series of negative emotions into society—bitterness, unhappiness, sadness, and disgust. Used to an atmosphere of polite sociability, she felt a need for connection to others. But the newly rancorous tone of Parisian high society made this impossible.[20]

Numerous authors also discussed how the factional hatreds of the Restoration destroyed personal ties. For instance, Charles Louis Lesur's *La France et les français en 1817: Tableau moral et politique, precedé d'un coup d'oeil sur la révolution* set out to describe the France of his day. He detailed its population, its social classes, its political institutions, and its place in a post-Napoleonic Europe. In a chapter titled "Des Moeurs et des opinions," he told the tale of two friends who had not seen each other since the Revolution. One had remained in France and was left-leaning, hence his name of Démophile. The other—the more aristocratically named Altamor—had emigrated and was on the right. After decades of separation, the two men were overjoyed to be reunited, but they quickly found they had little in common and could no longer be friends. Altamor thought Démophile to be a bloody republican hiding under a mask of liberalism, while Démophile saw Altamor as a prejudiced fool who wanted to drag France back to the Middle Ages.[21] Of course, this story was a parable for what had happened in France since the Revolution—the polarization of opinion and the fragmentation of society. But for Lesur, the tale of these two men provided a model of what factionalism had done to social relations. As he said, "How many miserable heartaches did this party spirit unleash into families! How many sacred bonds and happy unions did it destroy! How many children were torn away from their fathers, how many friendships were torn apart!"[22]

And indeed, many long-standing relationships were destroyed in the wake of the events of 1815. Béranger, for instance, ended two friendships because of politics, one with the composer Marc Antoine Désaugiers and another with the artist Pierre Narcisse Guérin, who would go on to paint idealized portraits of the leaders of the Vendée uprising. Béranger also belonged to a group of songwriters and authors called the Caveau that broke up in 1817 over politics.[23]

Both Mathieu Molé, a prominent official during the Empire and politician during the Restoration, and the marquis de Lafayette had love affairs that ended after 1815 because of differences of political opinion. In Lafayette's case, he and his mistress had been together since the days of the Revolution, but their relationship could not withstand the tumult of the Hundred Days and White Terror.[24] Chateaubriand, too, found himself cut off from others. He and Guizot had maintained a cordial—if formal—correspondence during the Empire, but the advent of the second Restoration severed this bond.[25] During the Empire, Chateaubriand was particularly close to Mme de Montcalm, but his opposition to her brother troubled their friendship.[26] In turn, Montcalm's relationship with her best friend, Mme d'Orglandes, an ardent ultra, foundered over politics. For Montcalm, a woman who was a committed if difficult friend, this made her doubt whether friendship itself was truly possible. In a journal entry from January 1816, Montcalm stated, "I tell myself with despair that after so much unhappiness and heartbreak, I must regard friendship as one of the number of treacherous illusions that is briefly offered so that one feels the painful absence of it more deeply."[27] For her, like for so many others, unhappiness and profound feelings of estrangement inaugurated the Restoration.

Thus, in the early years of the Restoration, politics was the great social dissolvent as elites had good reason to feel distrustful of and alienated from one another. The Restoration is often described as France's apprenticeship in political modernity, as it was the nation's first sustained period of parliamentary government. Yet many observers felt that something had been lost in the shift to a representative system. The process of politicization had torn apart French society. The Restoration may have educated political elites in the ways of representative government, but the lesson for many was that politics was a nasty, brutal, and divisive business.

DISTRUST AND THE RESTORATION POLICE STATE

In the years following 1815, observers suggested that neither the intense politicization of society nor the atmosphere of suspicion went away. One reason that the divides between right and left could not heal was that politically motivated denunciation came back into fashion. Many authors feared that denunciation prevented individuals from forming connections with others, and that it spread distrust within society. The Restoration state also continued many of Napoleon's practices of surveillance as well as his control of associational life. This state intervention was seen as responsible for putting individuals on their guard and further troubling social relations. Hence, the Restoration was a period when the sources of suspicion from the Revolution came together with those from the Napoleonic era.

After 1815, anxieties about denunciation spread through society, particularly among those who were not confirmed ultras. Numerous works of the time discussed this practice. The liberal dramatist Emmanuel Dupaty even wrote a book in 1819 titled *Les Délateurs; ou, Trois années du dix-neuvième siècle*, which was critical of the regime and the conservatives who supported it. That this work went through three editions in two years suggests that it found a ready audience. Like many others, Dupaty saw factionalism as driving denunciation. Individuals denounced their political opponents in order to advance their own position, and Dupaty accused ultras of denouncing those on the left in retribution for their perceived disloyalty during the Hundred Days. Because ardent royalists could no longer physically attack their political opponents, they fed information about members of the liberal opposition to a suspicious state.[28] Of course, this denunciation of denunciation was itself politically motivated, as it was a way to attack ultras as being mean-spirited and vengeful. But even those who were not especially politically engaged repeated the idea that the epidemic of denunciation had its origins in factionalism. Mme de Genlis, for example, held that the outbreak of denunciation in the Restoration was the sign of a divided society.[29]

Despite the widespread belief that denunciation was a common practice during the Restoration, it is difficult to assess its prevalence or frequency. Certainly, the police files reveal that denunciation did occur. There are, for instance, anonymous letters reporting on conspiratorial activity and assassination attempts against members of the royal family.[30] Yet not all such notes were necessarily preserved, and no doubt many individuals denounced others orally. Nor did such notes detail the motives of those who supplied information to the police. In some cases, the roots of denunciation were entirely personal, as denouncers leveraged the state's concern about the loyalties of its citizens to satisfy their private grievances.[31] In other cases, however, the political motivations are clear. One thick police file concerns Mme Roger, an ardent royalist who fed the government a steady stream of information about Bonapartist activity. She was from Toulouse, where the violence of the White Terror had been particularly brutal and where political passions ran exceptionally high. In her reports to the police, she claimed that she befriended the wife of an exiled Napoleonic general in order to gain her confidence. (To do so, Roger stated that she had to conceal her political views.) Roger then relayed the information she gained about the general to the government.[32] This was a clear betrayal of trust. Roger positioned herself as the confidante of a woman who possessed information about Napoleon's former collaborators. The general's wife trusted her, but Roger's obligations to the regime outweighed any loyalty to her supposed friend.

Authors of the time also described how denunciation spread distrust and ruptured personal bonds; anyone who had anything to hide lived in a state of anxiety and suspicion. For instance, in his *Les Délateurs*, Dupaty stated that denunciation "destroyed all ties, divided all hearts," and that "Everyone bottled up the secrets that oppressed them / Friends feared each other, the lover feared his mistress! / Brothers no longer considered themselves related to one another."[33] For Dupaty, the necessity of living in a state of constant suspicion took a terrible emotional toll, as it made it impossible for individuals to unburden themselves to those around them. Salvandy maintained much the same thing in his *Vues politiques*. He writes, "Denunciation . . . dissolves the ties of affection or the bonds of family, and corrupts public morality by constantly showing how many of the oppressors [i.e., those on the right] are actually cowards who defect [*transfuge*] in order to spare themselves from becoming victims."[34] As in Dupaty's account, the fear of denunciation strained the social fabric. Yet Salvandy went beyond a discussion of the reshaping of intimate relations to consider how denunciation compromised public life as well. Many individuals—presumably those on the left—renounced their true views and became more conservative to avoid being reported to the police. Such charges were not that different from those leveled at "girouettes" during the Hundred Days and its aftermath. Once again, the political struggles of the day were leading individuals to switch sides out of convenience. Only this time, it was liberals who accused their opponents of betrayal. The use of the word "transfuge" is also significant. This term can be used for someone who changes sides, as well as someone who deserts from the military—in other words, someone who goes back on his commitments. Thus, both the events of 1815 and the climate of denunciation that followed led to a belief that politics was a realm of dishonorable betrayal and that political loyalties were a matter of convenience, not true conviction.

The state had its own ways of gathering information about citizens. Throughout the Restoration, the government spied on both legal and illegal forms of political opposition out of fears about the loyalty of the citizenry.

After the Hundred Days, the government knew it did not have the allegiance of all French men and women or even all those in its own ranks.[35] To carry out this surveillance, the Restoration regime adapted the Napoleonic police state to its own purposes. Indeed, the first minister of the police was Fouché. Far too tainted by his collaboration with Napoleon, he lasted only a few months. Élie Decazes, Louis XVIII's favorite and a man allied with the doctrinaires, replaced him. Like Fouché, Decazes sent spies into cafés and salons. He also gave the position of head of the postal service to his protégé Dupleix de Mézy so that he could have access to personal correspondence. Decazes was concerned with both those on the left and those on the right. He kept a close eye on Napoleonic soldiers who might still be loyal to the emperor, as well as on the ultras who regarded him as a dangerous liberal.[36] The police paid special attention to Chateaubriand; two of his servants reported on his activities and copied his ingoing and outgoing correspondence.[37] They also detailed his relationships with both Claire Louisa Rose Bonne Lechal de Kersaint, duchesse de Duras, and Juliette Récamier, née Bernard.[38] Decazes, who became minister of the interior in 1818 when the Ministry of the Police was dissolved, lasted as royal favorite until a fanatical Bonapartist assassinated the duc de Berry in 1820, after which the government shifted to the right. Once the ultras were in power, the police focused their attention squarely on members of the liberal opposition. Police officers followed noted figures like Lafayette, Constant, Manuel, and Casimir Périer. Their reports to the minister of the interior remarked on the comings and goings of these men and with whom they traveled and met.[39] Spies were even sent on vacation to spas like Plombières and Baden to report on those with whom liberals were taking the waters.[40]

To obtain information, the police paid servants to report on their employers.[41] Spies also listened at doors and windows and occasionally went undercover to track a particular individual. For instance, in 1822, the police wanted to gain access to the house and garden of a banker who hosted gatherings of liberals. To do so, they claimed that they were interested in buying some of the orange trees that the gardener was selling.[42] Or they went to the homes of prominent liberals and pretended to be Napoleonic soldiers in need of money.[43] Authors of the time also stated that members of high society regularly reported to the police and that the government sent spies trained in the ways of elite sociability into salons, although these claims may speak more to the anxieties of the moment as opposed to the realities of Restoration-era police work.[44]

All of this surveillance was widely known and was the subject of considerable debate inside the Chambers.[45] These tactics of policing gave men and women good reasons to distrust those around them. Anyone asking for information about a neighbor or a friend might be a spy. The man who claimed to be a down-on-his-luck soldier asking for money might be telling the truth—or he might be working for the police. Speaking openly at a salon was also inadvisable. More generally, anyone who was a stranger was a potential spy and should be met with distrust and dissimulation. As in the Napoleonic era, many authors stated that the presence of spies created an atmosphere of suspicion. The liberal dramatist Étienne de Jouy spoke for many when he stated that "morality disavows spies; they destroy trust between citizens, the gentlest element of the social bond."[46] Here, Jouy's words echo the discourse of social dissolution, as individuals are estranged from one another, and social relations are under enormous strain. Jouy's statement also bears similarities to Salvandy's description of the effects of denunciation. Both men describe a lack of trust within the public realm. In this case, Jouy's use of the term "citizens" locates the problem as one that is essentially civic and political. That is to say that in his account, individuals are suspicious of and disconnected from those whom they encounter in the public realm, and they find it impossible to attach themselves to the nation as a whole. After all, those who engaged in politics often found themselves under surveillance, particularly if they were in the opposition. Undoubtedly, too, the fear that any stranger could be a spy could lead to the weakening of generalized trust among the members of society.

The Restoration also inherited much of the Napoleonic regime's attitude toward associational life, which compounded the problems of distrust and public cohesion. In general, the regime was generally more tolerant of associations than Napoleon was, but it did use article 291 of the Penal Code to dissolve one association—the Société des Amis de la presse—and refused to give permission to another—Aide toi, le ciel t'aidera—both of which were designed to promote liberal causes.[47] Other societies came under government scrutiny for a variety of reasons, including a liberal philanthropic association the doctrinaires founded and the Cercle de l'Union, a social club for conservative aristocrats from the Faubourg Saint-Germain. The former was suspect for its political leanings and for the presumed atheism of its members, while the latter was thought to be a center of gambling.[48] Not surprisingly, the police seemed to be particularly concerned about Freemasonry, and police records contain both detailed information about who attended Masonic reunions as well as transcriptions of conversations at the lodges.[49] Even outside the problem of government oversight, associational life in the form of social clubs was relatively weak during the Restoration and did not take off until the mid-nineteenth century.[50]

Hence, the Restoration was a period when public solidarity was difficult to imagine and when men and women had good reasons to be distrustful of one another. Speaking one's mind was an imprudent act, as the state made public forms of cooperation difficult. Both the regime and its supporters were actively engaged in trying to ferret out the secrets of those it suspected. The factional divisions of the era destroyed personal relationships and opened up a flood of bitterness and rancor. Those on opposing sides of the political spectrum thought of each other as fundamentally disloyal and immoral—and in some cases, ready and able to commit violence in order to pursue their quest for ideological purity.

If the politics of the Restoration disrupted private relationships, such as those between lovers and friends, it also led to a particular understanding of public life. Any generalized sense of trust that extended to all members of society was impossible. Politics was understood to be a hostile world of betrayal. Those who engaged in politics did so with the knowledge that their activities made them a ready target for denunciation and police surveillance. In the Restoration, then, the political struggles of the regime fed the sense of dismay at a crumbling social order.

THE JULY MONARCHY AND THE PROBLEM OF SELF-INTEREST

After 1830, some of the sources of division and suspicion became less prominent. Politics became less factionalized as many elites realized that the threat was not so much from one another, but from the lower classes. The state also policed high society less severely than it had before. Yet the sense of atomization and distrust did not go away in the July Monarchy. After all, once trust is destroyed, it is hard to rebuild. And this regime saw a new set of concerns about social relations—ones related less to ideological disagreements and more to the problem of self-interest. Now it was greed that was seen as responsible for destroying the social order and for isolating individuals from one another. Thus, while the sources of division were understood as being different in the July Monarchy than in the Restoration, trust and cohesion were still regarded as impossible in public life.[51]

During the July Monarchy, the government no longer took to spying on its elites—although many still suspected that police agents circulated in high-society gatherings. For example, in his memoirs, Rémusat discussed the reach of the police when he wrote of his short tenure as minister of the interior in 1840. Here, he took great pains to set the record straight about whether there were spies in high society. He stated that the Ministry paid servants in men's clubs for information. But otherwise, he maintained, the government did not send spies to report on elite social gatherings, despite what was generally thought.[52] The regime did crack down on associations, however, as it feared that clubs were hotbeds for political and social unrest. Thus the government passed an 1834 law tightening restrictions on associations and introducing stiffer penalties for violating article 291. While associational life grew in strength in the 1830s and 1840s, it was weakest among those studied here: Parisian political elites. Elite men's clubs were numerous in the provinces but less so in the capital, where salons continued to exert a powerful hold over elite social habits.[53]

The factionalism that was so prominent in the Restoration also began to wane after 1830. There were still clear ideological divides. Many ultras became legitimists who dreamed of returning the Bourbons to the throne, for example. Meanwhile, the liberal opposition during the Restoration split apart into a number of different factions. Some of these men aligned themselves with the juste milieu and became ardent supporters of the Orleanist regime. Others remained in the opposition and advocated for an enlarged franchise or even for a republic. Politics in the July Monarchy, however, were largely organized around personalities and patronage networks as opposed to sharp ideological distinctions. For instance, Guizot and Adolphe Thiers were two chief rivals during the 1830s and 1840s, but their political disagreements related primarily to differences over foreign policy and France's standing in Europe.[54]

Despite the slackening of ideological tensions, politics could still be a force for division. The political shifts that occurred after 1830 reorganized individuals' social networks. Béranger, for instance, found that he could no longer be friends with many of those to whom he had been close during the Restoration. Despite his professed republicanism, he initially supported the July Monarchy because he thought that a republic was not possible and that Louis-Philippe was the best hope for France.[55] But after the king's conservatism came to the fore, Béranger found himself estranged from some of his friends who supported the regime. He broke off relations with Barthe and

Dupin, both of whom had defended him during his trials in the 1820s, when they moved to the right during the 1830s.[56] In addition, his relationship with Thiers, to whom he had been close in the Restoration, was considerably strained. During the July Monarchy, the two continued to socialize with each other, but some of Béranger's letters to his other friends—and particularly those on the left—indicate that he felt personally and politically estranged from Thiers.[57] Others, as well, found that politics was still divisive. Guizot and Rémusat were close in the 1820s, but in the 1830s the latter balanced an attachment to the doctrinaires' center-right position with sympathies to Thiers's center-left politics. Their friendship ended dramatically in 1840 when Rémusat joined a left-leaning cabinet led by Thiers, one that Guizot came to oppose.[58] Political divides still led to social ones.

Politicians also continued to regard their work as a nasty business, existing in a realm where trust was impossible. For instance, in 1837, Guizot wrote the following to his mistress, the princesse Dorothea von Lieven, née Benckendorff:

> Between us, I have more than once regretted that I could not be as cordial, as benevolent with my political opponents as I would have liked. I know more than one whom I could have befriended or at least had a pleasant relationship with, were it not for politics. But my concern for my personal dignity, my duty to my cause, the demands and the suspicions of my allies, all that creates a coldness, a hostility between men, often without personal grounds. I must resign myself; it is the law of warfare, because politics is a war.[59]

According to Guizot, he would have liked to have been friends with some of his adversaries, but he was too intimately involved with political struggles to do so. He had to remain antagonistic to those who disagreed with him or else he would lose the fight. This statement can be read on a number of levels. For one, it was meant to reassure Lieven that the fact that she cultivated relationships with some of his rivals, including Thiers and Mathieu, comte Molé, did not bother him. It is also entirely true that Guizot had problems being friends with men whose views he did not share, and that his close male friends in this era were his political allies. Here, though, Guizot was talking about friendship not just as a meaningful personal relationship but also as a metaphor. It was not so much the possibility of friendship that was missing but the possibility of trust or open communication. After all, Guizot did not really want to be friends with men like Molé (whom he hated) or Thiers (for whom he had little respect).

The language of this passage is also telling. In Guizot's mind, politics follows the same laws as warfare and is thus a realm with clear allies and enemies; the ultimate goal is to defeat the other parties. However, Guizot's view of politics as warfare was not an accurate or astute understanding of parliamentary life in the July Monarchy. Alliances between factions were a central element to the political maneuverings of this era. For example, in 1836, Guizot aligned himself with the center-right Molé, while two years later he joined with the center-left Thiers and Odilon Barrot, the leader of the dynastic left, to oust Molé from power.[60] Thus politics was transacted at this time by both fighting against and allying with other factions. In other words, politicians often needed to cooperate with one another. But rather than adapting intellectually and politically to the new ways of the regime, Guizot relied on a Restoration-era understanding of politics: political adversaries were implacable foes with whom no compromise was possible. Guizot's inability to be friends with politicians from different factions or to imagine that he could trust them should be seen as one of the continuing legacies of the Restoration.

Yet when individuals of the 1830s and 1840s talked about the strain placed on social relations, they tended to focus less on ideological concerns and more on the issue of self-interest, which was in turn infecting the political realm. Many authors maintained that France was a nation entirely consumed by greed, one in which citizens engaged in brutal forms of competition with one another. Interest destroyed social bonds and made it impossible to connect with others. Despite this fundamental shift from a concern about politics to one about money, the problem was still a lack of trust and cohesion. Individuals no longer betrayed one another because of ideological conviction, but because being loyal was not in their interest. Maintaining any connection with others was simply not worth it.

These concerns about the destructive nature of self-interest were part of a larger set of anxieties about the effects of economic growth in the early nineteenth century. For many, this new, wealthier society offered a depressing sight, as they held that money had become the exclusive preoccupation of the French.[61] In turn, this pursuit of self-interest was corroding the political realm. Many authors maintained that the very foundation of the government was self-interest—the bourgeois king Louis-Philippe was ruling because the bourgeoisie benefited from his rule. The royal family, despite their vast wealth, was frequently accused of being corrupt and consumed by greed. In turn, this self-serving government was teaching its citizens to be avaricious and materialistic.[62] For example, the salonnière Virginie Ancelot suggested that the motto of the July Monarchy should be "The king serves our interest and we serve the king!" In her account, too, money had become the nation's only guiding principle.[63]

Thus, for many observers, the problem of the July Monarchy was not factionalism, but the degree to which political life had become bound up in questions of self-interest. This shift from a concern about the divisiveness of ideology to the corrosive nature of greed is aptly portrayed in an 1840 short story by Honoré de Balzac titled "Z. Marcas." Part of Balzac's *Scènes de la vie politique*, this work condemns the regime for its mediocrity, its exclusion of the youth of France, and its materialism. Set between 1836 and 1838, it tells the tale of Zéphirin Marcas, a journalist of intense ambition. Marcas is poor and dreams of obtaining power through his innate intelligence and political skill. He allies himself with a rich deputy in the hope that his patron will enable him to acquire enough property to become a deputy himself. But the unnamed deputy fears that if Marcas becomes too prominent, he will outshine him and so decides to hinder Marcas's career and oust him from any position of influence. Marcas is forced to eke out his living as a copyist and resides in a boardinghouse for students, where he meets the narrator and tells his tale to him. At the end of the story, Marcas's patron rehires him and then just as quickly dismisses him again. Marcas dies soon afterward, worked to death and impoverished.

As a tale about political life, "Z. Marcas" has a somewhat surprising understanding of politics. First, ideological questions are hardly the point. The reader gets no sense of what Marcas's politics are, or where his patron lies on the ideological spectrum. Nor does conviction drive Marcas; the reason he enters politics is that he sees it as a path to influence and riches. In Balzac's words, "When he dreamed of power, he also dreamed of luxury."[64] Indeed, the narrator mentions this very lack of ideological commitment on Marcas's part. In describing his entry into political life, the narrator states that Marcas did not "espouse the doctrines of a man in the opposition, as they would later hinder him if he came to power."[65] For Marcas, the appeal of politics is that it is a path to upward mobility. In this, he is no different from the narrator, an aspiring lawyer, or Juste, the narrator's roommate, who wants to become a doctor. All three are from modest provincial families and all came to Paris to make their fortune and satisfy their ambitions. This notion that politics is an arena of personal advancement can also be seen in the description of the difficulties that the narrator and Juste face in their quests for positions. The narrator details the frivolous lifestyle of the two roommates and then states:

> The reason for our dissipation was related to the most serious political problems of the time [*politique actuelle*]. Juste and I could not conceive of establishing ourselves in the two professions that our parents forced us to take up. There are a hundred lawyers, a hundred doctors for one place. The crowd blocked these two paths which seemed to lead to fortune and which are really two arenas in which one kills, one fights, not with steel and fire, but with intrigue and calumny.[66]

This is the first mention of the word "politics" in the story. Yet the problem that the narrator describes seems to be an economic—not a political—one, as it is a situation of too many applicants for too few spaces. After all, these men's chosen professions did not require one to work for the state. Why, then, should the difficulty of upward mobility be tied to politics? One reason is that the limited prospects for ambitious young men mirrored the electoral structure. In the narrator's account, any available positions went to those with family connections or money, as opposed to the most capable applicant. Likewise, in the July Monarchy, electoral rights and political positions were limited to the wealthy, shutting out men like Marcas. The talentless oligarchy that took up all places in the political system monopolized all other positions. In Balzac's view, such a regime can only lead to revolution. As Marcas states, because so many young men are shut out of the system, they "are pushed into being republicans because they think that the republic will liberate them."[67] In other words, for both the supporters of the regime and its opponents, interest is the motor of politics.

This description of the "most serious political problems of the time" also brings up the central issue of competition. The young men who crowd into Paris with dreams of fame and fortune are all fighting with one another because there are only a few places for many aspirants. As the narrator states, such combat is profoundly vicious—the wounds that these men inflict on one another can be mortal, even if they fight with words and not physical blows. The same is true in politics, with Marcas as a prime example. He and his patron are locked in a struggle that only one can win. If Marcas becomes too prominent, the deputy will become a nonentity.

Marcas's patron is both dependent on Marcas and needs to destroy him, as he eventually does. As a result, these men are tied together but bear an intense animosity toward each other. In the narrator's words, "These two men, though they seemed united, hated each other."[68] Politics was shot through with anomie and distrust. For instance, at the end of the story Marcas's patron, now a cabinet minister, attempts to win Marcas back after realizing that he needs him. To do so, the minister makes a host of promises: "He gave his word to make a place for Marcas in the administration, to help him become a deputy; then he offered him a prominent position by telling him that from now on, he, the minister, would be the subordinate."[69] Although Marcas goes back to work for his patron, the minister never follows through. Returning to the boardinghouse, Marcas is more embittered than ever. The fact that this politician is never named—the reader is only told that he is a prominent one—means that he could in effect be any political figure. As a result, he becomes all of them. In Balzac's telling, the politicians of the July Monarchy are all untrustworthy. Their promises cannot be believed because self-interest will ultimately win out over any sense of loyalty or honor.

As in the Restoration, politics is a vicious, brutal business marked by inconstancy and distrust. Interest may have overtaken factionalism as the source of this problem, but in both cases political life is atomizing. The last words of the story highlight this problem, as the narrator ends his tale with the pronouncement, "We all know more than one Marcas, more than one victim of political devotion, rewarded by betrayal or oblivion."[70] In this case, "political devotion" is an utterly ironic phrase, for no such thing exists. Instead, the desire for self-advancement makes any bonds between political actors impossible and makes politics particularly cruel.

POLITICS, INTEREST, AND FRIENDSHIP IN HONORÉ DE BALZAC'S *ILLUSIONS PERDUES*: REKNITTING THE SOCIAL ORDER

The overwhelming materialism of the early nineteenth century was a consistent theme of Balzac's work. He regarded it as a central feature of the new society he set out to examine in the *Comédie humaine.* Throughout his works, greed so consumes his characters that they cannot maintain any social ties and do not have the least hesitation about betraying those who stand in their way.[71] His work *Illusions perdues* perfectly illustrates this model of an anomic and hostile society, especially in the section from 1839 titled *Un Grand homme de province à Paris.* Balzac, writing during the July Monarchy, chose to set his critique of Parisian social relations in the Restoration, and he depicts how both political tensions and the search for material gain pulled individuals apart. In this novel, Balzac also uses friendship as an idealized relationship that could heal political divisions and reestablish solidarity in an interest-dominated society. At the same time, discussions of this bond function as a way to illustrate the difference between the morally pure characters and the corrupt ones.

In this novel, friendship becomes a utopia—an impossible ideal separate from the modern world. Friendship unites individuals and quells political tensions, and thus establishes a positive form of individualism that includes self-development and free choice but excludes atomizing competition and destructive self-interest. Friendship thus becomes a prescription for a laundry list of ills that were seen as plaguing the social order of the early nineteenth century—suspicion, factionalism, individualism, and greed. Yet idealized friendship is always exclusive, for it can incorporate only a small group of individuals who were committed to excising political tensions and economic concerns from their affective lives. In essence, if public life was an arena of hostility, then trust and connection could exist only in private and among a select few.[72]

Illusions perdues is the story of Lucien de Rubempré, an aspiring poet from Angoulême. From a poor family, Lucien moves to Paris with his aristocratic mistress and hopes to make his name through her connections in high society. Once in the capital, she abandons him and he is forced to make his way by his wits alone. He is quickly presented with two choices. The first, devoting his life to his literary works, involves a slow, laborious process and years of poverty, but it might ultimately lead to the full development of his talent. The second is to become a journalist. At least in the short run, this option could allow him a life of ease. But it comes at a very high price. Lucien ultimately succumbs to the temptations of journalism and becomes destitute, betrays his principles and his friends, and watches his teenage mistress die.

In *Illusions perdues*, Balzac's characters confront the two forces seen as destructive of the early nineteenth-century social fabric: politics and self-interest. As a novel set during the Restoration that takes place among journalists, *Illusions perdues* contains a number of references to the poisonous political atmosphere. When Lucien thinks about switching his affiliation from liberal to ultra because he imagines it would speed his path to success, his friends warn him against this by referencing the deep political divisions in the country and the legacy of the White Terror. One friend tells him that if he starts professing ultra views in his writings, liberals will destroy him, and that he "will be carried away by the rages of factionalism which is still at a fevered pitch; only the fever has passed from the brutal actions of 1815 and 1816 to the realm of ideas and verbal struggles in the Chambers and debates in the press."[73] Politics, then, leads individuals to seek one another's destruction.

Lucien's shifting political affiliations and France's ideological divisions are not the focus of *Illusions perdues*, but they are used to illustrate the degree to which Lucien will do anything that he thinks might advance his career. Instead, the problem of greed is more central to the novel, which details how the pursuit of material success destroys social bonds, particularly among journalists who inhabit a world inextricably bound to the marketplace. Indeed, what initially attracts Lucien to this career path is the opportunity for gain and the apparent luxury that journalism affords him. Balzac writes that at a dinner full of journalists and actresses, Lucien "enjoyed the first delights of wealth, he fell under the spell of luxury, under the empire of good food; his capricious instincts revived, he drank good wines for the first time, he came to know the exquisite dishes of haute cuisine."[74]

Such luxury comes at a very high cost, however, for journalists sacrifice their personal ties to self-interest. As Lucien is introduced to this world, his contacts repeatedly warn him that friendship is impossible. One journalist advises Lucien, "I see that you are entering the literary and journalistic word with illusions. You believe in friends. We are friends or enemies according to circumstances."[75] Later, the newspaper publisher Finot gives Lucien the following advice about his comportment as a journalist: "Don't overwork yourself. And above all, don't trust your friends."[76] The journalistic profession is so competitive—and the path to success so narrow—that the only way to survive is to exploit and betray others. This is precisely what Étienne Lousteau, Lucien's mentor in journalistic affairs, does as he quickly sacrifices Lucien in order to maintain his own status. At the dinner party during which Lucien is definitively seduced by the worldly pleasures of the journalistic lifestyle, Balzac writes that Lucien looks at Lousteau and thinks, "There's a friend! without suspecting that Lousteau already feared him to be a dangerous rival."[77] And so Lousteau decides to deny Lucien any chance of real success; he "resolved to remain Lucien's friend and come to an agreement with Finot to exploit such a dangerous newcomer and keep him in need."[78] In these instances, Balzac uses friendship as a signifier of morality. The fact that journalists are incapable of true friendship indicates that they cannot escape from their own greed, naked ambition, and ruthlessness.

In contrast to this world of destruction and self-destruction is the space of friendship, represented by the Cénacle, a group of nine artists and thinkers dedicated to truth and beauty. The fact that these men are all devoted friends is a sign of their moral purity, as friendship serves as a metaphor that stands in for generosity as well as artistic and personal integrity. Indeed these men represent perfect friendship. In describing the bonds among them, Balzac states, "The charming delicacy that made the fable *The Two Friends* [by Jean de La Fontaine] a treasure for great souls was habitual among these men."[79] With such words, Balzac situates himself in the canon of French literature as another author constructing an ideal human relationship.[80]

Lucien initially thinks about joining the Cénacle, but decides that journalism is a quicker route to fame and fortune. But before he starts down this path, he is given a sense of what true friendship looks like, and his brief foray into this alternative universe of talented young men allows Balzac to propose his model of friendship. As he discusses the relations among these men, Balzac draws explicit and implicit comparisons between friendship and other types of social ties, with friendship always coming out the clear winner. For instance, he contrasts male friendship to romantic love, writing that "what makes friendships indestructible and doubles their charms is a feeling that is absent in love—certainty. These young men were sure of each other."[81] While love always includes doubt (the lover is capable of betrayal or abandonment), friendship is a unique space of trust. It is also an oasis of affection in the otherwise hostile environment of Paris. Lucien comes in contact with the Cénacle through one of its members, Daniel d'Arthez, and when he does so, Balzac writes that Lucien is "happy to have found in the desert of Paris a heart which abounded with generous feelings in harmony with his."[82] D'Arthez is appealing because he is so unlike the others that Lucien encountered up until that moment, and emotion signifies this difference, given the sentimental vocabulary Balzac employs. Thus friendship exists as a utopia in the middle of an otherwise vicious Paris.

Crucial components of Balzac's model of friendship are the generosity, solidarity, and unity among the members of the Cénacle. For instance, he writes, "the enemy of one became the enemy of all, they would have broken with their most urgent interest in order to obey the sacred solidarity of their hearts."[83] Although these men have self-interest, their bonds with one another have primacy as they take on one another's concerns, even to the point of self-harm. At the end of the novel, these men show that they will defend one another whatever the consequences. When Lucien is forced into writing a negative review of d'Arthez's book, one member of the Cénacle, Michel Chrestien, spits in Lucien's face, provoking a duel. D'Arthez's enemy has indeed become his enemy, and he is willing to die for his friend. Balzac writes of the smaller, yet constant, sacrifices these men make for one another and the steady gift exchange among them. When Lucien initially befriends d'Arthez, the latter's first act is to pawn his watch to buy firewood so that he and Lucien can be more comfortable in his quarters. Balzac also describes that on an unseasonably cold autumn day, five of the members of the Cénacle bought firewood to take to d'Arthez's quarters, where they all meet.[84] Such acts of spontaneous generosity demonstrate the solidarity that exists among these friends, as they share one another's burdens and sacrifice money for the sake of love. Nothing could be farther from the competitive, atomized world of journalists.

Yet Lucien is unable to integrate himself into this gift economy. When the members of the Cénacle perceive that he is in financial difficulty, they all make sacrifices to come up with 200 F to give him. Lucien imagines that he is conscientious when he pays them back promptly, but they are insulted. One member says to him, "If you loved us like we love you, would you have been so eager and so emphatic in returning to us what we had so much pleasure in giving you?" Another states, "We do not make loans here, we give."[85] By thinking of the gift as a loan, Lucien shows that he does not share their values and that he can only think in terms of market calculations.[86] Theirs is an economy of sentiment, one that exists outside the realm of self-interest. The problem, however, with this perfect human relationship is precisely that it is a utopia—impossible to achieve, as Lucien cannot understand the rules of these men's relationships.

If friendship stands in for generosity, Balzac also uses this bond to figure the cessation of ideological hostilities. He states the following about the men of the Cénacle:

> Esteem and friendship made peace reign over the most opposing ideas and doctrines. Daniel d'Arthez, Picard gentleman, believed in the monarchy with a conviction that equaled Michel Chrestien's commitment to his European federalism. Fulgence Ridal made fun of the philosophical doctrines of Léon Giraud, who himself predicted the end of Christianity and the Family to d'Arthez. Michel Chrestien, who believed in the religion of Christ, the divine legislator of Equality, defended the notion of the immortality of the soul against the scalpel of Bianchon. . . .

> They had no vanity whatsoever, as they were their own audience. . . . Did it have to do with an important matter? The challenger abandoned his own opinions in order to enter into the ideas of his friend.[87]

The views of these men range from the far-right to the far-left. But an ideological flexibility allows them to transcend political divisions. In their discussions, these men help one another out by adopting alternate views, as any one of the members can "enter into the ideas of his friend" to improve the other's argument. Given Balzac's reference to the notion that those with opposing political views during the Restoration generally wanted to destroy one another, ideal friendship opens up the possibility of political reconciliation. One reason friendship wins out over politics is the notion of audience. These men are more interested in speaking among themselves than to members of the public, in contrast to journalists who strive for public recognition. Hence, friendship can exist only through some form of privacy and removal from the world.

Here Balzac uses the possibility or impossibility of friendship as a way to describe the problems France was facing. This bond is imagined as an ideal relationship that allows for pleasure, choice, and self-development, and restrains the forces of competition and egoism. In essence, friendship is a model of voluntarily restrained individualism. These men have their own talents and their own views, but they willingly suspend their self-interest for the sake of those whom they love. Friendship becomes a utopia within an individualistic society and is one solution to the anxiety about post-revolutionary social dissolution. It serves as a model of how free and equal citizens could come together, trust one another, and find happiness. Yet ideal masculine love could only be imagined as a refuge from the wider world. The bonds that connect the men of the Cénacle are particularistic and exclusive. Because public life—in the form of either politics or the market—was seen as too isolating and too hostile, individuals could come together only in private.

3

FRIENDS WITH BENEFITS

I hope that you miss me a little, for I miss you terribly. As I get older, I need fewer people, but I need them much more. . . . Each day the number of those with whom I take pleasure in communicating, those to whom I can truly, freely express myself, gets smaller. As a result, sympathy and moral fiber become at the same time all the more necessary and all the more rare.

So wrote François Guizot to Victor de Broglie in September 1832.[1] Although the two men were best friends, their correspondence was rarely affectionate. But in the fall of 1832, France was undergoing a political and social crisis. Cholera was ravaging the population and Casimir Périer, the man whose strong leadership had stabilized France after 1830, had died of it in May. For Broglie and Guizot—men whose fathers had both been guillotined during the Terror—the specter of political instability was always unsettling. The anxieties of the moment led Guizot to reflect on his relationship with Broglie. According to him, one of the great advantages of this bond was that he could say anything to a true friend. In his account, friendship is a relationship built on trust, one in which individuals can speak the unguarded truth and reveal all of their thoughts and feelings—it is this that makes friendship special and different from all other social relations.

This chapter explores how early nineteenth-century elites described their bonds with one another, focusing on the pleasures of friendship. It looks at the connection between friendship and sexual desire in an era without a sharp distinction between erotic and platonic love. Friendship was also seen as a source of psychic satisfaction, as friends explored with one another the dimensions of their selves and their psychology. Men and women of the time did not write of themselves as enclosed beings who acted or felt in isolation. Instead, they posited that they were permeable creatures who were deeply imbricated with one another, both physically and emotionally. Crucially, too, friendship was understood to be a source of trust. Normative sources such as novels and conduct books praised friendship as a site of transparency, while friends celebrated their ability to communicate openly in their letters. Friendship, then, became a source of trust, pleasure, and cohesion, all of which were seen as lacking in an otherwise hostile and suspicious society. As did Guizot in his letter to Broglie, men and women often made sharp distinctions between the world of friends and the wider social scene where suspicion was the only possible attitude. This is not to say that friendship was the only space of intimacy in the early nineteenth century. Brothers and sisters were often close, for instance.[2] But by definition friendship cannot exist without some level of intimacy and trust, in contrast to the ties of kin. For this reason, discussions of friendship are a particularly interesting window into the affective imaginations of post-revolutionary elites.

Beyond the general connection between friendship, cohesion, and trust, the specific workings of friendship were highly gendered. Bonds between men revolved around the notion of similarity, connection, and generosity. Friendship was supposed to motivate men to act outside their narrow self-interest. As a result, male friendship was seen as establishing trust in the form of loyalty. Male friends were to act in solidarity with one another and be faithful to their commitments to one another. In contrast, bonds between men and women were linked less to action and more toward interiority. These ties attached men to a private world of the affections and self-reflection as women and men served as each other's confidantes. Women also helped situate men in their social milieus. They maintained bonds among men and channeled male emotions. These dimensions of friendship illuminate the gendering of social relations and sentiment in the nineteenth century. Historians have suggested that after the Revolution, both privacy and the emotions were feminized, as men were understood to be rational, public actors. Yet the picture that emerges here is more complicated. While male friendship was bound up in discussions of public affairs, not private feeling, men's friendships with women could be highly emotionally expressive. Thus the qualities of emotionality and interiority were gendered, but were attached more to relationships than to bodies.

In order to look at the inner workings of personal ties in the early nineteenth century, this chapter draws on novels, conduct books, memoirs, and letters. To a remarkable degree, there is a confluence between normative descriptions of friendship and the expectations that the men and women studied here had of their bonds as revealed in their life writings. This similarity highlights a shared set of cultural expectations about how friends were supposed to act, although of course individuals did not always behave according to cultural norms. For one, there were certainly plenty of times when they disappointed their friends; alternately, although they might have stated that they were revealing their innermost thoughts and feelings to their intimates, we cannot know whether they actually did. What this chapter is primarily interested in, then, is not what friends felt for one another, but how they spoke about their bonds. Thus I rely largely on correspondence because letter writing was central to defining, creating, and maintaining personal ties as well as analyzing the self and its relationship to others. Yet letters, like memoirs, were not transparent reflections of correspondents' feelings. They followed clear conventions, some of which are discussed below. Scholars of epistolarity are also interested in the fictions of personal correspondence—that letters are particularly honest and open effusions of the heart, or that they serve as a substitute for conversation and thus can shrink the geographical distance between separated friends.[3] Indeed, the men and women discussed here often claimed to write the unvarnished truth to one another and wrote of their desire for one another's physical presence. But what is interesting is not the emotional truth of these statements, but rather what they say about a cultural understanding of the workings of friendship.

In particular, this chapter draws heavily on the letters of those in Guizot's circle, due to the great quantity of available correspondence between his friends, both male and female. Many of the patterns of epistolary communication discussed here are visible in the correspondence of Chateaubriand, Béranger, and their intimates, however. It also examines discussions of friendship that range from the Napoleonic era to the Third Republic, as the individuals studied here communicated with one another in ways that remained consistent over time. Thus I do not claim that friendship became linked with cohesion and trust only in the period between 1815 and 1848. Rather, because of its strong association with these qualities, friendship was one way to imagine a solution to the problem of an atomized and suspicious society.

A RECIPROCAL AND SINCERE TRUST: FINDING AND REVEALING THE SELF

The connection between trust and friendship is visible in novels and conduct books where friends appear as each other's confidantes, sharing all their thoughts, joys, and sorrows. For instance, in the 1816 *L'Honnête homme à la cour et dans le monde*, the author states the following in a chapter titled "Des Avantages de la véritable Amitié": "And what is sweeter than this reciprocal and sincere trust, where the friends share their most secret thoughts with each other?"[4] Alternately, consider a passage from Mme de Souza's 1801 epistolary novel *Charles et Marie* in which the author ties together friendship, personal revelation, and the self. The novel opens with a letter from Charles to an unnamed friend, one that begins by describing a journal Charles had been keeping: "I followed your advice: each day I give an account of the different sentiments that I felt. I thought that you would read my journal and I told myself: My friend will be a second conscience for me; I will speak to him or will speak to myself with the same sincerity."[5] In this case, self-reflection went hand in hand with friendship, as Charles wrote his diary at the instigation of his friend and with his friend in mind as he composed his entries.[6] In this novel, accessing one's interiority was constructed as a dialogic process, one that was undertaken with another. Charles scrutinized his moods, emotions, psychological makeup, and anxieties for his friend. In other words, it was not just that he was revealing everything to his friend; it was also that without his correspondent, there would be far less to reveal.

Friendship was also commonly associated with the term "épanchement," or the verb form "épancher," meaning effusion or outpouring, as authors and friends spoke of the "épanchements d'amitié."[7] This was how friends were supposed to communicate with one another, as they were to reveal everything. Hence, in the epilogue to Eugène Sue's *Les Mystères de Paris*, the German prince Henri d'Herkaüsen-Oldenzaal writes a letter to his best friend in which he states that he needs to "épancher" his heart into his friend's.[8] And toward the end of this letter he claims, "I have never hidden my most secret thoughts, good or bad, from you."[9] The friend was one's confidante, even more, perhaps, than the lover, and was willing to receive whatever one needed to disclose. As such, the trust between friends was supposed to be absolute, for one had to believe that the all-knowing friend would keep the details of such *épanchements* to him- or herself. Such a vocabulary of friendship also established that the friend was the recipient of parts of the self. In pouring one's heart out, one was placing elements of oneself in the friend's body. Indeed in much of the language of friendship, the body is figured as permeable, as if men and women did not see themselves as enclosed selves, but open to their chosen intimates.

Letters between friends also celebrated personal revelation as a special property of friendship, a notion central to Guizot's statement to Broglie from 1832. Many of the same attributes of this bond can be seen in an 1841 letter from Dorothée de Courlande, duchesse de Dino, to Guizot's friend Barante, who was returning to France after an unhappy term as ambassador to Russia. In Dino's letter, she states she was looking forward to his arrival and then writes, "Retired enough to be able to give time to my friends, but not too retired to be ignorant of the things that would interest you, you can unload your judgments, opinions, reprimands, and surprises into my heart with complete security. And you will find in the relaxation and the total abandon of your trust and our communication a tranquility and a well-being that you probably searched for in vain elsewhere."[10] Mme de Dino was here offering herself as a confidante to whom Barante could tell anything. In her account, such communication would do him a world of good, as Dino associates a host of positive qualities like "relaxation," "tranquility," and "well-being" with their relationship. To our twenty-first-century ears, such language makes it sound as if their friendship was an extended therapy session. She wanted him to find a kind of psychic calm after a difficult period. Of course, such a notion is highly anachronistic, but Dino's letter makes friendship central to self-revelation and emotional well-being. Alongside such a statement about the benefits of their friendship, Dino also invoked the idea that Barante's ability to be open with her made their bond a unique one. In her reckoning, Barante had no doubt sought such relief elsewhere, but only in the context of their friendship could he find another who would accept the outpourings of his heart. Friendship was thus a haven in a heartless world.

MALE BONDS AND THE SEARCH FOR LOYALTY AND CONNECTION

While friendship in general produced trust and cohesion, it did so in distinctly gendered ways. The ties of male friendship revolved around notions of similarity and union, as men spoke of each other as another self or as part of their very self. Friends were to act in each other's interest and with generosity; they proved their loyalty by offering direct financial assistance or by activating patronage networks. Hence, these bonds were to establish solidarity in an otherwise anomic society. Yet, except at moments of extreme personal stress, male friendship did not demand emotional expression or personal intimacies.

Instead, the free communication between men was frequently confined to discussions of public affairs. While these bonds often involved a play between distance and proximity, the language of male friendship can also sound strikingly erotic to our ears. In a period before homosexuality emerged as an identity, the fluidity of social and sexual boundaries allowed men to describe their desire for one another in physical terms.

Although novels and conduct books depicted the exchange of confidences as central to bonds between men, in practice, their correspondence was not particularly personal. Letters between the men of the doctrinaire circle typically revolved around discussions of political and scholarly matters—that is to say, news of public life. They sent lengthy reports to one another about the Parisian political scene, making personal correspondence a crucial source of information for those outside Paris. Friends in the provinces thus thanked one another when receiving the latest political news, stating that without such correspondence, they would have been in the dark as to what was happening in the capital.[11] During the Restoration, when many of the doctrinaires maintained active scholarly agendas, these men also discussed their writing projects, gave advice to one another, and offered editorial assistance.[12] Given that shared politics and intellectual endeavors held these men together, correspondence was clearly an important medium for political and intellectual cohesion. Yet, although they sent each other lengthy letters at regular intervals, their correspondence contained relatively little in the way of personal news. Information about the writer's family life was often confined to a brief comment at the end of the letter. Indeed, it might even be as short and nondescriptive as a sentence like "Everyone around me is well," as Guizot wrote to Barante in 1832.[13]

The Guizot/Barante correspondence is especially revealing because their friendship was conducted entirely by letters during the 1830s, as Barante was living abroad during this decade as an ambassador. His only tie to his friends was through letters and he often expressed a desire that Guizot write him with more frequency. But what he wanted was not outpourings of intimate revelation, but an exchange of news on domestic and foreign affairs. For example, in 1834, he requested that Guizot "tell me your news and converse a bit with me. It has been a long time since I have heard anything from you."[14] His letter focused on a discussion of politics and diplomacy, suggesting that it was this that gave Barante pleasure. His epistolary exchange with Guizot was a form of intellectual sustenance and a way to maintain a tie to his intellectual milieu in France. The content of these letters may not have been intensely personal, as only one paragraph at the end of this letter contained information about how he and his family were doing. Nonetheless, their correspondence was still intended to build forms of connection and allow friends to reaffirm their commitments to each other.

Similarly, these men were rarely openly affectionate in their letters. As with personal news, loving words tended to be confined to the end of letters and were often very brief. In many cases, such expressions of sentiment were formulaic, such as the closings "tout à vous" or "mille amitiés."[15] In other instances, although they were short, they might refer more to the specific nature of the relationship or to the content of the rest of the letter. For instance, in June 1826, Rémusat sent Guizot a long, six-page letter with information on the political situation in Grenoble, his writings on the subject of education, and his thoughts on religious affairs, a topic intimately connected to the state of the French educational system at this time. At the end of this letter, Rémusat included a short paragraph in a different vein. In it, he wrote, "A thousand affectionate feelings to everyone around you. . . . I love you with my heart and my reason."[16]

This last statement referred to the nature of the two men's relationship, as Guizot was Rémusat's mentor during the 1820s. It was also a reference to their shared political and theoretical project, and to their commitment to the sovereignty of reason.[17] Lastly, loving Guizot with his reason was an allusion to the content of his letter. Both men were concerned that Catholic educational institutions inculcated passion and hatred and did not develop students' rational faculties. This statement of affection was, however, relatively restrained; Rémusat did not, for instance, describe why he loved his friend, detail the history of his affection, or go into much depth concerning the exact nature of his feelings. This was also the only explicit discussion in this letter of the sentiments Rémusat had for Guizot, except for the use of the salutation "mon cher ami." But by all accounts, this was a close and significant friendship for both men. In his memoirs, Rémusat returned again and again to a discussion of the exact nature of his bond with Guizot. After the two men split over politics in 1840, their estrangement led Rémusat to question whether Guizot ever really loved him. Concluding that he did, Rémusat repeatedly proffered as proof of Guizot's affection a statement that Guizot made to someone else. According to Rémusat, Guizot had once said that "the two men he [Guizot] had loved the most were [Pierre Paul] Royer-Collard and myself."[18] That he displayed a scrupulous attention to the state of his relationship with Guizot in his memoirs implies that his friendship with

Guizot meant a great deal to him. In their letters, however, the affection has to be read between the lines. The writing of the letter itself was to serve as a sign of how much the correspondents cared for each other and valued their intellectual, political, and personal partnership.

Although male/male correspondence was usually governed by restraint, there were a few instances where these men's letters were openly—even wildly—emotionally expressive. During moments of great anxiety or personal distress, such as after the death of a loved one, friends often included outpourings of sentiment and exchanges of confidences in their letters.[19] In these cases, friends offered support by allowing one another to grieve. Guizot's 1832 letter to Broglie in which he spoke of his need for his friend and the importance of their relationship occurred at one such moment. In a correspondence that lasted for more than fifty years, this was the most emotionally laden discussion of their tie. The illness and death of Guizot's first wife, née Pauline de Meulan, in 1827 also occasioned an extraordinary series of letters between Guizot and his male friends, ones that were meant to be both deeply emotional and extremely revealing. For instance, in a letter to Barante, Guizot wrote the following about his mental state:

> I feel detached from myself, without any intimate personality; I belong entirely to activity. . . . Events, ideas, how much influence each one of us can exercise, all this occupies me and will continue to occupy me. It is the interior that is lacking. You know what it is for an honest worker who has finished his workday, who returns to his home, to find his wife, his children, his room, his fire, to rest in the center of this personal and pleasant space where he does not have to think of anything other than himself, his emotions, and his happiness. I will never finish my day, I will never return home. . . . I will always live outside, I will always be working.[20]

At one level, this passage was meant to reassure Barante. Despite his devastating loss, Guizot would not give up his work as a scholar, political activist, and journalist. But in Guizot's account, this was all that was left. He had been hollowed out; his sense of public duty remained but not his interiority. Part of the problem was precisely that his wife had helped him access his private life and the world of the affections. Now that she was gone, he could not find any respite from the realm of public activity. To be sure, this was an elaboration of the separate-spheres model, as his wife had been the guardian of his interiority who provided him with a refuge from his working life. At the same time, even if his discussion focused precisely on this lack of an inner life, he was still describing his mental state to his friend. In this case, Guizot was acting as if he could understand and come to terms with the extent of his loss through engaging in such intimate revelation. Such a statement also shows how mourning reversed customary epistolary practices between men. Most of the content of this letter is personal; a discussion of political matters was relegated to two short paragraphs at the end of the letter.

In turn, Guizot's male friends responded in kind. They wrote of their love for him and stated that they, too, shared his grief. This was a particular theme of Rémusat's letters. In one written just before Guizot's wife died, Rémusat writes, "I suffer knowing that you are still worried and unhappy. What can I tell you that your heart cannot guess and your reason does not already know? I have only one need, and that is to repeat that everything, fears, anxieties, hopes, everything is shared by my brotherly love, and that my heart unites with yours a thousand times a day."[21] Rémusat had been close to Guizot's wife, for she had served as a surrogate mother to him after his own mother died in 1824. Less than a year before, his first wife had also died.[22] Rémusat was here saying that he could empathize with Guizot's feelings and enter into his emotional life as a result of his own losses. While the control of one's emotions was seen as a necessary masculine attribute in this era, there were moments when it was acceptable to appear weak and at the mercy of one's feelings. During these times, friends needed to provide one another with manifestations of affection and remembrance. This was what Rémusat was offering here, for he was stating that he not only mourned Pauline Guizot but also shared the burden of Guizot's grief.

Rémusat's letter illustrates some of the conventional ways in which men talked about their friendships with one another. When, for instance, he stated that "that my heart unites with yours," he posits an essential connection between himself and Guizot and a physicality to their relationship that joins their bodies together. This was another instance in which individuals saw themselves as permeable beings. As an element in the language of male friendship, this convention made male bonds into sources of connection in an otherwise atomized society. Such terms also described how friends were similar to one another, as their identities and emotional lives were bound up with one another. The physical intimacy contained within the language of male friendship here is also notable. The men of the period frequently wrote of their desire for a bodily connection with one another and did so in terms that strike us as remarkably homoerotic. Men demonstrated restraint in discussing their affections, but not in describing their desire for one another's physical presence. Such a language speaks to a particular understanding of the boundaries between love and friendship and to the nature and possibilities of same-sex love in the post-revolutionary era.

Consider, for instance, a passage in Ludovic Vitet's biography of his best friend, Charles Tanneguy Duchâtel, when he writes of how they became close during the Restoration. Both men were doctrinaire politicians during the July Monarchy and close friends of Guizot. In this posthumous biography, Vitet writes:

> From our first encounter, . . . by an almost simultaneous movement, he came to me just as I came to him; then we sought out each other's company in preference to others, and in just a few days our lives were united: between our spirits and our hearts an absolute trust was quickly established which nothing ever troubled. We had such a need for one another that soon we could hardly spend a day without exchanging our thoughts, and yet in everything we had to have the same tastes and the same needs.[23]

Vitet's biography, written long after his first meeting with Duchâtel, should be seen less as an accurate description of their relationship than an engagement with the language of male friendship. Here, friendship revolves around a trust and similarity that arose from a simultaneous desire to be with each other. Vitet also conveys this notion of sameness by using the word "exchange," as he presents a model by which his thoughts become those of Duchâtel and vice versa. Indeed, their friendship can be complete only after the two achieve this similarity.

Vitet's description of his relationship with Duchâtel relies on two sources that were central to how the men of the early nineteenth century imagined their friendships. The first was Cicero's *De Amicitia*, a widely reprinted work in the era. Cicero defines friendship as "nothing else than an accord in all things, human and divine, conjoined with mutual goodwill and affection."[24] Friendship also unites individuals together, or in his words, it makes "one soul out of many."[25] Vitet's passage calls on this idea of similarity, as well as the conception of the friend as another self, as he and Duchâtel were so alike that they could serve as twins. Many of these notions would be taken up by Michel de

Montaigne, whose essay "Of Friendship" served as *the* model for writing about the relationship in the early nineteenth century.[26] For Montaigne, friendship created powerful forms of connection that joined men together. He writes, "In the friendship I speak of, our souls mingle and blend with each other so completely that they efface the seam that joined them."[27] Montaigne also focused on the simultaneity of desire, as did Vitet. He describes his bond with Étienne de La Boétie in the following terms: "We sought each other before we met. . . . And at our first meeting . . . we found ourselves so taken with each other, so well acquainted, so bound together, that from that time on nothing was so close to us as each other."[28] Montaigne's essay employed terms of physical permeability, with words like "mingle," "blend," "bound," and "close," a language that men of the nineteenth century would use to articulate how the friend became a part of the self.

Vitet language is strikingly homoerotic (as was Montaigne's) as he wrote of the exclusivity of his relationship with Duchâtel and how both men desired each other's presence. Vitet also writes of their "same tastes and the same needs"—words generally associated more with sexual desire than with political belief. Of course, we will never know what the two men felt for each other or what they did behind closed doors, as is the case with Béranger and Manuel, two other best friends whose devotion to each other may have surpassed the boundaries of platonic friendship. Yet this passage was not meant for a private audience but for a very public one, as it was in a biography that celebrated Duchâtel's political career. Speaking in such terms established Vitet's right to write of his friend's life; as his best friend, he knew the man's thoughts better than anyone else did. But it also points to a lack of self-consciousness about the language of male friendship and its connection to sexuality, one that would mark other early nineteenth-century writings about these bonds.

Crucially, the early nineteenth century fell between two eras of repression. In contrast to the Old Regime, homosexual acts were not criminalized during this time. Nor did homosexuality exist as a fixed identity that was connected to medical and criminal pathology, as would be the case at the end of the century. As a result, there was a space—though limited—for toleration of men whose sexual preferences were for other men. Many elites might condemn homosexual behavior at the same time as they were willing to accommodate it on occasion. Napoleon, for instance, relied on the talents of both Cambacérès and Joseph Fiévée and gave them considerable positions of authority in his government, despite the fact that both men were open about their same-sex inclinations. Indeed, the latter lived with his lover Théodore Leclercq, a fact that did not prevent him from becoming prominent in ultra circles in the early years of the Restoration. The case of Astolphe de Custine—the son of one of Chateaubriand's close friends—is also instructive. When his preference for other men became clear, some of his high-society connections cut off contact with him. But not all did, and he was still received in some of the salons of the Faubourg Saint-Germain as well as in Parisian literary circles.[29]

More generally, the post-revolutionary era was one in which certain boundaries—whether between male and female or between forms of affection—were not necessarily fixed. Historians have shown how the social and political upheaval that began at the end of the eighteenth century made way for a great deal of sexual and affective experimentation. For instance, Victoria Thompson states that the unrest of the 1830s and 1840s meant that "sexuality and gender often appeared as fluid." This was, after all, the era in which George Sand dressed as a man. Many novels and plays written during the July Monarchy featured homosexual and bisexual love, cross-dressing, and other acts of gender nonconformity.[30] Likewise, the boundary between love and friendship was porous. Speaking of the pre-Freudian affective understanding, Carroll Smith-Rosenberg writes that the "tendency to view human love and sexuality within a dichotomized universe of deviance and normality, genitality and platonic love, is alien to the emotions and attitudes of the nineteenth century."[31] Thus friendship was often the language of homosexual love; Custine, for instance, called his longtime lover Edward Sainte-Barbe "my best friend."[32] Alternately, the culture of military friendship that grew out of Napoleon's Grande Armée—one that echoed throughout early nineteenth-century literature—encompassed "a broad spectrum of masculine affection and intimacy" that included erotic as well as platonic attachments.[33]

While this fluidity of affective and sexual categories made articulations of same-sex love possible, it also meant that men could discuss their homosocial desire without being seen as necessarily deviant.[34] This is true even among men whose erotic affinities were for women, as was the case with Rémusat and Molé, two of Barante's friends. For instance, in 1831, Rémusat asked Barante, "When will we see each other again? It will make me very happy. . . . It seems that one of the reasons why I cannot come back to myself is that I do not have the conversations like those I had with you. Come back, my dear friend, if only to complete me."[35] Two years later, Molé told Barante, "I miss you more that I can say, with my reason, my spirit, and my friendship. When I am with you, I vanish with you and without you I am a sterile instrument."[36]

Both men described that they needed Barante to make them complete. In Rémusat's case, he stated that he was not whole without Barante and was incapable of being or knowing himself without his friend. In the absence of their conversations, he claims to be unable to think and function properly, a formulation that tied male friendship to intellectual endeavors. In Molé's account, Barante was his animating spirit, and without his friend he was not truly alive. But when he and Barante were together, they could fuse their existence. Here, the friend appears not much as a double, as for Cicero and Vitet, but as a necessary component of the self and its functioning, revealing both notions of the porous self and the openness with which men could discuss their need for each other's physical presence.

Yet while these discussions of the need for the friend convey considerable affection and were meant to indicate the importance of this bond for the letter writer, such statements are not quite the same as the open and profuse descriptions of love that were so common in correspondence between men and women. In this respect, the language of male friendship could contain some elements of restraint. These bonds were not constructed around detailed revelations of sentiment, but rather around closeness. Statements of similarity indicated that there was no mental or emotional divergence between friends, as did the assertions that the friend's physical presence was required in order to ensure the proper functioning of the self. In an atomized society, friendship was to fight against the forces of isolation. The idea that a friend was a twin, another self, or an element of the self made the friend into a unique, chosen companion. Indeed, the notions of union and similarity also help explain the culture of male emotional restraint: if the friend was another self, he had no need to be told what his friend was feeling.

These understandings of male friendship also help explain some of the ways that bonds between men functioned in practice. Men provided financial support for each other and access to patronage networks. They were to prove their love through action and not necessarily through scrupulous accounts of their affections. In a world where many feared that narrow self-interest was the only motivation, male friendship served as an exception. Because emotion was understood to be a force that compelled action, love could lead men to act outside the bounds of their own self-interest.[37] Hence, male friendship offered the prospect of loyalty and the promise of assistance when needed. This is what Balzac imagines in *Illusions perdues*, in which he creates a world of masculine solidarity within the confines of the Cénacle.

Providing for friends in times of need was a clearly defined cultural norm in the early nineteenth century. One conduct book from the period told the male audience that we are to "share our money with our friends when they are poor and when we become rich."[38] The male friends of novels are also figured by their generosity. Early on in Stendhal's *The Red and the Black*, Julien Sorel's friend Fouqué, a timber merchant, offers to make Julien his business partner; Julien refuses, dreaming of a grander life. Later, when Julien is in prison, Fouqué thinks of giving all his money to help Julien escape. Male friendship and generosity went hand in hand in Balzac's novels as well. Such is the case in *Illusions perdues*, while in his *Le Cousin Pons*, written between 1846 and 1847, the title character wills his valuable art collection to his best friend, Schmucke, the one man who treats him with kindness and generosity. Certainly some of the men studied here saw aiding each other as important acts of friendship. For Chateaubriand and Béranger, the connection between friendship and financial assistance was particularly noteworthy, as both men lived much of their lives under the constant threat of penury. In 1820, when Chateaubriand was in considerable monetary difficulties, his friend Hyde de Neuville proposed that he lend Chateaubriand 800 F per year until Chateaubriand achieved financial stability (Chateaubriand did not accept Hyde's proposal).[39] In the years of the July Monarchy, he and Béranger offered to provide pecuniary assistance to each other. Both men declined such aid, but each regarded the gesture as a proof of the strength of their bond.[40] Béranger was also famous for both his generosity toward his friends and his reliance on them. For instance, during the Restoration he supported his friend Rouget de Lisle, the author of "La Marseillaise," who had fallen on hard times, while in the 1830s he helped his friend Louis Bérard who was experiencing financial difficulties.[41]

Beyond such direct monetary exchanges, the men studied here frequently asked for and received favors from one another. During the July Monarchy, Béranger's letters to his friend Pierre Lebrun contain a steady stream of requests on behalf of Béranger's friends and acquaintances. As director of the Imprimerie royale, Lebrun had any number of positions he could fill with Béranger's contacts.[42] Béranger also arranged for Rouget de Lisle to have a state pension from the government right after the Revolution of 1830, which had the secondary benefit of ensuring that he was no longer responsible for supporting a troublesome and depressive friend.[43] But it was Guizot's friends who benefited the most from their relationships with him, and he typically took seriously his duty to provide for his friends. For instance, in the early years of the July Monarchy, he created the position of Inspector general of historical monuments for Ludovic Vitet and put Vitet on the Conseil d'État. Guizot also helped Barante's sons find positions in the diplomatic and the prefectorial service.[44]

In their requests for favors and positions, men used a sentimental vocabulary to motivate their friends to take action, and the performance of favors offered proof of love. This is visible in a series of letters from the 1830s from Barante to Guizot in which Barante sought a position for his children's tutor, a man named Louis François Bellaguet. When Barante first hired Bellaguet, he promised that once the children were grown, he would find Bellaguet a post as a *fonctionnaire*, and in 1834 Barante began to search for such a position. Because he was serving as an ambassador, he needed to rely on his friends who remained in France, and he asked Guizot, then minister of public instruction, to aid him. Presumably, Guizot could provide a position to a promising young man. When Barante made this request, he appealed to Guizot in two ways. The first was by describing Bellaguet's merits, such as his intelligence and good character. But he relied primarily on personal appeals, telling Guizot that his aid would be "a true service of friendship." In another letter, Barante described it as "a benefit of friendship that I ask of you."[45] As Barante's requests continued through the years, he touched more on the emotions and less on Bellaguet's qualities, indicating that he considered the obligations of friendship to be the stronger argument. Thus, in 1837 he asked Guizot to "give me this sign of recognition"; in another letter, he called the favor a "special sign of your remembrance."[46] Here, Barante suggested that if Guizot did not perform the favor, he did not value their friendship.

At the same time, Barante articulated that his own obligation to Bellaguet arose out of affection. In one letter, he wrote that Bellaguet "has given me proofs of affection and devotion that have created a real obligation for me."[47] Barante needed to obtain a post for Bellaguet because not doing so would be a failure of honor—he had given his word—and a failure of the demands of love on Guizot's part. Here, Barante both connects and distinguishes love and honor, a crucial attribute for elite men of the nineteenth century. Both created obligation, as Barante was trying to create a chain of duty that connected Bellaguet to him and himself to Guizot. Love and duty were powerful motivators for action that also existed outside of interest. Speaking in these terms allowed Barante to request that Guizot act for his benefit and not Guizot's own while using a language that was more culturally acceptable than that of self-interest. Despite these similarities, honor was generalized, as men were to behave honorably at all times, whereas friendship was a particularized affection that bound intimates. Notably, Barante does not discuss whether he had any affection for Bellaguet; his duty toward the tutor arose only from his desire to fulfill his promises and not from sentiment. In contrast, Guizot was to take on this request because of the reciprocal love that tied him and Barante together, one that placed special claims on Guizot. In the end, Guizot did find a place for Bellaguet, but in 1839 he replaced Barante's protégé with his own. Barante indicated that this act was a clear sign that Guizot did not reciprocate his love and he gave Guizot an ultimatum: if Guizot did not find a post for Bellaguet, Barante would break off their friendship.[48] When Guizot failed to do so, Barante put an end to their friendly correspondence. One year later, though, it recommenced—but only after Guizot honored Barante's request for a position for his son.[49]

Barante used affection as a way to activate assistance, and this exchange shows how individuals relied on sentiment to solve the problem of individualism in an interest-driven society. The prospect of a world where men and women pursued nothing but their own gain was a distressing spectacle for observers of the time, one that Barante discussed in his scholarly works.[50] It also provided a practical problem: how could one persuade others to undertake tasks that were not necessarily in their immediate self-interest? In this instance, Guizot had provided one of his own protégés with a position as a *fonctionnaire*, but Barante wanted him to reverse his actions and aid someone in his entourage. For Guizot, this would be to act in Barante's interest and not his own. Doing so would take time and effort; he would then need to find another place for his protégé. Barante's solution was to appeal to love and duty, two acceptable spurs for action, unlike self-interest. Guizot's failure to bend to Barante's appeal offered evidence that his affection was not reciprocated. Once Guizot aided Barante's son, their friendship could be restored. This act offered proof of love and remembrance. No doubt he regarded procuring a position for his son as more important than finding one for the son's former tutor.

Male friendship, then, was understood to create cohesion and trust in the form of loyalty. Men were to support one another and saw their ties as leading one another to action. Providing benefits to a friend was a form of activity that was both self-interested (in that the friend was another self) and took one outside the self (because, in fact, the friend was not the self). As a result, bonds between men were understood to create solidarity within the confines of an individualistic social order. For men, however, action was to provide more proof of affection than was intimate revelation.

MEN AND WOMEN IN A WORLD OF EMOTION AND INTERIORITY

In both novels and conduct manuals from the early nineteenth century, friendship was usually described as uniting two or more members of the same sex. Certainly Balzac's vision of friendship in *Illusions perdues* was of an all-masculine fraternity. Yet the men and women studied here hardly lived in such a gender-segregated world; Chateaubriand, Guizot, and Béranger all had close ties to women. Indeed, both Chateaubriand and Guizot maintained that their relations with women were easier and more pleasant than were those with men. In Guizot's words, "All things being equal, a woman is always more amiable than a man."[51] In these friendships, men searched for confidantes who were to help them access their emotions and interiority. Male/female friendship established bonds of trust through the open exchange of intimate thoughts and feelings. If men provided each other with psychic relief during exceptional moments, such as after the loss of a loved one, men and women were to do the same for each other on a more consistent basis.

Women also frequently conveyed affection between men and managed their emotional lives. Such patterns of communication reveal that the men of the early nineteenth century did have authorization to discuss their inner lives and emotional states. After all, this was the era of Romanticism, a cultural and literary movement that praised the expression of emotions and personal self-reflection.[52] Because men were generally more restrained with one another than with women, it was women who were to anchor men in a private realm of the emotions and social ties. While the construction of male/female bonds challenged a division between a masculine public sphere and a feminine private one, it also relied on the notion that the realm of the emotional and the social belonged to women. Women served as gatekeepers to men's private lives and social milieus.

Many of the differences between men's bonds with each other and their ties with women are articulated in a conduct book titled *Nouveau guide de la politesse* by Louis Damien Éméric. Written for a male audience, it contains the following statement about friendships between men and women:

> Friendship with women is sweeter, pleasanter, and more soothing than friendship between men: the female friend pardons our frailties with gentleness, and every day her counsel pierces the heart with such delicacy that she makes us feel the charms of hope. Friendship between men is stronger and perhaps more useful during important events. One

> is the flower that every day brightens our moments of peace by alleviating our troubles; the other is a robust and vigorous plant whose wondrous sap gives us new life even if it does not follow the rules of good manners.[53]

What is immediately apparent in this telling is how easy, enjoyable, and emotional friendships between men and women are, hence Éméric's use of terms like "sweeter," "pleasanter," "soothing," "heart," and "charming." In this case, too, the functions of consolation and lifting psychological burdens are particularly gendered. With a female friend, a man can open up and reveal his private, flawed self. It is this that makes these relationships so restful, as the ability of men to talk about their troubles with women has psychologically calming effects. By contrast, male friendship is less pleasant. Éméric's assertion that these bonds are not conducted according to the rules of politeness implies that honesty and roughness characterize male friendships. These relationships, however, connect men to masculine virtues as they make men stronger and more vigorous. Éméric uses a remarkably homoerotic phrasing when he describes how the "wondrous sap" of masculine ties restores men. Such terms point to a lack of self-consciousness about language in a pre-Freudian era, one in which open expressions of male desire were permissible. This was, after all, a normative work, one intended to map the contours of friendship for a literate public. But the benefits of male/male friendships have little to do with interiority. Instead, they help men succeed in public life; they are useful "during important events." In this respect, Éméric's account fits with the patterns of male friendship traced above, as men aided one another and proved their love through action.

Éméric's description of the functioning of male/female friendship is also born out in the correspondence patterns of the individuals studied here. For one, relations between men and women involved expressions of distance, fitting with Éméric's notion that these ties "follow the rules of good manners." Thus, unlike male bonds, they require some level of formality. Indeed, the forms of address that men and women used with one another indicate a respectful distance. While men used "mon cher ami" with one another, they often used "chère madame" or even "madame" with their female friends, while women frequently employed the salutation "cher monsieur" in their letters to men.[54] The play of distance and intimacy between men and women—and the way in which distance could facilitate intimacy—can be seen in the correspondence between Hortense Allart and Sainte-Beuve from the 1840s. The two were former lovers turned best friends; according to her side of the correspondence she was still in love with him, but he wanted only a friendship. Their letters contain detailed descriptions of their views on literature, philosophy, religion, politics, their mutual friends, as well as their emotional lives and their feelings for each other. They also spoke of the love affairs they were pursing; in Allart's case at least, she discussed her sex life, as when she wrote that her relationship with Henry Bulwer-Lytton contained "the delights of a delicate and powerful sensuousness."[55] Yet in her letters, she often called him "monsieur"; had this salutation been used between men, it would have indicated the absence of a personal connection. Here, though, this formality did not preclude the intense exchange of intimacies. Instead, it served as a mark of respect for both him as a person and for the nature of the relationship, as she was signifying that she understood and accepted the fact that they would not reignite their love affair. In this case, the hallmarks of distance allowed them to have the relationship they did have—a close friendship.

As was true with Allart and Sainte-Beuve, men and women wrote to each other as confidantes and men turned to women to be the bearers of their secrets. For instance, Chateaubriand's letters from the 1820s to his former mistress Cordélia Greffulhe, comtesse de Castellane, are filled with the details of his health, financial situation, personal preoccupations, and likes and dislikes. Likewise, Béranger relied on Hortense Allart and his friend Judith Cauchois-Lemaire for such revelations. In 1834, he wrote to the latter about his melancholy and his increasing sense of isolation as he aged. He then stated, "You know that I have always had the pleasure of confiding my thoughts to you, as I am sure that I can count on your complete discretion as well as your friendship."[56] Such a statement was intended to reveal how special she was to him, as well as the degree of trust that he placed in her. She would not betray Béranger's confidences to others. Guizot had a string of female confidantes—Mme de Broglie, then after she died in 1838 Gabrielle Henriette Catherine Laure de Daunant de Gasparin, and then Juliette Dutilleul, comtesse Mollien, after Gasparin's death in 1864. Broglie and Gasparin were two of the only friends with whom he discussed his disappointment with his younger son, Guillaume, and his correspondence with Broglie includes what were meant to be exhaustive reflections on his mental state and family life.[57] Thus one letter from 1835 describes an inability to achieve true happiness. He states, "During the moments when I have been the happiest, I always felt that I could not attain all the happiness that was given to me. . . . It always seemed that a part of the blessings fell to the ground before they were able to penetrate into my soul."[58] And while he was relatively terse about the state of his family life with his male friends, his letters to women were considerably more detailed. In the same letter, he told Mme de Broglie about his children who had just returned from a trip taking the waters: "They are doing wonderfully. The baths and showers fortified my little Pauline more than I could have hoped for. Guillaume is very well, always a good and sweet creature who does not suspect and will never suspect what the pure blue of his eyes means to me. Henriette is more lively and serene than ever."[59] Guizot's reference to the blue of his son's eyes is not clear; he may have been referring to his son's resemblance to Guillaume's mother, née Elisa Dillon, who had died two years earlier after giving birth to Guillaume. But certainly this was something that Mme de Broglie would have known, as if this letter was part of an extended conversation about his personal and sentimental life. In this case, correspondence was intended to serve as a form of self-exploration. Guizot's memoirs were not particularly introspective, and instead focused on his public life, while his letters to his male friends were typically not as personal as those to his female friends. Thus female confidantes were to facilitate reflections on interiority and a scrupulous detailing of the state of his soul.

Broglie's letters in which she responded with descriptions of her mental state matched the tone and content of Guizot's letters. During the 1830s, she was increasingly melancholic, and in one letter from 1837 she claims to have diagnosed what was wrong with her. In her words, "I was tired when I left Paris, not bodily or spiritually, but in an intermediary region; at least for me, it is precisely the link between the mind and the body that becomes exhausted, even though neither my health nor my rational capacities feel it, I hope, but it still makes me incapable of many things."[60] Broglie and Guizot were united by their shared Calvinist faith, and the introspective nature of their letters may have owed something to a Protestant sense of self-examination. Yet Guizot was not the only individual to whom she turned for such revelation; in the 1810s and 1820s, when she was especially close to Barante, he specifically asked her to write to him about her mental state and her sorrows.[61] Her letters to her female friends, including Mme de Castellane (the same woman who was Chateaubriand's mistress and then friend) and Mme Anisson du Perron (Barante's sister), also contained statements of similar introspective intensity.[62] Likewise, men often relied on their sisters to serve as loving confidantes, as did Barante and Chateaubriand.[63] In this respect, women—either as friends or as sisters—set the patterns of male/female bonds. Men had to play by women's rules in their correspondence. Women had different expectations of friendships than men did with each other. Friends were not to come to each other's aid in the public realm, but to provide psychological relief by giving each other the opportunity to describe and understand their mental states.

Similarly, if profusions of affection were not typical in letters between men, they were both customary and expected in letters between men and women, as they were in female/female correspondence.[64] Chateaubriand's letters to Mme de Castellane and to his adviser Mme de Duras consistently contained expressions of how much he valued their friendship and how much he cared for them.[65] Likewise, Mme de Broglie's letters to Guizot were intensely affectionate. In one she states, "I can tell you that in thinking of the gifts I have received from God, I placed friendships like yours at the top of the list."[66] In return, his letters to his female friends were intended to read as being highly emotional and even wildly, almost passionately, loving. For example, in one from 1845, Guizot wrote the following to Gasparin when at his country home:

> When are you coming to see me? I want precise details. I like to think about our conversations. You must know how much pleasure it gives me to see you, to talk with you. I know you well, and I want you to know that no one thinks more highly and affectionately of you than I do. The more I know you, the more rare and special I find you to be. I like only what is rare. But I appreciate these things a great deal. The truth, the truth, the truth which is perfectly free, hearts and spirits entirely exposed, the interior and the exterior completely identical and merged, without any lies or difficulties, only this is good, gentle, and charming. But it is charming. I have this with you. And then do you know that you are very witty and that this is also rare and charming? We have so much to say to each other! I have thought of many, many things since we last saw each other. I have told you a few of them. I hold the rest in reserve.[67]

This veritable torrent of affection occupies much of the letter. Here, Guizot makes claims about how much he loves, misses, and needs Gasparin, how special she is to him, and what it is that makes her so unique. She is charming, she is full of life; their conversations are particularly easy and free. According to Guizot, he can be completely himself with her and can achieve a perfect and entire communication—some ultimate transparency—in her presence. Most obviously, he repeats the term "truth" three times to emphasize the fact that the two communicate to each other with total openness. He also reinforces the unspoiled nature of this truth, that it is "perfectly free" and without any shadow of falsity or hindrance ("without any lies or difficulties"). Additionally, there is the phrase "hearts and spirits absolutely exposed." He and Gasparin are to bare their souls to each other and hide nothing from each other. The next phrase reinforces this notion of transparency, as he states that with her, he finds "the interior and the exterior completely identical." According to Guizot, the fact that this is a relationship that is entirely without dissimulation is a special quality, one he can find with few others. As in so many other epistolary testaments to friendship, this bond is constructed as unique.

Chateaubriand's letters to his female friends, including Duras and Castellane, could also be emotionally expressive; crucially, much of his correspondence with the latter constructs an emotional permeability between himself and Castellane. When she set out on a voyage to Italy in 1825 he sent her frequent letters in which he described an emotional attachment to her in two ways. The first was through straightforward descriptions of his affection, as in one letter in which he wrote, "You will see by this that even beyond the mountains your friends follow you with their greetings and that there is no distance for the hearts that are attached to yours."[68] The notion of the attached heart reveals the same idea of physical permeability and connection that pervaded the rhetoric of male friendship. In other letters, Chateaubriand wrote as if Castellane had an emotional influence on him. He described his anxieties that arose when she was in danger or unwell, and wrote of how her sadness made him sad or her happiness gave him a sense of pleasure. For instance, in response to a letter in which she discussed going to a ball, he wrote, "I like to think that you are enjoying yourself. . . . I delight in everything that can make the ones I love happy."[69] This was another manifestation of the notion of the open self that pervaded descriptions of friendship, for here Castellane was understood to be molding Chateaubriand's psychological state through her actions and emotions.

Much of this language is notably erotic as well. After all, Guizot spoke of a longing for Gasparin, while Chateaubriand wrote of his bodily attachment to Castellane, a woman with whom he had recently had a passionate affair. As was true between men, the boundaries between romantic love and platonic friendship were not necessarily sharp. For instance, Guizot and Gasparin's relationship was never physical, but they considered becoming lovers in the mid-1830s.[70] Alternately, Chateaubriand had a habit of remaining close with his ex-mistresses, including Castellane as well as Delphine de Custine, née

Sabran, and Hortense Allart. His relationship with Mme Récamier is illustrative as well. The two had an affair that began in the early years of the Restoration, but by the regime's closing they were no longer physically intimate. Yet she remained his companion and the two considered marrying each other after his wife died.[71] Such a relationship does not fit with our notions of what a love affair should be nor what a friendship is; in this case, our own categories cannot contain the dimensions of this relationship.

Men and women could even be open about their romantic interest in one another, as were Hyde de Neuville and Mme de Montcalm, two of Chateaubriand's friends. In one letter from August 1817, she wrote the following to him when he was ambassador to the United States: "Our relations have a romantic tinge to them, one that might be dangerous if we were younger and if a thousand ties did not separate us and if you were less absorbed by a mistress who has taken over all of your affections and who is so terribly jealous of all of your thoughts that you are not allowed the least bit of distraction; this mistress is politics."[72] Their letters spoke of an erotic affinity that never developed into an affair. But if they were not lovers, they could be friends, ones who wrote as if their tie might have had a different cast in different circumstances.

Nor did these men and women have difficulty with relationships that included unreciprocated love. This was the case in the bond between Allart and Sainte-Beuve; her love went unreturned but not her friendship. Similarly, the bond between Duras and Chateaubriand straddled the border between love and friendship. By all accounts, she was in love with him, but he was uninterested in becoming her lover. Except for a lack of physical intimacy, however, they behaved liked lovers. He told her that he loved her more than he loved anyone else and she was constantly jealous of his ties to other women.[73] When he and Récamier began their affair, he hid the relationship to assuage Duras's suspicions.[74] Such an insistence on the monopoly of his affections seems outside the rules of friendship, a bond that is generally not so exclusive. Certainly, these men and women conceived that there was a distinction between friendship and romantic love. After all, without such an understanding, Montcalm's statement to Hyde de Neuville would make no sense. But as was the case between men, individuals did not see these forms of attachment as being sharply different from each other. As a result, the friends studied here could speak of physical attraction and erotic desire without either one disrupting the relationship. Rather, as in the case of Montcalm and Hyde de Neuville, the erotic frisson could strengthen their bond and add to their sense of mutual devotion. Romantic love and platonic friendship were not understood as arising from separate impulses, but as two manifestations of affection.

WOMEN'S SOCIAL ROLES: MAINTAINING CONNECTION, MANAGING EMOTION

Just as women were to aid men in accessing their emotions and interiority, so, too, did they integrate men into their social milieus and help them maintain their personal networks. Notably, letters between men and women frequently contained a mixture of society gossip, political news, and information about the friends and allies of the correspondents. In this respect, as well, these letters are more similar to those between female friends than between men.[75] Thus, when Hyde de Neuville was ambassador to the United States in the early years of the Restoration, he received relatively short, impersonal letters from his male friends. But his letters from Mme de Montcalm and Mme de La Trémoïlle were filled with the latest Parisian scuttlebutt, as well as both personal and political news.[76] Mme de Broglie's letters to Barante also contained information about political, diplomatic, and literary matters, as well as a fair amount of society chatter. In one from 1824, she mentioned that although he had asked her for gossip, she had relatively little, except that pertaining to a society marriage that was attracting a great deal of mockery.[77] Likewise, letters from men to their female friends were much more wide-ranging than those between men. In the 1840s, Guizot wrote Mme de Gasparin long letters that included information about politics, his social life, his family, his health, and his servants.[78]

Women also maintained contact between men. Thus it was Mme de Broglie, and not her husband, who wrote letters to his friends reporting on his doings.[79] In the 1830s, she and the princesse de Lieven, Guizot's mistress, were also in charge of informing Barante about what was happening in Paris when he lived abroad as an ambassador.[80] Mme de Dino, too, sent Guizot letters with information about her companion Talleyrand, as well as the news of two doctrinaires to whom she was close—Théobald Piscatory, who was briefly her lover in the 1820s, and Royer-Collard, who was her neighbor.[81] If correspondence between men situated men in a political and intellectual milieu, letters from women integrated men into a social one.

Moreover, women frequently conveyed and managed affection between men. Once again, it was Mme de Broglie who was tasked with communicating how much her husband cared about his male friends. In a letter from 1828, she wrote the following to Guizot about his upcoming visit: "I would like you to come as early as possible. I wish it for myself and I wish it just as much for Victor. You know that you are indispensable to him and that his spirit is incomplete without yours."[82] Victor de Broglie was rarely affectionate; Guizot's memoirs (published while Broglie was still alive) call him "the least demonstrative of men."[83] But he did not have to be, for he had his wife to interpret and convey emotions to others.

The relationship between Béranger, Chateaubriand, and Hortense Allart is also instructive in this respect. During the Restoration, Allart and Béranger were good friends who circulated in the same liberal milieus. In 1829, she began an affair with Chateaubriand when the two were both in Rome. At the same time, he was flirting with the liberal opposition. In early 1830, after both Allart and Chateaubriand had returned to France, she decided to orchestrate a meeting between Béranger and her lover, and it was this encounter that eventually led the two men to become friends. From the beginning, they called on Allart to facilitate their relationship. After their initial meeting, Béranger wrote Allart a letter in which he stated, "M. de Chateaubriand just left my home. In truth, it is more than I deserve, even if you find me too humble! I do not know how to admit such kindness. Please be my interpreter, for I am so stupid that I fear he did not understand the feelings that he inspired in me."[84] Béranger was writing as if he was overawed at meeting the literary lion and so needed Allart to convey his emotions to Chateaubriand; as a woman, she was to have an emotional intelligence that he lacked. Even after the two men started corresponding with each other directly, Béranger still charged her with helping him communicate with Chateaubriand on particularly sensitive matters. For instance, when Chateaubriand proposed to nominate Béranger for a seat in the Académie française, the latter asked Allart to convey to Chateaubriand that he had no interest in becoming an *immortel*.[85]

These patterns of male/female correspondence relied on both new and old understandings of the inner workings of gender and the emotions. The salon culture of the seventeenth and eighteenth centuries made women responsible for interpersonal interactions, a role they would continue to play here as they maintained social networks and helped men cultivate their ties with one another. At the same time, the content and tone of letters between men and women fit with the new emotional regime and the new understanding of male psychology in the post-revolutionary era. In the early nineteenth century, emotional expression was feminized, in contrast to the eighteenth century, when both men and women could be highly emotive. Because men could not always express their feelings, they often turned to women to do it for them. Moreover, the men of the post-revolutionary age could not always engage in personal revelation with one another. The new psychology of the time, founded by Victor Cousin, emphasized men's rational capacities. Although Cousinian psychology stressed the importance of introspection, this psychological system offered limited guidance on *how* to look inward.[86] Because women demanded and authorized personal and emotional revelation, men were to turn to female friends for scrupulous accountings of their interiority. These correspondence patterns thus relied on an understanding that women were private actors and men public ones. Because they belonged to private life, women could receive the intimate thoughts and feelings of men. Among one another, men had to be preoccupied with public affairs, whereas women were concerned with social relations, the cultivation of personal ties, and emotional states—although chapter 6 will show the political application of these roles. At the same time, of course, male/female ties helped men access their private selves. In these relations, men came to behave like the women around them—emotional, reflective, and connected to their social milieus.

For the men studied here, the benefits of friendship—physical, psychic, and material—were many, but were for the most part highly gendered. Relationships with women were understood to provide men with the ability to give and receive affection and personal confidences. They could connect men to their social worlds and allow for psychic relief. In contrast, friendships among men supplied tangible benefits, such as financial assistance and the activation of patronage networks, as well as intellectual and political companionship. In many respects, the construction of bonds among men relied on the old understanding of the friend as a companion in arms, as these men fought for the same causes as one another and acted in solidarity with one another. In both cases, however, friendship was bound up in the creation of trust, as male friends were to act with loyalty toward one another and as men and women were to serve as confidantes and the bearers of one's most intimate thoughts. Friendship was thus imagined to be a key location of trust in an otherwise suspicious society and a primary source of connection in an atomized world.

4

POST-REVOLUTIONARY SOCIAL NETWORKS

If patterns of epistolary communication highlight a series of understandings about the workings of friendship, social network analysis offers another perspective. Looking at the networks of Chateaubriand, Guizot, Béranger, and some of the women to whom they were close illuminates crucial structural differences between men and women's ties. This chapter focuses on two moments in time—the 1820s and the 1840s—to show the degree to which political affiliations shaped social ones. In the Restoration, politics had a profound effect on men's personal ties, as factional allegiance was a force for both cohesion and division. But in the July Monarchy, social bonds began to be depoliticized among the political classes. In this respect at least, the divisions spawned by the Revolution began to heal. For Béranger and Chateaubriand, two men who had ceased their political activity, ideology was only one of a number of factors that shaped their friendships. In contrast, Guizot's bonds with other men remained bound up in factional considerations. However, throughout both regimes, women's networks were not determined by political affiliations, and they had little difficulty maintaining ties across the political spectrum. As a result, it was they who served as bridging actors between different factions and social groups. In the face of the upheaval of the revolutionary and post-revolutionary eras, women maintained the unity of Parisian high society and served as forces for social cohesion.

METHODOLOGY AND SOURCES

Network analysis, a technique pioneered by sociologists and mathematicians, has become increasingly popular in recent years. The explosive growth of the

Internet and the rise of social media have led to an understanding that we live in a networked world, one where our social connections influence what we think, how we behave, and what opportunities open up to us. Among historians, network analysis has been hailed as a way to revive social history after the challenge of post-structuralism, as it makes questions about individual agency central to empirical research.[1] Because it focuses on systems of relationships, as opposed to attributes of institutions or individuals, network analysis can also bring new issues into focus, such as the transmission of ideas and the transformation of social habits over time. In this instance, social network analysis illuminates the forces for division and cohesion among early nineteenth-century Parisian political elites. For this reason, friendship is particularly interesting. By definition, family relationships cannot be destroyed; even if two relatives stop talking to each other, they are still related. But looking at friendship networks provides insight into whom individuals chose to have around them and with whom they communicated on a regular basis. Hence, at some level, it shows what men and women wanted in their relationships with others.

In order to compile information on the networks of Béranger, Chateaubriand, Guizot, and the women around them, I rely on the enormous quantity of documentation about their social lives. All three men wrote memoirs in which they discussed their friendships to a greater or lesser degree, and they left extensive collections of letters, either published or unpublished. Biographers have also been interested in these men's social ties.[2] We also have considerable information about the lives of some of the women with whom these men were friends. The networks of Mme de Montcalm, Mme Récamier, and Mme de Duras, all of whom were in Chateaubriand's circle, are relatively well documented. For Guizot, we have some information about the relationships of his friends Mme de Broglie, Mme de Dino, and Mme de Castellane, as well as those of Mme de Lieven, his mistress from the late 1830s on. Works on Béranger's friend Hortense Allart provide detail about some of her social ties.[3] The information about some of these women's networks is extensive, as in the case of Broglie and Montcalm, who both have published correspondence. Récamier's social circle has long been a source of fascination, while works on Allart, Duras, and Dino have examined their closest friendships. However, we have only some indications of the relationships of Castellane and Lieven. As a general rule, there is far more information about the social worlds of the men studied here than the women. Nevertheless, there is enough to provide a sense of some of the essential differences between men's and women's networks.[4]

This chapter relies primarily on correspondence to track the personal relations of the men and women studied here. By definition, letter writing is a social act. Parisian elites also spent approximately half the year outside the capital and at the same time expected their friends to stay in regular contact with them. Thus friendship could not exist without a paper trail in this era (unless friends were staying with one another).[5] Another advantage of using letters is that correspondents of the time often had clear ways of signifying who was a friend and who was not. For instance, Guizot and his male friends consistently used the salutation "mon cher ami" with one another, a term that Béranger and his male friends often used as well.[6] Salutations are more complicated in women's correspondence, however. Female friends typically called one another "chère amie" in their letters, and in some cases men and women used "mon cher ami" or "ma chère amie" as a form of address.[7] Yet in other instances, men and women did not use a salutation with one another or used salutations that would have indicated formality and distance had they been employed between friends of the same sex, as was the case with Hortense Allart and Sainte-Beuve. In these instances, it was not the form of address that signified the nature of the relationship. Rather, it was the frequency of the letters and the fact that the correspondence was personal, affectionate, and sustained over a long period of time. Men and women also discussed the fact that they were friends in their correspondence with one another even in cases where the salutation did not indicate the nature of their tie.

For the purposes of this chapter, correspondents who used the formulations that signified friendship are counted as friends. Additionally, relationships between men and women who did not use these terms are considered to be friendships if their correspondence otherwise discussed their friendship and was personal in nature. Frequency and duration are also factors. Friendship is sustained over time, and there must be some indication that the contact between individuals was not limited to just one or two letters. Likewise, to be counted as a marker of friendship, letters must have some affective or personal content, such as news about the writer's health or family.[8] This weeds out those who wrote to Béranger requesting his literary advice or to Guizot asking for favors. Biographies and memoirs have been used to supplement the collections of letters in cases where a relationship cannot be tracked by correspondence.[9]

This study also pulls in two additional types of data to give us a fuller picture of these networks. First, it examines the relationships among these individuals' friends. Thus it takes note of the fact that Béranger was friends with both Manuel and Dupont de l'Eure *and* that Manuel and Dupont themselves were friends.[10] In general, we have a great deal of information on the interlocking friendship ties in Guizot's circle and somewhat less for Chateaubriand and Béranger. Additionally, a limited number of other types of relationships are included in this study. Ties between lovers and some family members, including spouses, are noted, but only where such relationships were integrated into their friendship networks.[11] For example, Guizot's brother is not included because none of Guizot's friends was close to him. However, the relationship between Mme de Broglie and her brother Auguste de Staël is included because he had ties with many of her friends. In these instances, showing the family connection or love relationship can illuminate the conditions under which certain individuals became friends with one another. Of course, as discussed in the previous chapter, the boundary between love and friendship was often porous. For the sake of simplicity, I have placed bonds where there was significant ambiguity in one of these categories, based on whether the parties acknowledged their relationship as a love affair and whether there is evidence of sexual activity, at the same time as I recognize that these labels can be reductionist.

These sources must be approached with considerable caution. Memoirs, for instance, were typically written toward the end of a life and are thus subject to the vagaries of memory. Moreover, individuals might have wanted to downplay (or hide) certain ties to shield themselves from embarrassment.[12] One advantage of using letters is that they capture relationships at particular moments in time. But the codes of nineteenth-century correspondence, the way in which these sources have been made available for future generations, and the very meaning of the terms "friend" and "friendship" complicate any notion that individuals' letter collections provide uncomplicated access to their social networks. For one, we do not possess the complete correspondence of any of the men or women studied here. With some individuals—such as Mme de Dino—we have only a small sampling of their letters. In contrast, Guizot's personal papers contain well over ten thousand letters that he either wrote or received, while Béranger and Chateaubriand's correspondence both take up many volumes. Yet even in these cases we do not have their complete correspondence, as many letters—probably most—have been destroyed or lost. Some that were too personal or revealing were burned at the sender's request. Heirs also pruned these collections in order to protect their relatives' reputations.[13] Chateaubriand and Béranger's available correspondence largely consists of letters they wrote, which means that we are dependent on the recipients having saved these men's letters (and having been willing to make them available to the editors of these men's correspondences). There are also considerable lacunae; Chateaubriand's correspondence after 1830 remains largely unpublished, while we have relatively few letters from Béranger written during the Restoration. In Guizot's case, there is little from before 1826.

Thus, despite all the available material, the networks analyzed here are not necessarily complete. For the women studied here, it is certain that we are missing significant information about their social ties. In general, we know the most about Guizot's network and should regard this as closest to complete. Thanks in part to the painstaking efforts of Béranger's biographer Jean Touchard, we have a great deal of information about the songwriter's most important relationships, but relatively little about the connections between his friends. In Chateaubriand's case, we know a lot about the network of Récamier, but less about the man himself. In part, this is a reflection of his personality: he had none of the warmth of Guizot or Béranger, nor their need for companionship. Nevertheless, despite these limitations, the available evidence provides us with a general sense of these individuals' social ties, the types of relationships possible for them, and how different social groups were connected to one another.

A second set of issues relates to the connection between language, emotion, and authenticity. After all, letters were written for a specific purpose and in an environment where calling someone a friend provided access to patronage networks and political favors. Thus one problem with using letters and memoirs to derive data about personal networks is that doing so requires taking individuals at their word. There were also social conventions that led correspondents to use terms of friendship with those who were not friends. Hence, it is important to know the cultural codes of the time and to be aware of how these men and women used the words "friend" and "friendship." On the one hand, it is easy for an individual to claim to be linked by friendship to another; this is a tie that requires no formal method of affiliation. Yet on the other hand, the men and women of this study were relatively conservative in their application of the terms "ami" and "amitié." "Ami," for instance, was not an appellation for those who merely knew each other socially, as individuals of the time often made careful distinctions between who was a friend and who was not. Take two statements that Guizot made in his *Mélanges biographiques et littéraires*, a collection of essays about notable personalities, most of whom he knew personally. In discussing the friends of Mme Récamier, he writes, "The comtesse de Boigne became one of her closest and most constant friends; without the same intimacy and in a more passing relationship, the duchesse de Luynes and the duchesse de Chevreuse, her daughter-in-law, enjoyed the charms of her company."[14] Later, while writing about Mme de Boigne herself, Guizot states, "I never entered into one of these intimate relationships with her that leads to mutual confidences and makes people privy to one another; I only knew the pleasures of her mind and her society."[15] In both passages, Guizot carefully qualified who was a true friend and who was a mere social acquaintance. Récamier might have spent a considerable amount of time with Mmes de Luynes and de Chevreuse, just as Guizot frequented Boigne's salon. This was not considered enough to create a friendship, however, as such a bond would require an intimacy and a perceived knowledge of the other.

Individuals of the time also made clear distinctions between "amis" who were merely political allies and "amis" with whom they shared a personal connection. For example, Mme de Broglie wrote the following to Barante about Victor Cousin in 1824: "You will see our new friend, M. Cousin, *friend* whom I do not like that much."[16] Likewise, correspondents might discuss whether and why they could consider themselves friends. Thus, in 1868, Guizot and the comte de Montalembert—a former political adversary—began calling each other "ami" in their letters. This provoked Montalembert to write, "You are right to call me your friend; it is a title that I deserve and that I will bear with sweetness and pride, friends! We were already friends even when it seemed that we fought with each other the most."[17] These two men were immensely proud that they had turned their political differences into a personal friendship. In their discussion about why and how they could call each other "friend," Montalembert gave careful deliberation and consideration to this issue.

Despite these calculations about who was and was not a friend, there were certain occasions when correspondents used terms of friendship with those whom they did not regard as friends in the fullest sense of the term. For instance, elites sometimes used the word "ami" to refer to high-status servants in their households, such as secretaries. Chateaubriand thus called his secretary Jean Baptiste Le Moine a friend in his letters.[18] Chateaubriand may have had affection for him and placed a great deal of trust in him, but the core of the relationship was an economic transaction. In practice, however, it is not difficult to determine who was a servant and to weed out these types of relationships. Alternately, as is discussed in chapter 5, politicians occasionally used words of friendship strategically in negotiations to signify a political allegiance and did not do so to make claims about their feelings.[19] Fortunately, these empty expressions of love deployed between politicians are relatively easy to locate. For one, the terms of affection tend to be extremely formal and elaborate and even violated the codes of communication between male friends. The claims of friendship were offered only once, and the remainder of the correspondence shows the hallmarks of distance. As with secretaries, then, these instances of empty words of friendship are relatively easy to find and exclude.

Further, it is important to note that the appellation "friend" did not always describe a deep emotional connection. Some of the relationships discussed in this chapter were by all accounts important to the men and women involved. This is the case with Béranger and Manuel, who were buried together, and with Guizot and Mme de Broglie, who treated each other as confidantes. But some of these friendships seem to operate on the level of social convention and do not appear to be close. For instance, Mme de Broglie and Mme Récamier maintained a correspondence with each other for many years; we only have the former's side, but Broglie called Récamier her friend in it. However, Récamier's biographer states that Broglie did not actually like or understand Récamier.[20] Likewise, in the 1820s, Mme de Dino and Guizot corresponded with each other on a regular basis and called each other friends. In reading her letters, however, one gets the impression that there is little genuine warmth to them.[21]

Both of these relationships have all the hallmarks of friendship—regular contact and the employment of forms of address used between friends—but they seem to have arisen out of a desire to appear to be a friend more than anything else. Broglie and Récamier were both noted salonnières; they had some friends in common, such as Prosper de Barante, and Broglie was the daughter of Mme de Staël, who had been close to Récamier. It was perhaps easier for them to claim to be friends than to state that they were not. For her part, Dino's relationship with Guizot probably arose from her efforts to facilitate the political career of her uncle-in-law, companion, and occasional lover, Talleyrand. Certainly, many of the women whose networks are discussed here were salonnières and might have had a whole host of reasons to act as friends toward those for whom they did not have a great wellspring of affection. They might wish to attract prominent personalities to their salon, for instance. In this chapter, I make no judgments about the authenticity of a particular relationship as long as there is evidence that the parties treated each other as friends over a sustained period of time. That is to say, if their letters employed the conventional signs of friendship, I count them as friends. In other words, my aim is not to understand the innermost feelings of these individuals or the sincerity of their expressions. Instead, it is to examine with whom individuals thought they could be friends and with whom they were in regular contact.

THE POLITICAL DIVIDES OF THE RESTORATION

Figure 1 shows the social networks of Béranger, Guizot, and Chateaubriand from 1825 to 1829; it also includes information on the ties of Hortense Allart, Mme de Broglie, Mme de Dino, Mme de Duras, Mme de Montcalm, and Mme Récamier. This four-year window was selected because it offers the most information about these individuals' social ties. However, to be included here, the individuals do not have to have been friends for this entire period, but only to have had a relationship during these years. Thus, for instance, Mme de Duras is shown here, even though she died in 1828. Likewise, Chateaubriand's relationship with Hortense Allart is included, even though the two met in 1829. The names of some individuals featured prominently in this study are provided here; a full list can be found in appendix B.[22]

Despite their quite different political positions and social milieus, all three men's networks were connected to one another in some way. Hortense Allart is the only direct tie between Chateaubriand and Béranger, although Mme Récamier also linked their social worlds, since she was friends with a number of those in Béranger's circle. Mme de Dino connects the extended networks of Guizot and Béranger to each other, as she was friends with Thiers, a friend of Béranger, and with Guizot and a number of other doctrinaires. There are more bridging figures between Guizot and Chateaubriand's networks, including Mme de Catellan, Mme de Récamier, and Mme de Castellane. Crucially, most of the individuals who connect different networks are women. A number of them, including Récamier, Catellan, and Dino, hosted notable salons of the day. Salonnières had the aim of sparking conversation among individuals who did not necessary know one another, and they might pull in artists, intellectuals, foreign visitors, and politicians from different

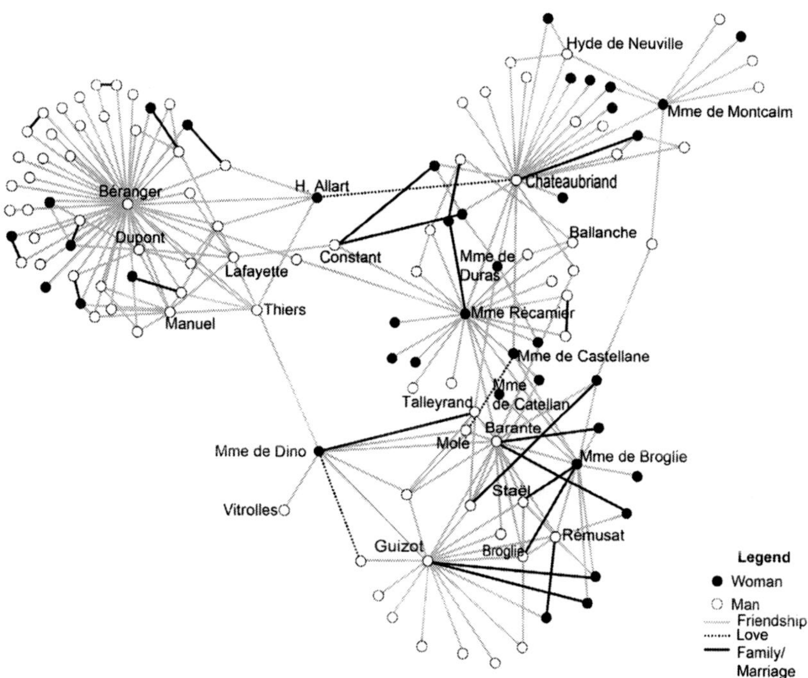

FIGURE 1 Social networks, 1825–29

factions.[23] As a result, it was up to them to cultivate ties with individuals who belonged to different social groups.

Récamier is a good example of this, for her network is made up of a number of different subnetworks. Some of her friends—like Benjamin Constant, Mme de Broglie, and Prosper de Barante—were essentially legacies of her friendship with Mme de Staël during the years of the Empire, as they had all been close to Staël. Récamier was also friends with a number of members of the Bonaparte family, as well as with the young men who grouped around Jean Jacques Ampère and Pierre Simon de Ballanche. At the same time, some of her closest relationships were with conservative politicians, such as Chateaubriand and Mathieu de Montmorency. Many of these individuals knew one another, but were not necessarily friends; instead, they were largely connected through Récamier. Thus, insofar as these men and women's networks represent a slice of Parisian high society (with Guizot and Chateaubriand definitely belonging to an elite stratum and with Béranger having strong connections to notable elites of the day), it is clear that it was women who ensured the unity of the Parisian monde. This is but another example of women's social roles, for they both maintained connections among men who were friends with one another and tied different elite circles together.

It is also notable that there are many friendships between men and women and that women were well integrated into men's networks. Such bonds should challenge the notion that nineteenth-century sociability was divided along lines of gender, or that the concept of separate spheres was a sociological fact, as some scholars have claimed.[24] Historians have also described the prevalence of gender mixing in this era as an aristocratic phenomenon deriving from the social habits and salon culture of Old Regime elites.[25] Indeed both Chateaubriand and Guizot attended salons and circulated in largely aristocratic milieus. But Béranger is a different case. His background was decidedly nonaristocratic—yet he, too, had friendships with a number of women.

However, male and female networks were different, a fact that is particularly visible in figure 2, which sorts individuals into the four basic political camps of the time—the liberal opposition, doctrinaires, center-right moderates, and ultras. Liberals were those in the opposition since 1815. In terms of their ideology, they ranged from liberal monarchists to republicans to Bonapartists, but they were nonetheless generally united in this period.[26] The doctrinaires were a relatively small, cohesive faction that occupied a position in the center-left. More conservative than other members of the liberal opposition, they wanted to serve as a moderating force between the left and the right.[27] To their right were moderates, who were committed royalists opposed to the excesses of the ultras. These men and women of the center-right had often supported the policies of Louis XVIII, but not those of his more conservative brother Charles X. Within this camp was a faction known as the Defection. This group was made of up politicians like Chateaubriand and Hyde de Neuville who had been ultras in the early years of the Restoration but who moved to a more centrist position in the mid-1820s.[28] On the far-right were the ultras who opposed all gains of the Revolution and supported Charles X.[29]

There are some individuals, such as Mme Récamier and her friend Pierre Simon Ballanche, who do not fit neatly into any factional camp. Récamier, for instance, claimed to be neutral, but she did have some political orientation. In the early years of the Restoration, when Chateaubriand was an ultra, he considered her too sympathetic to liberals, while Benjamin Constant thought she was too tied to conservatives. Her niece and adopted daughter, Amélie Lenormant, née Cyvoct, spoke of her as a good royalist who found the

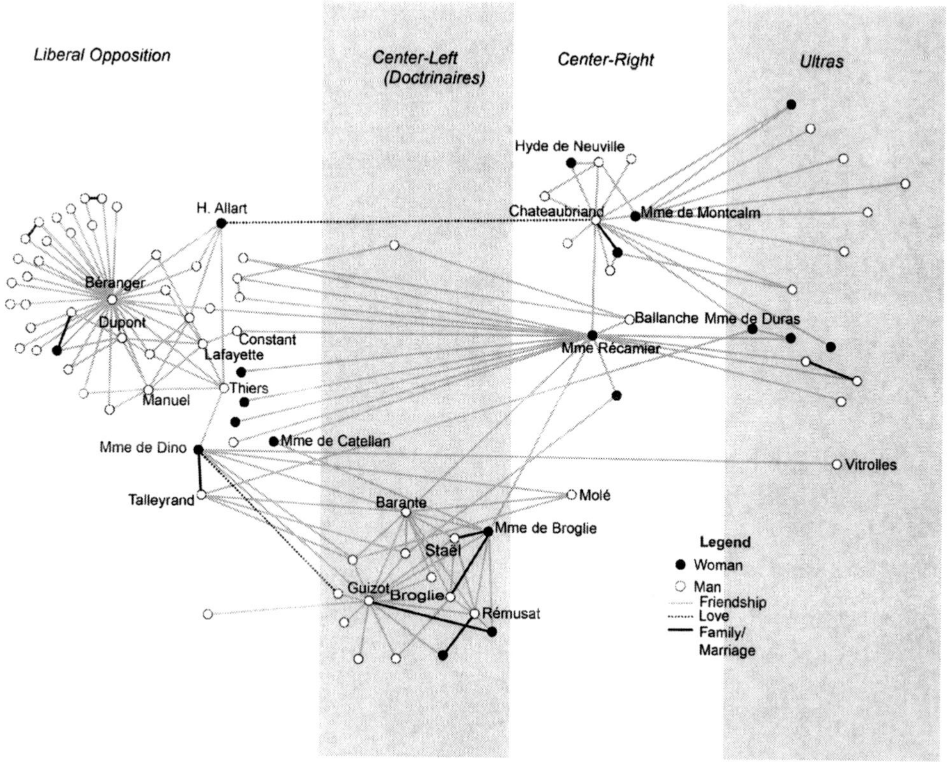

FIGURE 2 Social networks and political affiliations, 1825–29

ultras too conservative. For this reason she has been placed in the center-right camp.[30] Ballanche presents an even thornier case, as he was a political thinker with idiosyncratic views. He was committed to a counterrevolutionary philosophy, but one that allowed for progress and radical change. His friend and biographer Jean Jacques Ampère suggests that he was never an ultra, and that by the end of the 1820s he thought that the Restoration regime was incapable of governing. For lack of a better way of understanding his politics, he, too, has been placed in the moderate camp.[31] Individuals whose political views are unknown have been excluded from figure 2, as have Guizot and Chateaubriand's British friends, since their political positions did not necessarily align with French factional divisions.

Figure 2 shows that men's networks were determined largely by political affiliation. All of Béranger's friends were liberals, while Guizot's male friends overwhelmingly belonged to the doctrinaire camp. Chateaubriand had some connections to ultras, but for the most part his male friends belonged to the center-right, as did he. To be sure, some men were able to maintain ties across factional divisions, including Talleyrand, Barante, and Ballanche. But as a general rule, it is clear that shared ideological affiliation was a constitutive element of male friendship. This is hardly surprising, given the fact that male friendship centered on notions of similarity and public allegiance.

Indeed, in a number of cases, political commitments were central to the formation of ties between men. For Guizot, three of his most important male friendships were formed in the first few years of the Restoration—that with Rémusat, Barante, and Broglie. All four men were friends with one another and they were all tied together by their similar political views.[32] It was also after 1815 that Béranger became friends with Manuel and Dupont de l'Eure, two men who shared his far-left politics.[33] Thus, during this era, men's social ties were highly politicized, and factional commitments were a force for both cohesion and division. For men, the notion that France was a nation divided by ideological tensions fit with their personal experience.

Just as male social networks were highly politicized, so, too, were their political networks deeply social. This is striking in the case of the liberal opposition; its most prominent politicians, including Lafayette, Constant, Manuel, and Jacques Laffitte, were all either Béranger's friends or friends of a friend. Indeed, the liberals are interesting precisely because they functioned as a united front without a set of shared ideological positions. For instance, these politicians orchestrated electoral campaigns in concert with one another with great success in the late 1820s. What united these men was a hatred of the existing regime, but also strong personal connections. Hence, in an era before official political parties, men's social networks often served as networks of political affiliation.[34]

In contrast to the intense politicization of men's personal ties, politics did not bind women's networks, and many women had friends who belonged to other factions. For instance, Mme de Dino shared the politics of her uncle-in-law and companion, Talleyrand, who was in the liberal opposition.[35] In the closing years of the Restoration, she cultivated a friendship with Thiers, also a liberal, and had many ties to the men of the doctrinaire circle. Her closest friend, however, was the baron de Vitrolles, an ultra.[36] Similarly, Récamier had many connections to ultras, but also to liberals like Constant and Ampère and to exiled members of the Bonaparte family. Hortense Allart's network was also politically extensive. She herself was firmly in the liberal camp and had male friends who shared her factional commitments, but she was also Chateaubriand's lover.

Even women who were politically engaged had social ties that transcended factional divisions. Mme de Duras was Chateaubriand's most important political adviser, but she maintained a relationship with Talleyrand in the 1820s. Her biographer also asserts that in the early years of the Restoration—when factional tensions were at their height—she supported the moderate Richelieu government, to which Chateaubriand was bitterly opposed.[37] Despite their political disagreements, their relationship was untroubled and she remained his confidante and tireless advocate. Mme de Montcalm was another politically active woman whose friendships crossed factional lines. A moderate who worked on behalf of her brother, the duc de Richelieu, she also maintained a number of close ties to ultras. There are exceptions to these patterns of female friendship; Mme de Broglie's intimates were largely confined to the doctrinaire circle, for example. Nevertheless, in general, political affiliation was less determinative of women's networks than men's. Thus, not only did women connect different social milieus to one another, they also served as links between different factional groupings.

One reason women could have more diverse social networks than men was their official exclusion from politics. Men had to remain loyal to their particular faction, both because it represented their political views and because it was a path to power. For example, when Chateaubriand's faction triumphed, it raised the possibility that he could become a cabinet minister. Because this option was not open to women, they were less invested in the success of any one political grouping. Additionally, while a male politician had to have an opinion on every issue up for debate in the Chambers in order to vote on it, a woman could choose to remain silent on an issue or to suggest that she did not have an opinion on the matter. Thus some women, like Récamier, claimed to be neutral, although she was not necessarily so.[38] Likewise, in 1829, Mme de Dino stated in a letter to her best friend, the baron de Vitrolles, that "politics does not interest me at all anymore."[39] This was hardly true, for at the time, she was actively involved in promoting Talleyrand's political career. But she did not want Vitrolles, an ardent ultra, to know this, for Talleyrand was aligned with liberals at the time. However, Dino's claim of political disengagement was plausible only because of her gender: no man as close to Talleyrand as she could have held such a position. A few other women, such as Montcalm and Allart, did have fixed political views, but were seen as capable of having personal as well as political loyalties. As public actors, men found this less possible. Moreover, the fact that bonds between men and women were not constructed around similarity enabled women to be friends with men whose politics did not match their own.

Thus, while the men and women who inhabited Parisian political circles did not live in separate social worlds in this era, they did have very different experiences of friendship. Politics shaped the personal lives of men but not those of women. For men, politics was a clear force for division, but it also brought them together. Shared political views were responsible for the formation of lifelong friendships for both Béranger and Guizot. This was not as true for women, however. Politics was not what tied Chateaubriand and Allart together, nor was it what bound Mme Récamier to her friends. In this respect, women's social lives did not match the notion that early nineteenth-century France was a nation torn asunder by politics. Their networks show the persistence of old ideas about female sociability, and in practice they held Parisian political society together. In contrast, men's social lives were far more shaped by the upheaval of the revolutionary and post-revolutionary eras.

THE 1840S: PERSISTENT AND DISAPPEARING DIVIDES

After the Revolution of 1830, the political landscape shifted. New factions appeared and others split up; many ultras became legitimists, while the liberal opposition of the Restoration broke apart. Some of its members, such as Thiers, supported the new regime, while others, including Béranger, maintained an oppositional stance to the July Monarchy. Many of the old political flash points died down as well. It was now clear to all but die-hard legitimists that some of the gains of the Revolution would remain in place and that France would not be an absolute monarchy. At the same time, the issue of popular participation in politics—and the degree to which the working classes would have their demands met or repressed—became central to the politics of the new regime.

Historians have also stated that this period was less factionalized than was the Restoration. After all, fears of popular unrest led many elites to feel that the threat did not come from within the ranks of the wealthy, but from those who were excluded from the political system. In turn, this opened up opportunities for reconciliation within the ruling class. And indeed, politics was less a force in Béranger's and Chateaubriand's networks in the July Monarchy than it was before. Both of them had largely retired from political life, and to some extent their personal ties were depoliticized. Nevertheless, politics could still be a force for division. This was especially true for Guizot, the only one of the three who remained active in politics. Once again, however, women had no trouble maintaining ties to politicians of different stripes, and they continued to connect factional groupings to one another.

Figure 3 maps the social worlds of these three men from 1843 to 1847, a period for which we have a great deal of information about Guizot's and Béranger's networks. This is not the case for Chateaubriand, however, as the documentation regarding his relationships after 1830 is relatively scarce. He was also in considerable decline in this period and was far less sociable as a consequence. As with previous mappings, this figure incorporates information about the networks of some of the women to whom these men were close: Récamier, Allart, Dino, Castellane, and Lieven. I have not assumed any continuity between these men's and women's relationships in the 1820s and their ties in the 1840s. For example, while there is much evidence that Chateaubriand and Mme de Castellane were friends in the 1820s, there is no information about whether they remained so in the 1840s. As a result, no relationship is indicated here.

This figure shows a number of changes since the 1820s. The personal networks of Chateaubriand and Récamier have diminished greatly in size. Both were ailing at this point and had social lives that were considerably less active. However, Chateaubriand and Béranger's networks have come closer together. They were joined by their friendship with each other, and both were close to the abbé de Lamennais. Meanwhile, the number of Guizot's friendships increased. Being connected to the head of the government could be a lucrative prospect in this era. His network also appears to be less dense than it was during the Restoration, but this is primarily due to a lack of sources. Much of the information about the relationships within the doctrinaire coterie during the Restoration comes from Mme de Broglie, who died in the 1830s, and Rémusat, who was no longer friends with Guizot in the 1840s.

Figure 4 maps the friendship networks across the political divides of the period, placing individuals into four general groupings. On the right-hand side are legitimists who advocated the return of the Bourbon monarchy. To their left are those in the juste milieu. In power during the 1840s, this faction consisted of conservatives who supported the Orleans branch of the monarchy and opposed any opening up of the parliamentary franchise.[40] A number of different factions opposed this government, including liberals and liberal

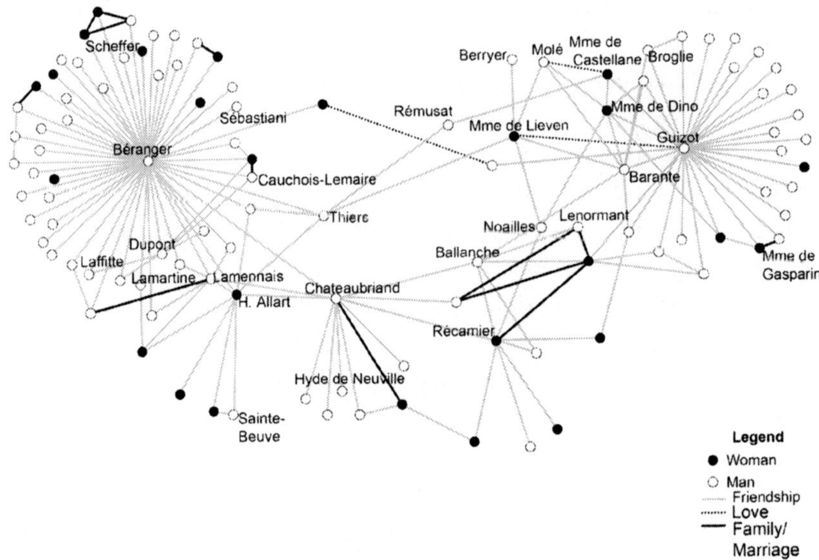

FIGURE 3 Social networks, 1843–47

Catholics, those who supported Thiers, and republicans and socialists on the far-left. For the sake of simplicity, I have consolidated these factions into two basic categories—the far-left and the center-left. The former group includes republicans, socialists, and all those who wanted to dramatically alter the nature of the regime. In the latter category are those who were generally happy with the structure of the parliamentary monarchy, but who advocated some opening to the left, such as parliamentary reform or an expansion of the franchise. It should be said that within these categories, there were many different shades of opinion. For instance, Thiers's politics were hardly the same as those of liberal Catholics, despite the fact that they are in the same left-of-center grouping.

As before, the women around Béranger and Chateaubriand had politically extensive networks. Two of the men closest to Récamier during the 1840s were Chateaubriand, on the far-right, and Pierre Simon Ballanche, who was drawn to liberal Catholicism. Even more strikingly heterogeneous is Allart's network. She had friends across the political spectrum. She herself was an unwed mother, a feminist, and a proponent of radical political views. Many of those around her had also turned their backs on the establishment. Her friends included Marie d'Agoult, who left her husband and her life in high society for Franz Liszt; George Sand, who dressed as a man; and Lamennais,

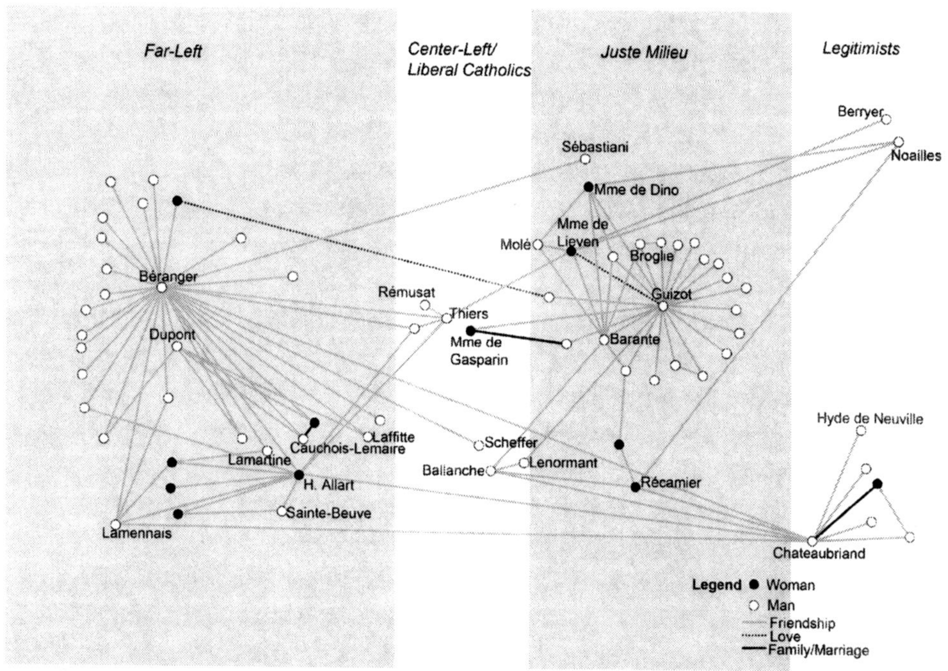

FIGURE 4 Social networks and political affiliations, 1843–47

whom the Catholic Church had condemned. But she was also friends with Thiers, a man who gave up radical politics after 1830. As one of the most important politicians of the July Monarchy and a member of the Académie française, he was as close to the establishment as one could get.

Béranger's and Chateaubriand's social ties also changed shape, for they were depoliticized to a certain degree. Many of Chateaubriand's male friends were legitimists as was he, but others were liberal Catholics or on the far-left. Likewise, Béranger continued to circulate in a radical milieu, and, as during the Restoration, shared politics remained a force for cohesion. This was true in the case of his relationship with Alphonse de Lamartine. The two men were particularly close when their politics aligned with each other.[41] Nevertheless, Béranger had friends across the political spectrum, including Ary Scheffer, who had affinities with liberal Catholics, and Horace Sébastiani, part of the juste milieu. Béranger had been friends with all of these men during the Restoration, and their differences of opinion after 1830 did not fundamentally disrupt these ties. Yet he also had close relationships with those to whom he had been opposed during the Restoration, including the legitimist Chateaubriand and the former ultra Lamennais.[42] If male friendship was based on similarity, by the 1840s this similarity could be constructed in a variety of fashions. It might involve shared political views, a shared history, or a shared set of literary preoccupations.

However, quite particular circumstances enabled these connections between men on opposite sides of the political spectrum. After all, Chateaubriand was an unusual legitimist, for his sense of honor more than any real attachment tied him to the Bourbon branch. In his account, his political career ended after the Revolution of 1830 because he felt that swearing an oath of allegiance to the new regime would have involved a betrayal of his previous oath of loyalty to the Bourbons.[43] In 1831, he also stated that he was a "republican by nature, a monarchist by reason, and a legitimist by honor"—but such political heterodoxy was hardly characteristic of others who shared his loyalty to the Bourbon branch.[44] Indeed, the very fact that he was friends with Béranger shocked many of those on the far-right. In Chateaubriand's memoirs, he spoke of receiving a letter from another legitimist who decried the fact that Chateaubriand was being praised by "he who attacked your king and your God."[45] Such a reaction only triggered an outburst of pride from Chateaubriand; he discussed his relationship with Béranger as a way to show his independence and open-mindedness, and to demonstrate that as a legitimist, he was not one of the stultifyingly dull ones. Likewise, Lamennais was hardly typical of those on the far-left. During the Restoration, he had been an ultra and had contributed to the far-right *Le Conservateur*, along with Chateaubriand. Certainly his friendship with Béranger was shocking to some of his other friends.[46] If there were increasing opportunities for ties across political lines during the July Monarchy, the extent of Chateaubriand and Béranger's networks were not necessarily typical of the time.

In contrast, the shape of Guizot's network was not fundamentally different from his social world during the Restoration. His male friends continued to be political allies.[47] A key reason for this difference is that Chateaubriand and Béranger were largely absent from the political life of this period. Political differences mattered much less to them than to Guizot. As the dominant politician of the time, Guizot knew that at any moment his rivals were trying to weaken his position. Anyone not an ally was a potential threat. The factionalized nature of Guizot's network was also intimately connected to his temperament and his view of politics. His biographers maintain that ideological similarity was an essential element of his relationships with other men, and that his approach to personal relations could be rigid and uncompromising.[48] His view of politics as a form of warfare also shaped his inability to be friends with men from different political groupings. In the midst of war, one does not consort with the enemy.

Yet as in the Restoration era, Guizot's female friends had ties that were not bound by shared ideological commitments. He was close to Mme de Castellane who was in turn friends with Rémusat, a former doctrinaire who had moved into the opposition. Moreover, Castellane's long-time lover was Mathieu Molé. Although Molé's politics were not that different from Guizot's, the two men were bitter rivals, largely because they were both vying for control of the conservatives in the Chambers. Mme de Dino, too, continued to have ties to the doctrinaires, including to Guizot, Royer-Collard, and Barante, as well as to the duc de Noailles, a legitimist. Meanwhile, Lieven was Guizot's mistress and yet she maintained friendships with legitimists like Berryer and Noailles and the center-left Thiers.

These women tended to be neutral or relatively disengaged from politics. Castellane did not care much about political struggles, although she did step in at times to help her lover Molé.[49] Dino had been politically active until Talleyrand's death in 1838. She was probably a centrist, as Talleyrand had been, but in the 1840s she was spending more and more time outside of France.[50] For her part, Lieven was heavily involved in diplomatic affairs. Although she claimed to be politically neutral, she was not, and she moved Guizot to the right in the 1840s, especially in matters of foreign policy.[51] For these women, claims to neutrality or to disengagement facilitated their relationships with men of opposing factions.

Yet Guizot was also able to be friends with a woman who had clear political differences with him. From the 1830s until her death in 1864, one of his closest friends was Mme de Gasparin. Despite being his confidante, she was clearly to the left of Guizot politically. For instance, in 1840, she supported Thiers's left-leaning government, one to which Guizot was adamantly opposed.[52] Indeed, she and Rémusat probably had more or less the same politics. But while Guizot's ideological differences destroyed his relationship with Rémusat, the same was not true for his bond with Gasparin.

For his part, Guizot recognized this difference between male and female networks. In the 1837 letter to Lieven in which he spoke about his inability to maintain bonds with men whose politics did not match his own, he admiringly described her capacity to decouple politics and friendship. He wrote, "You, Madame, you should without hesitation make the most of your privilege as a woman; be fair to everyone, good to everyone, friendly to all those who deserve it. What is better and more rare than fairness and friendship!"[53] In Guizot's estimation, this ability to have friends across the political spectrum was not exclusive to Lieven, for this quality belonged to her sex more generally ("your privilege as a woman"). In his mind, women could be friends with men because of their qualities as persons, connecting with individuals based on whether they "deserve" friendship. By contrast, he had to consider other traits. Politics overrode all other considerations in the formation of his bonds with men.

For Guizot, then, the basic pattern of his network was fixed in the Restoration; he needed to find ideological similarity in his relationships with men, but not in those with women. The same was not true of Béranger and Chateaubriand. Similar political views could still aid in the formation of their friendships, but were no longer necessary. In general, then, the July Monarchy saw the partial depoliticization of personal networks. This indicates that the members of the political classes were beginning to recover from the Revolution, as the ideological divisions it engendered were no longer as central to men's lives as before. In this respect, some of the men who lived during the July Monarchy were catching up to the women who were consistently able to maintain ties across the political spectrum and ensure the cohesion of Parisian political society.

5

THE POLITICS OF MALE FRIENDSHIP

Filed among Guizot's personal papers are letters from other prominent politicians of the July Monarchy, such as Molé and Thiers. Guizot's relationships with these men were never easy; they were his rivals for power, and if he occasionally allied himself with one of them, he was more commonly their adversary. Unlike the letters he wrote or received from his friends, any correspondence occurred for very specific purposes, such as to obtain information or to seal an alliance. Consider, thus, an exchange from February 1836 between Thiers and Guizot, in which two master politicians navigated post-revolutionary politics using sentiment. The letters were written just after Thiers replaced Victor de Broglie as the head of the government. Guizot had been minister of public instruction in the Broglie cabinet and had no official place in the new government, but he did give it his support. Guizot and Thiers now had to reassure each other of their sincerity and loyalty, and they sealed their alliance through correspondence.

For his part, Thiers was obliged to state that he would not veer to the left. Hence, in his letter, he wrote, "Events have separated us, but I hope that the feelings aroused by so many years working together facing the same dangers will remain. If I can help it, much of our union will continue."[1] In order to state that he would not forget their joint commitment to the causes of liberalism during the Restoration and order during the July Monarchy, Thiers called on the emotional realm. In his account, he had an affection for Guizot, one that arose out of a shared past. He and Guizot were also bound together by their essential similarities in the way that male friends were. In other words, Thiers was indicating that he and his government would not swing too far to the left because of his affection for his doctrinaire colleague.

In his reply Guizot had to set Thiers's mind at ease that he would not work against the new ministry, and that he accepted the ouster of Broglie, his close friend and ally, from power. Guizot also marshaled the language of friendship to describe his loyalty to Thiers. Indeed, Guizot wrote a draft of his response, one that shows the precise calculations in which he engaged. It was the salutation in particular that allowed Guizot to express his commitment to Thiers. Thiers had begun his letter with the words "mon cher monsieur Guizot," a greeting that indicated some degree of distance, but was relatively warm. Guizot, however, was inclined to indicate considerably more attachment to Thiers than Thiers had to him—but because the political situation called for it, not because he felt any deep affection for his rival. As a powerful politician with no place in the cabinet, Guizot would be at the top of anyone's list of those who might try to bring the government down, and thus he needed to signal that he would do his utmost to be loyal to the new ministry. To do so, he opted for a warmer salutation than the one Thiers had chosen. The draft of his letter shows that he first thought of referring to his rival as "mon cher ami et collègue" (the word "collègue" referred to the fact that both men were members of the Académie française). Yet this did not satisfy Guizot. Adding the word "collègue" to the phrase "mon cher ami" made the salutation more formal and distant, while he wanted to show affiliation and proximity. And so, as Guizot revised his draft, he crossed out the phrase "ami et collègue" and wrote in the word "ami," making this the warmest of all possible greetings: "mon cher ami."[2]

Such a salutation made an extraordinary claim. Guizot never used this phrase lightly, and for him, as well as other correspondents of the time, it indicated a real friendship in the fullest sense of the term. He reserved it for his closest friends, men like Broglie, Barante, and Rémusat. Thiers and Guizot, though, were rivals, and if they intermittently maintained good relations with each other during the 1830s, this is because they were often allied with each other in this decade. Certainly Guizot's draft indicates that he used the salutation "mon cher ami" not because it represented the spontaneous outpourings of his heart, but out of pure calculation. Nor was this statement meant to deceive Thiers into thinking that Guizot regarded him as a friend. For Guizot to have thought that such a profession of affection would fool Thiers would suggest that Guizot regarded Thiers, a man known for his craftiness, as being exceptionally naive. Guizot was hardly such a poor judge of character. Rather, this statement served a purpose of which both men were aware; here friendship functioned as a trope, not an actual, meaningful personal relationship. By claiming to be friends with Thiers, Guizot was really stating that he would act as a friend would. He would not betray Thiers or his ministry, and he was not upset about the fact that he had been ousted from a cabinet position. In essence, descriptions of personal feelings stood in for political allegiance.

This exchange provides an entry point into the political culture of the Restoration and July Monarchy, one that was based around friendship, both as a relationship and as a metaphor. Because male friendship was founded on notions of similarity, politicians used male friends as proxies in ministries, elections, and political negotiations. This was another example of how men were to offer support and act in solidarity with one another. In other cases, politicians who were decidedly not friends used terms of affection with one another to indicate allegiance, as Thiers and Guizot did here. Likewise, they relied on a language of friendship during moments of conflict. In the Restoration and July Monarchy, words of love could be used to persuade, assuage, and signify a whole host of qualities seen as missing in political life, such as loyalty, trust, and free communication. Such a reliance on friendship in the political realm stands in contrast to any notion of a separation between public and private in the early nineteenth century. Men and women at the time may have imagined and wanted their friendships to be entirely private relationships that served as refuges from the harsh and unpleasant public sphere. But friendship had so many political uses precisely because this bond was seen as so different from other ties and so closely connected to trust and affiliation.

In many respects, the use of personal ties to transact politics demonstrates considerable continuity with Old Regime political practices. Ties of friendship cemented political alliances, as they had at the court of Versailles, just as questions of political affiliation were often framed in terms of affection. As chapter 6 discusses, women in the early nineteenth century were negotiators and go-betweens in ways that recalled the practices of the Old Regime. Thus the period between 1815 and 1848 was one when politicians were learning how to practice parliamentary politics and resorted to familiar patterns from the past to do so. After all, many politicians of the era were aristocrats from social milieus that recalled the political practices of the Old Regime, even if they themselves had little personal experience of it. There were also structural similarities between pre- and post-revolutionary politics that made political life so personalized. In both cases, actors were working without the support of impersonal political institutions, such as political parties. Similarly, high politics in the Old Regime and the era of parliamentary monarchy were both a matter for elites, whether they were the courtiers at Versailles or the residents of Paris's aristocratic neighborhoods.

Nevertheless, there are considerable differences between the pre- and post-revolutionary uses of personal ties, ones that gave friendship a special significance in the early nineteenth century. Notably, the new parliamentary system presented a whole series of new problems regarding cohesion and coordination that friendship could solve. In the sixteenth, seventeenth, and eighteenth centuries, personal connections helped men and women appeal to their superiors and obtain the attention of important patrons or the king. But politics in the post-revolutionary era was a much more horizontal affair. And whereas a host of structures—corporate bodies, aristocratic lineages, privilege—supported political life in the early modern era, the Revolution left only individual actors on the scene. As a tie between individuals who were relative social equals, friendship was crucial because it was one of the only relationships that could build cohesion and facilitate politics in this environment. Additionally, there is the issue of ideology. The ideological divides of the Revolution made politics a much more fractious business and made the problem of trust more acute. Beyond the domain of sheer personal competition, politicians had a whole host of reasons not to like one another. Thus one of the principal functions of friendship in post-revolutionary political life was managing ideological divisions, as friendship could be used to prevent ruptures or build alliances among politicians who did not agree with one another. Men's ideological loyalties also meant that political roles were much more divided along the lines of gender after the Revolution than they had been before. Because of the circumscribed nature of their personal affiliations, men were especially suited to serve as allies and backers of factions, whereas women's relative impartiality and access to the emotions helped them work among political groupings. In contrast, neither of these roles was heavily gendered in the Old Regime.

PARLIAMENTARY POLITICS IN THE ERA OF THE NOTABLES

The Restoration was France's first sustained experiment with modern politics in the sense that this was a period of relative stability during which politicians were learning how to operate within the constraints of a parliamentary system. As a result, the political elites of the time had to acquire a whole new set of skills: how to negotiate with one another, how to organize factions, how to form alliances among political groupings, and even how to fight with one another. In this climate, friendship provided a set of powerful norms that governed interpersonal relationships as well as a way to understand allegiance. The July Monarchy built on this legacy of the Restoration, particularly since the structure of parliamentary government did not fundamentally change after the Revolution of 1830. Notably, like its predecessor, this new regime lacked official political parties. Many of the dominant politicians of this regime, including Guizot and Thiers, also received their political education during the Restoration and so continued to rely on the political practices they had learned before 1830.[3]

As they became proficient in the ways of parliamentary government, the politicians of the post-revolutionary era faced the a lack of trust and cohesion, key requirements for all of these new types of political activity. Indeed, far more than presidential forms of government, parliamentary systems need trust in order to function. After all, the government can survive only if it has the backing of politicians in the parliamentary body.[4] Ministers, too, came from within the parliament, and the composition of the cabinet was generally the product of negotiations among members of the Chambers.[5] All these negotiations required some form of trust. Factions needed to know that the men they nominated for cabinet positions would not betray their views once in power. Many of the ministries in the period between 1815 and 1848 were coalition governments as well. In these instances, the different political groupings had to offer reassurances of their loyalty to one another and to a shared set of principles.

However, the structure of parliamentary politics in this era made the question of cohesion especially thorny. French politicians rejected the British model that relied on parties, but in many cases factions functioned like parties did. Many of them had clear leaders; Chateaubriand served as the head of the faction known as the Defection in the late 1820s, while Guizot was de facto party leader of the doctrinaires during the July Monarchy. French politicians also had to negotiate both within their own factions and with members of rival groupings, as did their cross-Channel neighbors. The problem, however, was that French politicians had to come up with an alternate understanding of allegiance. Markers such as salon attendance became one way to do so, but unlike belonging to a party, going to a salon or a political reunion entailed no real obligation to be loyal to a certain faction. Nor was there any enforcement mechanism to deal with politicians who were unreliable allies, such as party whips, who are dedicated to maintaining discipline within formal political structures.[6] The lack of official parties created exceptional complications during the July Monarchy, an era that saw a profusion of factions organized around prominent politicians, such as Guizot or Thiers, instead of around clear ideological positions.[7] As a result, negotiations over the composition of cabinets and legislation were extraordinarily complex and lengthy.[8]

Because of the structural deficits within post-revolutionary politics, trust and cohesion were vital political commodities. Without these interpersonal qualities, politicians could neither maintain the cohesion of their own factions nor work successfully with other political groupings. Yet the members of the political class were operating in an era beset by the problems of distrust and individualism, one when public life was seen as particularly divisive and anomic. This was one reason why friendship was so important, for invocations of the affection between friends served as a way to build trust and create solidarity between political actors. In turn, as the epilogue will discuss, the practices of relying on personal ties within political life left a significant legacy for French political culture even in an era of official political parties, as parties in the Third Republic emerged out of clubs and friendship networks.

The use of social ties within a political context was also intimately connected to the narrow dimensions of political life in this era. From 1815 until 1848, France was governed by a tiny oligarchy. During the Restoration, electoral rights were limited to a mere ninety thousand of the wealthiest citizens. After the Revolution of 1830, the electorate increased to only two hundred thousand. Voters thus traveled in similar social circles and relied on social spaces to transact politics. For instance, in the provinces, men's clubs were gathering places for liberals, while salons were the locus of conservative politics.[9] In Paris, salons served politicians of all political stripes, and throughout the period of post-revolutionary monarchy they were a central location of extra-parliamentary activity.[10] Because of the lack of official political parties, ideological affiliations were generally understood through social ones. The salons that politicians attended frequently identified their political orientation. In an 1817 letter to his wife, Hercule de Serre, then aligned with the doctrinaires, stated that there were three basic divisions among Parisian political elites of the time: moderates who went to "the reunion at M. Ternaux's," those on the left who went to Laffitte's, and ultras, who had a variety of salons to attend.[11] During the July Monarchy, the doctrinaires gathered at the salon of Mme de Broglie or that of Lieven, while those allied with Thiers went to that of Eurydice Sophie Matheron Dosne, his mother-in-law. Salons also gave politicians a place to share information and discuss and disseminate strategy.

In an 1817 letter to his wife, Joseph de Villèle stated, "Reunions . . . are entirely necessary so that our little regiment can be put together."[12] For Villèle, who would become the effective party leader of the ultras in the 1820s, the cohesion of his faction was created through social activity. Hence, as politicians were learning how to organize parliamentary life, they relied on institutions of sociability and they adapted preexisting social forms to serve the new needs of this era.[13] In this respect, the period of parliamentary monarchy was one in which the political and the social were collapsed.

MALE FRIENDSHIP AND POLITICS: ALLIES AND PROXIES

The essential lack of division between the political and the social is visible in the language that politicians used to describe factional allegiance, as well as some of the uses of male friends in political transactions. In both elections and the negotiations surrounding ministerial combinations, friends were stand-ins for one another. For instance, if the leader of a government did not or could not include a prominent politician in his ministry, he often called on a friend of the politician to serve in the cabinet. This use of friendship in politics arose out of the set of understandings about the way in which male friendship functioned. Male friends were so similar that they could serve as one another's proxies; the closest one could come to a double of a prominent politician was his friend. Because ties between men created obligation and solidarity, politicians were assured that they would have a representative in the cabinet to look after their interests. In these instances, friendship created public forms of loyalty—a task that was both difficult and necessary in the political climate of the time.

At the most basic level, politicians used the vocabulary of friendship to stand in for political affiliation, as members of the same faction employed the term "ami" with one another. For example, speakers at the tribune used the phrase "honorable ami" to refer to their allies. Politicians also used this salutation in their letters to members of the same camp.[14] As one of the secondary definitions of "ami," such a usage was hardly new to the post-revolutionary period. In the Old Regime, the term "ami" had been used for allies, backers, or patrons. British politicians also used the phrase "my honorable friend" to refer to their allies in their parliamentary speeches.[15] In this case, the French borrowed from their past and their cross-Channel neighbors who were more experienced in the ways of parliamentary government.

In practice, too, a politician's closest friends were often his political allies. The ties among Guizot, Barante, and Victor de Broglie were those of political and personal allegiance. Likewise, Béranger, Dupont de l'Eure, and Manuel were bound by their shared political affiliation and their friendship. Many of Chateaubriand's male friends were also his allies, including Hyde de Neuville and Clausel de Coussergues. Like him, they were all ultras in the early years of the Restoration, and they followed him into the political center in the mid-1820s. Indeed, in the political climate of the Restoration, it was hard for men to be friends without a shared political allegiance.

Bound by similarity and solidarity, male friends were also proxies in political campaigns, when friendship became shorthand for political affiliation. Take, for instance, an 1824 letter from Manuel to his friend Dupont de l'Eure after an election campaign in which Manuel had stood as a candidate in the department of the Seine. One year earlier, Manuel had been expelled from the Chamber of Deputies for a speech that seemed to condone regicide. Re-electing Manuel to the Chamber became a rallying cause for those on the far-left. His return to the Chamber would indicate that the electorate disapproved of his expulsion, the ultras who led the charge, and the regime as a whole. Unfortunately for Manuel, the electors of the Seine were hesitant to vote for him; doing so would be a step too far. Instead, they cast their votes for Dupont, who had campaigned heavily for his friend. In writing to Dupont after the results were announced, Manuel reassured his friend that he was not upset about his loss to Dupont. Indeed, Manuel stated that he was not wholly displeased with the result of the election. After all, the electors had shown that they agreed with Manuel and Dupont's common cause of far-left politics. As Manuel wrote, the electors "clearly proclaim . . . that they have adopted the cause that I upheld in our shared fight. . . . In a word, all of France knows that you are, in the Chamber of Deputies, in my political career, my closest and most faithful friend [*mon plus intime et plus constant ami*]."[16]

These references to their friendship indicate that Manuel understood that if the electors of the Seine had not voted for him, they had voted for the next best thing—Dupont. Manuel's evidence that Dupont was his stand-in was that Dupont was widely known as his "closest and most faithful friend" in political life. In this, Manuel relied on the fact that "ami" is the term for both ally and friend. His statement referenced both the political realm (their shared work in the Chamber of Deputies) and the personal, as he uses the term "intime" to describe their bond. This word meant both close and private; in this case, it signified that the two men were close political collaborators *and* devoted personal friends. In other words, of all his political allies, Dupont was the one to whom he was personally closest. Such a statement was meant to reassure Dupont that his efforts to get Manuel elected had not failed, since he very nearly succeeded. If the electors of the Seine did not feel they could vote for Manuel, they cast their votes for his substitute. To phrase it another way, in voting for Dupont, the electors had come as close as they could to voting for Manuel, because Dupont, as a friend, was essentially Manuel's twin.

Friends were also used as proxies in negotiations surrounding the composition of cabinets. Calling on personal networks was a common tactic to ensure support from various factions and to neutralize potential opposition to ministries. For instance, in 1828, Joseph de Villèle was ousted from power after serving as the head of the government for seven years. The vicomte de Martignac led the new cabinet, one that was more centrist than Villèle's ultra-dominated one. In order to have any hope of surviving, Martignac would have to placate various conservatives. Villèle was one threat: it was not hard to imagine that he would be opposed to the Martignac government, both because it was too moderate and because he wanted to return to power. Just as dangerous were the men grouped around Chateaubriand who occupied a position in the center-right of the political spectrum and were used to voicing opposition to the government. But although Martignac needed to reach out to Chateaubriand, he could not include him in the cabinet. Chateaubriand was too much of a troublemaker and too proud to be part of any ministry of which he was not the head. He was thus appointed ambassador to Rome, which both gave him a position in the government and removed him from France. At Chateaubriand's suggestion, Hyde de Neuville was made minister of the navy, while the comte de La Ferronnays became minister of foreign affairs in the new cabinet. Both men were members of the Defection and personal friends. Martignac hoped that Chateaubriand would avoid criticizing a government in which his allies served. Meanwhile, the comte de Montbel, one of Villèle's closest friends, also joined the cabinet. In this way, Martignac also placated Villèle and his allies.[17]

These efforts went beyond attempting to ensure that Chateaubriand and Villèle's factions were represented in the new cabinet. Because Hyde de Neuville and La Ferronnays were Chateaubriand's friends, it was possible to imagine that Chateaubriand was in fact a member of the government; the same was true with Montbel and Villèle. Of course, Chateaubriand and Villèle would never have agreed to serve together in a ministry, for their animosity toward each other ran too deep. Nor would Martignac want them to do so, as they were too prominent in their own right. But if he could not have them, their friends were valuable substitutes. The nature of the Chateaubriand/Hyde de Neuville and the Villèle/Montbel relationships are also significant. Undoubtedly, Chateaubriand suggested that Hyde de Neuville join the cabinet because of his merits as a politician. Hyde was also one of Chateaubriand's closest and most loyal friends. He could be considered the one who was most like him and who could best serve as a proxy. Likewise, Montbel was not just any politician from Villèle's faction. The two men were close friends, both were from Toulouse, and both had served as mayor of that city.[18] Montbel and Hyde were the closest that one could get to Villèle and Chateaubriand respectively without having these two men in the cabinet.

Politicians of the July Monarchy would use many of the same tactics, as can be seen in the negotiations surrounding doctrinaire participation in Thiers's cabinet of 1840. After years of ministerial turmoil, the king asked Thiers to form a new government. To do so, Thiers called on both the center-left and the dynastic left. This was the most left-leaning cabinet of the July Monarchy. Not surprisingly, Thiers was concerned about how Guizot, the leader of the conservatives in the Chambers, would react to its formation. Fortunately, Guizot had been made ambassador to Britain under the previous ministry and so could simply retain this posting. For Thiers, this had the advantage of keeping him out of Paris and made him less able to act against the ministry. Nevertheless, he was still a powerful politician who needed to be appeased. Hence, Thiers selected two doctrinaires to serve in his cabinet—Hippolyte François Jaubert and Rémusat. Just after the ministry was formed, Thiers wrote Guizot the following about the government: "You will see that two of your friends are among its members."[19] As in the Martignac ministry, the relational quality was key. Rémusat in particular was meant to assuage any of Guizot's fears about the cabinet and to ensure that Guizot felt represented in it. Rémusat was made minister of the interior, a job that was generally second in importance only to that of minister of foreign affairs, Thiers's position. Rémusat was valuable because he was one of the few politicians who had been able to strike a balance between the doctrinaires' center-right position and Thiers's center-left one. But while there were other left-leaning doctrinaires, Rémusat was the one who was personally closest to Guizot. He had known Guizot since the early days of the Restoration and had been very close to Guizot's first wife. Rémusat was useful because his emotional proximity to Guizot would make the latter feel that his views were represented in the cabinet. As a male friend, he would serve in Guizot's stead, look after his interests, and behave with loyalty.

Rémusat's role as a stand-in for Guizot placed him in an enormously difficult position, for he would be at the epicenter of all tensions between Thiers and the doctrinaires. In order to secure his ties to the latter group, he went to see Broglie and asked for his support. Broglie gave Rémusat his blessing, as he had consulted with Thiers on the formation of the cabinet. Just as he backed the new ministry, he also backed Rémusat's role in it. Rémusat wrote of this encounter, "I opened myself up to Broglie, who showed me more friendship than he ever had before."[20] Broglie's support was crucial because, with Guizot in London, he was the most prominent doctrinaire politician who remained in France. He also tended to get along better with Thiers than Guizot did.[21] Moreover, he was Guizot's best friend. The Broglie and the Guizot families were deeply intertwined; until Guizot bought his property of Val-Richer in the Calvados, Guizot and his kin spent their summers with the Broglies in their chateau in the Eure. Indeed, these summers and his connection to the Broglies were the reasons that Guizot eventually settled in Normandy, rather than in his native South.[22] Securing Broglie's backing was as close as Rémusat and Thiers could come to obtaining that of Guizot himself. As a friend, Broglie was a stand-in for the absent politician. Here, friendship functioned as both a relationship and a way to reference political loyalty. It was the bond that linked Rémusat, Broglie, and Guizot, but when Rémusat stated that Broglie showed him friendship, he was not necessarily (or not solely) referencing Broglie's personal feelings for him. Instead, what was crucial was Broglie's political backing and declaration of support.

These negotiations regarding the composition of cabinets reveal the political applications of a set of ideas about bonds among men. Centered on loyalty and a notion of shared burdens, male friends were bound to look after one another's interests. Coalition government thus called on friendship networks to ensure that prominent politicians felt represented in ministries in cases where these men could not or would not serve. Such uses of friendship could neutralize potential opposition and build trust between factions. Chateaubriand could trust the Martignac ministry because two of his friends were in it, while in 1840 Thiers's selection of Guizot's friends was designed to reassure him about the politics of the cabinet. In 1836, too, when Thiers and Guizot sent letters to each other sealing their alliance through expressions of friendship, they were calling on the idea of the friend as proxy. Thiers would act as a representative of Guizot's interests in the cabinet, while Guizot would do the same for Thiers from within the Chambers. In an era without formal means to understand affiliation or ensure party discipline, it was personal connections that made up for the structural deficits of political life.

POLITICS IN THE LANGUAGE OF FRIENDSHIP: DESCRIBING AFFILIATION, MANAGING CONFLICT

The political uses of friendship are also apparent in negotiations in which political figures employed an elaborate rhetoric of affection to discuss the terms of their relationships with one another. Friendship offered a powerful and easily understood set of norms for interpersonal bonds. In these instances, politicians used a sentimental language of friendship with those who were in no way their actual friends. These affectionate words were not designed to make claims about the speakers' emotional states, as these politicians were not attempting to deceive their interlocutors. Rather, expressions of love were meant to be indicative of the attributes of friendship: they were promises of loyalty and statements of public affiliation. This language of affection was an adaptation of the language of patronage of early modern France, one in which clients employed a rhetoric of affection in their letters to their patrons. In the early nineteenth century, this vocabulary was adapted to the new needs of the post-revolutionary era. It was no longer used to negotiate dependence, but rather the terms of the relationship between prominent political figures who sought one another's backing or wanted to ward off the threat of ideological divisions. Thus this was a horizontal language of affiliation and not a vertical one. And in a period when oaths, intentions, and promises were thought to be meaningless and when political life was regarded as hostile and atomizing, politicians reverted to a vocabulary from the private realm to indicate their loyalty to one another, as friendship was understood to be a durable bond of devotion.

Politicians commonly used this affectionate language with one another during ministerial reshufflings, moments of great tension within the parliamentary body. These changes in cabinet makeup were a constant feature of parliamentary life in the Restoration and July Monarchy. The 1830s, for example, was an exceptionally unstable decade, one that saw a total of fourteen ministries. In other instances, a particular minister was replaced and the rest of the personnel of the government remained in place. As individual ministers were swapped out, leaders of the cabinets had reasons to be concerned about the loyalty of the men who had been divested of their posts. After all, a prominent politician had been informed that he was no longer an asset to the government and deprived of a source of income. Additionally, the formation of a completely new government often signified a political shift, and members of the previous ministry might have ideological reasons to oppose the new one. Understandably, these were moments when the leader of the government wanted reassurances that those who were no longer in power would not become his adversaries. In these cases, expressions of friendship and devotion served to indicate that the excluded politician would remain aligned with the government. This is precisely how Thiers and Guizot were using sentiment in their 1836 letters, as both men were operating within a cultural context in which friendship stood in for ideological affiliation and loyalty.

For instance, take an epistolary exchange between the duc de Richelieu and Élie Decazes in 1818. Since 1815, Richelieu had been leader of a cabinet in which Decazes served as minister of the police. Richelieu was aligned with the center-right and Decazes with the center-left and the doctrinaires, but the two maintained good relations up until the end of 1818.[23] The problem was that in the elections of 1818, the liberal opposition had won seats while the ultras had lost ground; as a result, Richelieu needed to make a decision as to where he would find backing from within the Chambers. He wanted to form an alliance between the center and the right, but Decazes, who was the king's favorite, preferred one between the center and the left. This occasioned a split between the center-right and the center-left, as well as a fight between the two men who came to regard each other with increasing ill will and saw each other as disloyal. After moving closer to the right, Richelieu eventually resigned from the cabinet and Decazes became minister of the interior as well as head of the new government. For Decazes, this created a problem: would Richelieu oppose him and his new ministry? After all, he hardly wanted a powerful and respected politician like Richelieu to shift from being an ally to being an adversary. Thus Decazes wrote the following to Richelieu after calling on him and being told he was unavailable: "Your door is closed to me and I greatly fear that your heart will also become closed to me." Ten days later, Richelieu replied, saying, "Assuredly it will never be my heart that is closed to you. A few miserable differences of opinion cannot destroy bonds held together by esteem and friendship."[24]

Although both politicians were speaking in a sentimental language with references to hearts and friendship, the issue here was hardly one of feeling. By this point the two men's relationship had soured considerably. In any case, what Decazes wanted was not a personal friendship with Richelieu but an indication of where his political loyalties lay. In his reply, Richelieu stated that while his political views were not those of Decazes, he still felt some attachment to his former colleague. In other words, he was reassuring Decazes that he would not betray him or work against him; he would act like a friend would in the political realm. Here then, questions of political allegiance and behavior were phrased in terms of personal affection—words of friendship were a metaphor, not an expression of deep emotion.

A September 1847 letter from Marshal Soult to Guizot called on much the same uses of affection in the context of a ministerial shift. The former had been president of the Council of Ministers since 1840, but while he was officially head of the cabinet, he was not politically active. Rather, he lent a luster of Napoleonic military glory to the government and helped hide the fact that Guizot—who was deeply unpopular—was the real leader of the ministry. Both men were staunch conservatives but hardly friends. All their correspondence was entirely formal and never personal. Nor did they even like each other. Guizot once called Soult a "vulgar muddle-head," and there was considerable tension between the two during the 1840s.[25] In 1847, Guizot and Louis-Philippe decided that they could do without Soult, and thus Guizot became president of the Council in addition to retaining his position as minister of foreign affairs. In a letter to Guizot accepting his ouster from the government, Soult wrote, "I have the honor to renew from my heart and soul the assurance of a friendship that will only end with my life."[26] Here, Soult used elements of the language of friendship, notably the references to the heart, to suggest that his affection for Guizot was deeply rooted. So, too, he wrote that his good feeling would last until death, as if the two men were similar to the lifelong friends idealized in novels of the time. Yet the letter and this statement were too formal to have been an exchange between friends. Soult's formulation is too stiff, and male friends did not speak of the honor of expressing their feelings. Given this and the long history of antipathy between the two men, Soult's letter was not meant to signify affect. This empty expression of emotion served to reassure Guizot that Soult would remain loyal to the conservative cause. He was indicating that he bore Guizot no ill will, despite his removal from office, and that Guizot could trust him not to betray him or his politics. Whatever his actual emotional state, Soult would act like a friend in the political sphere.

Politicians also used this sentimental language during moments of conflict. Two instances—one from the Restoration and one from the early years of the July Monarchy—illuminate how an empty rhetoric of friendship signified trust and allegiance in the political realm. In both cases, the individuals were somewhat estranged from each other and used expressions of love to sort out questions of affiliation and smooth over conflict.

One use of friendship as a metaphor to indicate cohesion can be found in a January 1829 letter from Benjamin Constant to Béranger, written in response to a letter from Béranger. This first letter has been lost, but it is clear from Constant's reply that the songwriter had rebuked Constant for his political views and activity and for an article he wrote in the *Courrier français*. In particular, both men were writing during a period of tension within the liberal camp between moderates like Constant and those further to the left like Béranger. During the center-right Martignac ministry, Constant was inclined to compromise with the cabinet, or at the very least cease his hostility. Indeed, he took to praising the government from the tribune when he approved of its actions.[27] The prospect of a union between prominent liberals and the government (what Béranger called "fusion") was, however, anathema to Béranger, for he considered that the entire Restoration regime was irredeemable and had to be overthrown. Indeed, Béranger had thrown down the gauntlet in 1828 with the publication of a new collection of songs that attacked the government. Imprisoned for sedition, Béranger had shown the limitations of the Martignac government's moderation. Anyone who was inclined to compromise with the ministry risked being seen as betraying Béranger, then at the height of his popularity.[28]

Constant's letter made these essential political differences between the two men clear while ceding no ground. The songwriter's letter had accused Constant of pursing a fusion between liberals and the ministry and seeking a position in the cabinet. For his part, Constant stated in his reply that he had no particular interest in obtaining a ministerial post and that "I will neither work toward nor oppose the fusion."[29] But of course he was not saying he would not accept a cabinet position were it offered to him, only that he did not seek one. Similarly, his statement that he was ambivalent toward the prospect of a fusion could be interpreted as indicating that he would agree to a fusion if the government, and not the liberals, were the ones who compromised. Constant was also forthright about his essential ideological differences with Béranger. He states, "I believe that we should remain a constitutional monarchy. I know or I think I know that old governments are more favorable toward freedom than new ones [i.e., republics]."[30] Thus he indicated that while he had no attachment to the Bourbon Restoration, he had no desire for a republic, as Béranger did.

For Constant, the problem was that these differences put him in a tight spot. He hardly wanted to cause a rupture among the liberals; nor did he want the immensely popular Béranger to turn on him. In order to win over Béranger despite their disagreement, Constant turned to a language of friendship and affection. He thus opened his letter with a statement describing his great love for the songwriter: "My dear Béranger, although your letter contains many things that could distress or hurt me, there is, especially toward the end, a wealth of friendship and interest that produced such a singular effect that I felt more pleasure than pain. You are one of the men toward whom I feel the most drawn."[31] Béranger could be a stingingly frank correspondent with those who disappointed him; Constant's opening indicated that the songwriter had not spared him. But Constant invoked the idea that the displeasure he felt in receiving Béranger's rebukes had turned into something sweeter. In the end, Béranger's letter demonstrated the affection the songwriter had for him and thus allowed Constant to show how much he loved the songwriter in return.

Toward the end of the letter, Constant continued in this same vein by stating, "This is a very long letter, my dear Béranger. I take great pleasure in talking to you with complete abandon. I would like it if this hassle . . . inaugurated a closer and more trusting friendship between the two of us. You are, I say again, the man in France who appeals the most to me. . . . I offer you a full and complete attachment. If we disagree on a few points, this is because our minds are differently made. This has nothing to do with affection."[32] Here Constant repeatedly invokes his love for Béranger, and as he did earlier in the letter he suggests that their quarrel has not so much demonstrated division as provided an opportunity for greater personal—although not political—union. He thus indicates that he hopes that the two of them will become great friends. Indeed, in the first sentence he describes how he has already begun such a move toward friendship. In stating that he writes with "with complete abandon," he makes it sound as if he was being especially honest and open, as if this letter was simply the outpourings of his heart and mind.

Instead of reading Constant's statements of affection as a reflection of his feelings, it is best to see that both men were operating in a context when a discourse of friendship served political ends. After all, Constant's letter was carefully crafted, and it is hard to imagine that his stated desire to become close friends with Béranger was in any way sincere. Given that he indicated that he was in fact open to some compromise with the government, Constant would have found a relationship with Béranger to be a liability. Rather, friendship functioned as a language meant to facilitate a political alliance that was in peril, for Constant was referencing the qualities of friendship, not his emotions. The two men had profound political disagreements, but the language of affection suggested that there could be some type of affiliation that overrode such differences. For one, Constant could claim that both men were united in a fundamental opposition to the Restoration regime, even if their views on the desirability of monarchy in general differed; friendship here stood in for similarity. Constant's invocations of emotion also assured Béranger that he would not betray the songwriter and that he would not go too far in his efforts to find common ground with the ministry. Notably, too, discussions of affection allowed Constant to articulate the idea of a loyal opposition: he understood and appreciated Béranger's different perspective even if he did not agree with it. This is most obvious when Constant states, "If we disagree on a few points, this is because our minds are differently made. This has nothing to do with affection." That is to say that he recognizes that their political disagreements arise out of their different natures and life experiences and are not the result of any deficits in Béranger's morality or intelligence. Historians have described that the problem of imagining a loyal opposition has bedeviled French politics since the Revolution. In this case, tropes of friendship were one way to signify difference without fundamental division, for they allowed Constant to state that he could not imagine betraying a man he wanted to treat as a friend.

This same reliance on a sentimental vocabulary is also visible in an October 1830 letter from Talleyrand to Molé at a moment of tension and conflict between the two men. Unlike in the Constant/Béranger exchange, the problem was not ideological. Both men belonged to the center-right and wanted to promote the interests of the new July Monarchy. Rather, the issue had to do with status and turf and whether these two men could establish a working relationship with each other. Although the men are somewhat outside the case studies on which this work concentrates, their remarkable exchange shows how a language of friendship established norms of communication and trust and smoothed over a conflict that threatened the stability of the newly established regime.

Soon after the Revolution of 1830, Molé was appointed minister of foreign affairs, while Talleyrand was made ambassador to Britain. This posting to London was both the most prestigious of all ambassadorships and, in 1830, the most important one. Talleyrand's job was to convince the British government that the July Monarchy was anything but revolutionary. If he could win acceptance for the new regime in Britain, all of Europe would follow. The upshot was that it was he who was really in charge of French foreign policy, more so than Molé.[33] Talleyrand was certainly the more experienced diplomat, and he met with considerable success in London. Dealing with Molé was another issue, for Talleyrand had no interest in showing deference to Molé or his position. Molé was technically his superior and the man through whom all communication with Louis-Philippe had to pass. Yet Talleyrand cut Molé out of the loop and reported to the king either through Mme de Vaudémont, a mutual friend, or through Mme Adélaïde, Louis-Philippe's sister and confidante. His dispatches to Molé were filled with useless information, such as reports on the tariffs for Portuguese wine.[34] In the words of one of Talleyrand's biographers, "Talleyrand behaved as if poor Molé did not even exist."[35]

By October 1830, Molé's frustration had become manifest and he was threatening to resign. Talleyrand felt that he had to mend fences, or at the very least give the illusion of doing so in order to prevent Molé from leaving the cabinet. After all, Molé's resignation would hardly have helped Talleyrand convince the British government that the Orleanist regime was a picture of stability.[36] He thus wrote a letter to Molé in which he stated:

> We know each other, we love each other, we want the same things, we understand them in the same way, we want them in the same fashion; our point of departure is similar, our goal is the same. Then why do we not understand each other on the route to this goal? This is something that I do not understand and that I hope will be temporary.—Our correspondence is neither friendly nor ministerial; it seems however that it should be otherwise between us, and I ask this of you with all my old interest. A less perfect trust, a less intimate understanding could damage, impede, stop our work, which would make me unhappy; our friendship could suffer, which would make me angry. If my way of seeing things is out of fashion, it would be easier to tell me plainly. We must be open with each other. We will only do well if we treat our affairs with

> the ease born of trust. You will find that I say everything except what I think to be of no importance.[37]

This is an astonishing letter, one that makes extraordinary claims about the relationship between the two men. Most notably, Talleyrand suggests that he and Molé are bound together by a great and strong friendship. He speaks of their love for each other and states that he is afraid that their friendship will be strained unless they learn to communicate better with each other. This letter is suffused with emotion terms like "sad," "angry," and "love" and he uses words like "friendship" and "intimate" to characterize their bond. The idea that male friends are bound by similarity also appears in the first sentence, where Talleyrand phrases everything in the first-person plural, stating the two men know each other, want the same things, have essentially the same views, and, of course, love each other. They are, more or less, twins who can substitute for each other. Likewise, toward the end of the letter, he maintains that the two men need to communicate more openly so that they can come to trust each other, and again raises the specter of an ideal friendship based on confidence and free communication.

As an account either of the relationship between the two men or of what went wrong between them, Talleyrand's letter is far from satisfactory. He did recognize that there was a communication problem between the two of them, but he suggested that the fault lay with both men, as he consistently used the first-person plural to describe the situation. He also stated that he did not know why their relationship was so strained ("This is something that I do not understand"). But, of course, the difficulties they were encountering had a clearly identifiable cause, for Talleyrand was violating the protocols of diplomatic communication. By so doing, he was implicitly asserting that he had no need of Molé, and that whatever their job titles, Talleyrand was master of the situation.

As in other epistolary exchanges between politicians, discussions of emotion were disconnected from actual emotional states. Though both men had worked with each other since the days of the Empire, they were hardly friends. Nor was this letter was meant to convince Molé that Talleyrand wanted to be his friend or that Talleyrand had some hidden wellspring of affection for him. Notably, Talleyrand's letter was *too* affectionate; this was not the way male friends communicated with each other. It was also without the trappings of epistolary communication between male friends, such as the use of "mon cher ami" as a salutation. And however Talleyrand regarded Molé, it was inconceivable that he would have thought that Molé would be taken in by such phrasings. The two men knew each too well for Talleyrand to have imagined that Molé would be deceived into thinking that this was the sudden and spontaneous outpouring of Talleyrand's heart.

Although these profusions of affection were empty, they were not meaningless, for this letter did serve a purpose. By using the language of friendship, Talleyrand was indicating that he would act like a friend. In this instance, he was promising that he would do a better job communicating with Molé and report to him as he should have done in the first place. It was the last sentence of the letter that was key, for here Talleyrand made a statement about how he would proceed in the future. He would tell Molé everything, leaving out only the trivial—those Portuguese wines, for instance. Such communication was Molé's immediate need. More generally, if Molé was going to remain in his position as minister of foreign affairs, the two men would have to have a functional working relationship and Talleyrand had to change how he treated Molé. He had to respect Molé and demonstrate that he was loyal to him, especially since ambassadors were considered political appointees who owed their allegiance to a particular ministry.[38] Talleyrand was promising that he would not work against Molé or seek to undermine him, as he had previously done by cutting him out of the chain of communication. In essence, he would have to trust that Molé knew what he was doing, while Molé would have to trust that Talleyrand was acting in the best interests of France and in accordance with their shared political principles.

Trust, loyalty, and respect were all requirements of friendship, and so useful here as these two men renegotiated the terms of their relationship. In using a language of friendship, moreover, Talleyrand was able to do more than merely suggest that he would act better in the future. Friendship is a bond of reciprocal obligation. If the two men were to be friends in the sense that they would act as such in the political sphere, Molé would be obliged to behave in a certain way as well. He could not undermine Talleyrand's position as an ambassador. While the king had great faith in Talleyrand's diplomatic abilities, Molé had the advantage of being in Paris and had had the king's ear whenever he wanted it. Speaking in the language of friendship meant that Talleyrand and Molé had to support each other.

Talleyrand's use of words of friendship was also extraordinarily canny in that it failed to resolve the central problem between the two men—who was really in charge. Friendship could indicate a vertical tie of dependence, as it did in early modern political discourse, and indeed Molé was Talleyrand's superior. But more commonly in the nineteenth century, friendship was understood as a bond among equals and Talleyrand's letter suggested that this is how he saw the nature of their relationship. Indeed, Talleyrand violated certain epistolary codes meant to indicate his own lower station on the diplomatic hierarchy in this letter, for diplomatic protocol required that Talleyrand address Molé as his superior. For example, in the Restoration, when Chateaubriand was ambassador to Britain, his letters to the minister of foreign affairs, Mathieu de Montmorency, showed clear signs of deference to Montmorency's position as his superior. Chateaubriand's letters were addressed "À Son Excellence, Monsieur le Vicomte de Montmorency," and he ended them with phrasings such as "I have the honor to be with a high consideration, Monsieur le Vicomte, your very humble and very obedient servant."[39] As a set of formulas, these indicated that Chateaubriand was Montmorency's subordinate. Montmorency was not, for instance, even required to include a closing statement in his responses to Chateaubriand; his letters could just end when the content did.[40] By violating these epistolary codes, Talleyrand was saying that he might keep Molé better informed in the future, but he would not recognize that Molé was his superior. Here, friendship signified Talleyrand's vision of the terms of their relationship: equality, obligation, and communication.

Thus, in all of these cases, politicians appropriated a language of friendship to describe political behavior. Friendship became a stand-in for trust, allegiance, and communication, and questions of ideological affiliation were personalized and sentimentalized. Friendship was useful because the duties of friendship were clear and well-known, and this bond presented a powerful set of norms for interpersonal relations. This use of the rhetoric of affection arose out of both the reworking of an old language of politics and the particular problems of the post-revolutionary era. With the birth of parliamentary government, politicians had to find ways to understand their relationships to one another at a time when it was no longer possible to imagine trust or loyalty as existing in the public realm. As a result, politicians appropriated a language from the private sphere to signify affiliation and cooperation.

The year 1815 reopened the wounds of the Revolution and ushered in a new chapter in France's political history, that of parliamentary monarchy. This conjuncture created a set of problems for the political class of France, as post-revolutionary politicians needed to find ways to establish and signify trust and cohesion. Although this context made ties between men and a language of friendship crucial to the political culture of the Restoration and July Monarchy, ultimately the uses of male friendship and this emotional rhetoric were quite limited. Words of friendship could serve to indicate that a politician intended to act in a particular manner, or could be deployed in an effort to persuade him to do so, but they offered no real guarantees. Empty of actual affection, they were only a statement of intention. Despite Talleyrand's claims to Molé, for example, he did not change his behavior. Placing male friends in a cabinet signified an alliance but could not create one—nor, in the end, could it offer substantial guarantees about the direction of the government.

One problem was that men's political loyalties were typically too circumscribed for them to be able to work between political groupings or build trust between factions. For example, Rémusat's task in the Thiers ministry of 1840 was to facilitate the relationship between center-left and center-right. Eventually, however, he had to make a choice as to whether his real allegiance was to Thiers or Guizot. When he chose the former, his friendship with the latter ended; Guizot and Rémusat were not on speaking terms until the 1850s. Since men's loyalties allowed insufficient room to maneuver, it was women who were called on to negotiate alliances and provide more lasting assurances of political loyalty.

6

THE BONDS OF CONCORD: WOMEN AND POLITICS

Because women could not vote or hold office during the post-revolutionary political regimes, they could not serve as proxies or allies in the way that male friends could. Yet despite this, many of the women studied here performed vital functions within the political system throughout the period of parliamentary monarchy. This chapter concentrates on three of these roles: helping politicians get along with one another, ensuring that factions remained united, and forming alliances. While none of these functions was an easy task in the fractious political climate of the time, politicians of the new parliamentary system needed to find ways to cooperate with one another. In order to do so, they relied on women's facility with male emotions and male interiority, as well as women's ability to socialize men. The fact that women could maintain personal ties that spanned political divides also helped them connect different factional groupings to one another. In essence, the particular nature of women's friendships made them especially able to build the trust and cohesion that allowed the parliamentary system of the post-revolutionary era to function. Hence, just as men gained access to the social and emotional through the women around them, women entered politics through their male friends.

To examine these issues, I focus primarily on the political negotiations of Guizot and Chateaubriand. If Béranger and his allies on the far-left are largely (although not entirely) absent, this is due to the nature of the documentary evidence, not to differences in how women functioned in republican circles. Guizot and Chateaubriand's maneuvers are especially easy to track because they often lived abroad as either exiles or ambassadors and so conducted many of their negotiations through correspondence. In contrast, while Béranger's friend Hortense Allart was instrumental in forming alliances during the Restoration, she largely did so orally and therefore left fewer traces of her political activity.

The scope of female political activity seems at odds with the idea of a strict separation between a private, female realm and a public, male one. Indeed, prominent political figures of the time voiced a desire to keep women out of politics. For instance, the duc de Richelieu, who was prime minister during many of the early years of the Restoration, thought that women had no business interfering in political matters. Mme de Montcalm, his sister, was inclined to agree with him. She regarded politics as a dirty, unpleasant business of which she wanted no part.[1] Guizot also maintained that women should refrain from any involvement in public life. At a speech in the Chamber of Deputies in 1842, he stated that women could not participate in politics because they "are dedicated to the family; as individuals, they are destined to develop through the affections of the home and through social relations."[2] This is as clear an articulation of the notion of separate spheres as any: women are domestic creatures who are connected to the emotional and the social and so cannot take part in public life. Yet both Richelieu and Guizot were dependent on women throughout their political careers, and Mme de Montcalm was highly active in politics—and quite successful at it. Whatever these men and women might think about the prospect of female political activity, they recognized that this was how the game was played.

Women's political roles arose in part from the legacy of the Old Regime when elite women served as crucial brokers and political intermediaries. Post-revolutionary politics did not see the elimination of female political activity so much as its transformation, as the functions of broker and go-between became feminized in the early nineteenth century. The new contours of early nineteenth-century politics and gender also facilitated the dimensions of female political engagement. Indeed, the seeming contradiction between women's official exclusion from public life and their de facto involvement in politics can be reconciled by recognizing that it was precisely the fact that women were outside of politics that gave them such important roles in parliamentary life. As private actors, they were connected to the emotions and so could use discussions of sentiment to spur men to action. Likewise, men could do the same with women, but not with one another. And because women were removed from political concerns, their networks could span factional divisions, which made them able to facilitate alliances between different political groupings. Yet the fact that women were regarded as private beings also limited the scope of their political activity. Because women accessed politics through the men around them, all final authority belonged to men. Women could offer advice, but it was up to men to decide whether to take it. Men's attitudes about the political activity of their female friends varied greatly. In some cases, they saw women as important and powerful political actors, but in others, they called on women to engage in politics only to help them achieve their own ends. Yet despite the limits on the degree to which women could exert influence, the roles they played were invaluable, as women made cooperation between politicians—and therefore the parliamentary life of the time more generally—possible.

ENSURING FACTIONAL UNITY

In the early nineteenth century, an era beset by anxieties about atomization and the anomie of public life, political thinkers often puzzled over what held factions together. After all, factional unity was necessary to the functioning of the political system, but there were no political parties to structure political life or enforce cooperation. What was it, theorists wondered, that allowed politicians to work in concert with one another? Was it a set of shared ideological positions? Or did interest and the pursuit of power lead men to unite with one another?[3] In practice, this matter was less perplexing, for women kept factions cohesive through their ability to maintain social networks and manage emotions.

One key female function was the circulation of information among politicians in the same camp. When he was ambassador to the United States, Hyde de Neuville received long letters from Mme de La Trémoïlle filled with news about the other ultra politicians with whom he was allied.[4] Likewise, Mme de Broglie's correspondence with Guizot contained important political news and information about her husband's activities.[5] Both women were highly partisan and committed to advancing the politics of their particular factions (the doctrinaires in Broglie's case and the ultras in La Trémoïlle's).[6] One way to do this was through conveying information between male allies, an extension of women's roles as communicators of affection and personal news between male friends.

At crucial moments, the unity of these women's political groupings also relied on Broglie and La Trémoïlle's abilities to access and manage emotions. For instance, in 1816, when Hyde de Neuville was in the United States, he was concerned about the state of the ultra camp. He was a relatively moderate ultra, but this was a moment when his more conservative and intransigent allies were making the most noise, unleashing a torrent of hostility onto Richelieu's centrist government. He wanted those who were like him and more inclined to compromise with the ministry to come to the fore. He also saw that an alliance between the far-right and the center-right would place the newly established government on a more secure footing. This was the task he gave to La Trémoïlle. In a letter from 1816, he wrote her with the following request: "It is you, Madame, who must guide our friends, and calm the impetuosity of some and the indecision of the others."[7] In order to accomplish Hyde's goal, La Trémoïlle was to play on the emotions of the other men in this camp. She was to pacify those on the extreme right so that they would give up their intense hostility to the ministry—to manage their emotions, in essence. At the same time, she was to reassure moderate ultras that they were on the correct course and move them away from their hesitancy.

This was an intelligent reading of the political situation, for, as will be discussed below, there was considerable common ground between moderate ultras and the center-right government; the real problem was precisely the ultras' overheated and rancorous tone. However, this was not a terribly good understanding of La Trémoïlle's personality or politics. She was famous for being intransigent and was aligned with the immoderate ultras of whom Hyde was so critical.[8] That Hyde made this suggestion indicates that he was either unaware of her political leanings or that he thought that whatever her views, she would still take his advice. The former possibility is unlikely. She was his friend and frequent correspondent, and, from all accounts, she was not shy about voicing her political views. More probably, it is that he understood her role as ensuring that the ultras were united, and that this task was to outweigh her desire to promote her own politics.

Mme de Broglie was another highly partisan woman who used her close connections to the men of the doctrinaire circle to keep them united in order to advance their position. This is particularly visible in a letter to Barante written in 1820 after a government led by the center-left Decazes fell to a more conservative one. Barante, who was allied with Decazes, was removed from his position in the government, thereby depriving him of an important source of income.[9] As a consolation, he was offered the ambassadorship to Denmark. Unsure of whether to accept this posting, Barante wrote to Mme de Broglie asking for her advice. Her response was an impassioned plea for him to stay in France. She stated that she could understand if he needed to accept the position due to financial exigency, but that otherwise he should not take the posting. Doing so would make him dependent on an increasingly conservative government and would remove him from France, where he was badly needed. In her account, the rapid shifts in the political terrain meant that the doctrinaires occupied a vital and necessary place in the political spectrum, as they were uniquely able to fight against the excesses of both the right and the left. In her words, "If we unite, if we draw together, we can become a core that attracts all those who love order and liberty." In other words, what she wanted was for the doctrinaires to be a cohesive faction that provided a voice of moderation. If Barante left France, this would be impossible. Such a desire was obviously close to her heart, and there is little doubt that her description of the doctrinaires as loving order and liberty was a statement of her own views. As a member of this political grouping, she was defining herself as a political actor, one attempting to exert influence on Barante to achieve her own aims. For personal and political reasons, she wanted to keep Barante in France and called on the emotions to do so. Toward the end of the letter, her prose became especially passionate. She wrote, "You have so many good reasons to give outside of political ones! Separate yourself from your loved ones, your family! Lead your wife to a terrible climate or be far from her! Your four children, to separate yourself from them or to take them who knows where! Even if the ministry did as much for you as it did against you, it would not merit such a sacrifice!"[10] Broglie's sentiments were here indicated by the liberal use of exclamation points and sentence fragments, as if she were so overcome by feeling that she could not write in full sentences.

Such an outpouring relied on Broglie's ability to express emotion, for the men of the doctrinaire camp could not have used such impassioned words to make the case that Barante should stay in France. Similarly, she also called on her ability to discuss his personal life. The last sentence provides a political reason why he should not go to Denmark—that he owed nothing to a ministry that had sacked him. But before that, she spoke of the personal sacrifices he would have to endure were he to go. Either he would be separated from his family or he would have to bring them to Copenhagen, a city that must have seemed like the back of beyond for a woman like Broglie. Given the norms of male correspondence, Barante's male friends could have supplied political justifications as to why he should stay in France. But she could make a fuller and more complex case, one that called on the political, the personal, and the emotional. As an argument for factional unity, this was bound to be more successful than one based solely on political considerations. In the end,

Barante refused the posting to Denmark, and while we do not have his response to Broglie's letter, his biographer states that her arguments may have had something to do with his decision to turn down the offer.[11]

La Trémoïlle and Broglie undertook the same task in the early years of the Restoration for much the same reason—because they believed ardently in the causes with which their factions were aligned. But these two instances show two different relationships between women's political activity and their ideological positions. For Mme de Broglie, her advice to Barante was a way to promote the doctrinaire cause and ensure that her male friends were effective in political life. In the case of Hyde de Neuville's letter, he sought to get La Trémoïlle to back his own vision of ultra politics, one that was dissimilar from hers. She was to facilitate his political program, not her own. These two instances show two models of female political engagement that will be seen throughout this chapter—that of women who exerted influence and achieved their own ends, and that of women who were called on to act as facilitators who could transmit information and cultivate politically useful emotional states in the men around them.

MANAGING POLITICAL RELATIONSHIPS

Female friends also played vital roles in helping politicians get along with one another in the Restoration and July Monarchy, a task that was often intimately bound up with the practice of ensuring factional cohesion. For instance, Chateaubriand relied heavily on the women around him to smooth over his relations with other politicians. Given his notoriously difficult personality, he was hardly beloved by the other political figures of the day, including Richelieu and Villèle, and so needed women to manage his relationships and thus advance his political career. Hence, during a term as ambassador to Prussia, he was desperate to return to Paris. To do so, he needed to have the support of Richelieu, the head of the cabinet, and so he turned to his friend Mme de Pisieux, who was also friends with Richelieu. In a letter from January 1821, he told her to "continue to look after my friendship with your prominent neighbor [Richelieu] if you want to see me returned to France."[12] If she could make Richelieu like him more, he would be able to end his glorified exile.

Similarly, Mme de Duras often reached out to Villèle on Chateaubriand's behalf while Mme Récamier ensured that Chateaubriand and her friend

Mathieu de Montmorency maintained a functional working relationship with each other despite their mutual antipathy. This was especially important in 1822, when Chateaubriand was ambassador to London and Montmorency was minister of foreign affairs and thus his superior. Yet Récamier was no ultra. Considerably more moderate than either Chateaubriand or Montmorency, she did her best to prevent a breach between them out of a personal loyalty to these two men.[13] Likewise, in the 1830s, Guizot called on his friend Mme de Castellane to facilitate his relationship with Mathieu Molé, then Castellane's lover. Although the two men were occasionally allied with each other, they hated each other and needed her to keep the peace between them.[14]

Two relatively well-documented instances provide substantive glimpses into this type of female political activity. The first comes from Chateaubriand's career and shows how his friend Mme de Montcalm tried to control his emotions in order to facilitate his relationship with her brother, the duc de Richelieu. In the second we can see how one member of the doctrinaire circle manipulated notions about female emotionality for political ends.

Chateaubriand and Richelieu were two prominent politicians of the Restoration who had a highly troubled relationship. The latter was a center-right moderate, while Chateaubriand was an outspoken ultra. Strictly speaking, the two men's political views were not that dissimilar. Unlike other ultras, Chateaubriand supported the Charter of 1814 and believed strongly in freedom of the press; in this respect both he and Richelieu were monarchists who accepted some of the gains of the Revolution. The real problem between the two men was one of tone. Richelieu was conciliatory, whereas Chateaubriand shared the ultras' inflammatory style of politics.[15]

In 1821, however, these two men wanted to reconcile with each other. Richelieu was head of a government that looked to the ultras for support, and he included two members of this camp—Villèle and Corbière—in the cabinet. He was considering replacing them with Chateaubriand, who was for his part desperate for a ministerial position. To effect this swap, Richelieu relied on his sister, Mme de Montcalm. She wrote Chateaubriand a note in which she said, "In the name of the friendship that I have for you, be careful and moderate in your speeches in the Chamber of Peers. You must not heighten party spirit at this moment. . . . I can assure you that if the two men leave [the cabinet], it will be good for you."[16] In essence, Montcalm was indicating that Richelieu was open to including Chateaubriand in the ministry if Villèle and Corbière were no longer a part of it. In order to join the government, though, Chateaubriand would need to change his behavior in the Chamber of Peers. He would have to moderate his tone and become less adversarial in public toward Richelieu and the political center. His devotion to his faction needed to give way to a more conciliatory attitude.

Here, Montcalm was not trying to change Chateaubriand's politics but to restrain his hostility. He was to do this both because this would get him the result he so badly wanted and because it would please her, for she began her note with a request that he moderate his tone for her sake. This was an act of emotional management as Montcalm attempted to cultivate Chateaubriand's positive emotions for her while at the same time tempering his aversion toward political moderation. Montcalm's advice was bound up in her gender, for as a woman she had access to his emotions. Her ability to maintain personal ties to both ultras and moderates made her able to argue that whatever their political differences, Chateaubriand should be a loyal friend and act in a way that made her happy. Unfortunately for Chateaubriand's sake, Montcalm's efforts did not bear fruit, and he was never included in any Richelieu-led cabinet. Nevertheless, the significance of this incident lies in how she made her case to Chateaubriand and how she tried to work between him and her brother.

One considerably more successful act of emotional management occurred in 1840, when Charles de Rémusat cultivated a friendship with a woman to secure his relationship with Adolphe Thiers after the latter became head of a new, left-leaning government. To win the support of the center-right doctrinaires, Thiers made Rémusat minister of the interior. In 1840, Rémusat knew that he might not be able to maintain his allegiances to both Thiers and Guizot. As discussed in chapter 5, he went to Broglie to secure his right flank. But he was also concerned that he would end up in a difficult position if Guizot and the other doctrinaires came to oppose Thiers's cabinet. In order to make sure that Thiers would continue to trust him whatever the other doctrinaires did, Rémusat went to Mme Dosne, Thiers's salonnière, mistress, and mother-in-law (!). In his memoirs, he writes that he spoke "for a long time about gratitude and friendship" and "beseeched her to be the bond of concord between us [i.e., between himself and Thiers] and the guardian of our mutual trust."[17]

What Rémusat wanted was a back channel to Thiers and a way to communicate with him in an unofficial fashion. He also needed to make sure that he had an advocate in Thiers's inner circle, someone who could smooth over any difficulties the two men might have. If he could make Dosne into his friend, she could be this figure. In this instance Rémusat's efforts were successful and the ministry did not founder over the question of factional loyalty. Indeed, in 1840, Rémusat moved from the doctrinaire camp into Thiers's center-left one.

In his memoirs, Rémusat suggested that he recruited Dosne through emotional manipulation, as he stated that he greatly exaggerated his anxieties about his place in the new cabinet in order to win her over.[18] Here, he was playing on the idea that men could reveal their innermost thoughts and feelings to women. If he could manipulate Dosne into thinking that he was deeply concerned about his relationship with Thiers, she could quell any of Thiers's suspicions about Rémusat's loyalty. As a woman she could claim to know Rémusat's true feelings toward her son-in-law, whereas Thiers would have less access to them—and so would be inclined to rely on Dosne's understanding of Rémusat's intentions. This self-conscious performance of emotion suggests that Rémusat's success was due in part to his ability to manipulate the emotional codes of the time for political ends. His calculations also lay bare the fact that he recognized the power of women's capacity to manage emotions, for he saw that Dosne's real role was not to be his confidante, but to keep the peace between himself and Thiers. Indeed, elsewhere in his memoirs he stated that he did not like her.[19] He did not want a friendship with her in any real sense of the term, but rather wanted her to act as female friends did in the political realm.

In both instances, what women did or what they were asked to do was create and manage trust between political figures so that ministries could function. This is most obvious in the case of Rémusat and Dosne, when he asked her to be the "guardian" of the trust between him and Thiers. After all, Thiers had plenty of reasons to be suspicious of Rémusat, for while the two men were friends, shared politics and long-standing bonds tied Rémusat to the rival doctrinaire camp. Indeed, his affiliation with Guizot was one principal reason Thiers selected him for a cabinet position. To make sure there was no breakdown in his relationship with Thiers, Rémusat needed to resort to Dosne, who had a facility with social ties and the emotions. Likewise, Chateaubriand and Richelieu had reasons to distrust each other, for Richelieu and the ultras had been opposed to each other's politics for years. But Montcalm could claim to be her brother's confidante who had access to his true thoughts and feelings, and in this way she could help these two men cease their mutual antipathy and work in concert with each other.

WOMEN AND ALLIANCE FORMATION

In the Montcalm/Chateaubriand and the Dosne/Rémusat negotiations, women helped politicians from different factions get along with one another. These female interventions came after an alliance between different political groups had been established, and when politicians were concerned about their ability to sustain the relationship. This task of alliance formation was crucial to the functioning of the parliamentary system. Indeed, most of the cabinets in the period between 1815 and 1848 were coalition governments. There were times when one faction dominated politics, as during the period from 1821 to 1828, when the ultras were in power, or from 1840 to 1848, when Guizot's ministry had the backing of deputies from the juste milieu. But even these governments occasionally needed to reach out to factions in the opposition to shore up their support in the Chambers, while political groupings that wanted to come to power had to secure the backing of other factions to do so. The problem is that coalitions require trust and assurances that the members of the factions who are allies will not betray one another. Moreover, the lack of a party system and the number of different political groupings engendered lengthier and more complex negotiations over both legislation and the composition of any new cabinet. In order to form a ministry, for example, one had to negotiate with politicians from many different factions, whereas in a two-party system, as in Britain, it was much easier to determine who would be included in a new government.[20] As a result, the stability of the parliamentary system relied on individuals who could work among factions and build trust among them; it was rare that politicians themselves could do this, as their political and social loyalties were typically too circumscribed. This was not the case for women, however, and it was they who created cohesion between factions and built chains of trust that made alliances—and thus the political system that depended on them—viable.

One notable—and surprising—alliance was between the center-right and the liberal opposition at the end of the Restoration. In the closing years of the regime, Chateaubriand was the leader of a center-right faction made up of former ultras who now opposed the government and often collaborated with the left. His mistress Hortense Allart was a key facilitator of contact between Chateaubriand and her liberal friends. She put Thiers and François Mignet, then liberal journalists, in touch with her lover. She also orchestrated a meeting between Chateaubriand and Béranger, one that showed the strength of the opposition to the Polignac government.[21] During the July Monarchy

Guizot relied repeatedly on women to help him form alliances. In 1840, just after the formation of the Thiers ministry, he asked Mme de Gasparin if any of the centrist politicians she knew were similarly opposed to the new government (he feared it was too bellicose) and whether he should write directly to any of them. Although Guizot did not spell out his precise intentions in this letter, he was undoubtedly trying to form an alliance with these men in order to topple the Thiers ministry.[22] Five years later Lieven helped him reach out to Thiers to shore up his support in the Chamber of Deputies.[23]

In all these instances, men called on women's abilities to maintain ties across factional lines. Allart was Chateaubriand's mistress and an ardent liberal; Gasparin was friends with Guizot and politicians to his left; and Lieven was friends with men to the right and to the left of Guizot. None of these negotiations left much of a paper trail, but there were two that did. Mme de Montcalm formed an alliance between ultras and moderates in the early years of the Restoration, while Mme Lenormant orchestrated another—among doctrinaires, Catholics, and legitimists—in 1848 and 1849. In both cases, men called on women's extensive social networks and their ability to convey information about their emotions and interiority. Indeed, the correspondence surrounding the formation of these coalitions allows us to see how women established bonds of trust between factions that either were highly suspicious of one another or had little experience working together.

One particularly illustrative example of this mediating role of female friends is the relationship between Mme de Montcalm and Hyde de Neuville. Indeed, theirs was a friendship that was born out of a desire for political reconciliation. At the beginning of the Restoration, the two knew each other, for it was Hyde who suggested to Montcalm that she keep a journal. Yet according to that same diary, they were not close at the time. But starting in 1816, they began a friendship that sprang out of an effort to effect a rapprochement between ultras and moderates. By all accounts, the two had a real affection for each other, but their expressions of sentiment were also politically useful and in some cases strategically deployed.

Montcalm's alliance between ultras and moderates was formed at a particularly difficult time. Early in the Restoration, factional tensions were at their height; this was when memories of the Hundred Days and White Terror were still fresh. One example of this is the division between the far-right ultras and the center-right moderates. The duc de Richelieu was the leader of the latter group; because of his conciliatory attitude, the ultras unleashed a torrent of hostility on him and his ministry. Yet there were some ultras, like Chateaubriand, who were ideologically moderate. Hyde de Neuville was another politician who had liberal views but who was known for his fierce temperament and hostility to the cabinet.[24] Nevertheless, he hoped that he could win Richelieu over to ultra politics; after all, Richelieu was an émigré from one of the great aristocratic families of France and had served the tsar of Russia during the Empire.

In March 1816, just before he took up his post as ambassador to the United States, Hyde visited Montcalm to ask her to approach her brother about collaborating with the ultra camp. In a letter written after their initial meeting, he deployed both a political and sentimental language to make his argument. He described the political difficulties ultras and moderates would face if the two camps could not agree. He also spoke about his affection and esteem for her and Richelieu. He wrote, "I do not know, Madame, if you realize the feelings that you inspire in me, my respect and attachment for you and for your brother." Later in the letter he stated, "You are kind, you suffer, I know that you have a good heart, I do not need you, but I greatly desire your friendship."[25] (Montcalm was very sick at this point and essentially an invalid, hence Hyde's references to her suffering.) Here Hyde used affection as a persuasive force. Because he liked her and her brother, she should try to reconcile the two men. He also used emotions to create trust. Montcalm and Richelieu had reasons to be suspicious of his efforts, given how opposed he was to the ministry, but by speaking of his feelings for her and Richelieu he indicated that he was acting in good faith and that his desire for an alliance was genuine. He was not yet friends with Montcalm, but he wanted to be so; he would therefore act as a friend would—with her best interests at heart. In this case, Hyde de Neuville's words of affection functioned as a metaphor, for he was promising to behave with loyalty in political life. At the same time, the expression of his feelings may have been genuine, as the two became close soon after this incident.

In her response to Hyde, Montcalm stated that she admired his loyalty to the monarchy and that she also desired a reconciliation between the ultras and her brother. However, she was quite clear that Richelieu should not be the one who did all the work, as both parties needed to come together. In other words, Richelieu would move to the right only if the ultras became more moderate. Although she offered advice to Hyde, she refused to intervene with her brother. She stated that she had no influence over him and that both she and Richelieu believed that women should not involve themselves in political matters.[26] Less than ten days later, however, she wrote Hyde another letter in which she conveyed an altogether different message. She reported that she had spoken with her brother and that if the ultras wanted to reconcile with him, they should be less hostile to him. In particular, they should visit him on a more regular basis. But she did not want Hyde to reveal that this suggestion came from her and indirectly from Richelieu, as that would demonstrate that Richelieu intended to ally himself with the far-right. Thus she asked him to "think about what I am telling you, but keep my secret; do not mention me in any fashion, and know that I am grateful for this trust which can only arise from a real attachment."[27]

Although we have no record of the conversation between Richelieu and Montcalm that precipitated this letter, she was clearly acting with his blessing. Brother and sister may have disliked the prospect of any female involvement in politics, but they also realized that women could be effective political actors. She could call on her social and emotional power for political purposes. By suggesting that the ultras should visit Richelieu more, she was organizing male sociability and telling men to behave with more courtesy. At the same time, by sending him a secret, she indicated that she liked and trusted him; in this respect, she was reciprocating Hyde's movement toward friendship. All of this would make Hyde more invested in trying to end the ultras' hostility toward Richelieu. If Montcalm and Richelieu felt friendly toward the ultras, shouldn't they reciprocate by ceasing their attacks?

Montcalm was quite conscious of what she was doing here. In her journal she discussed Hyde's character and focused on his hotheadedness. She hoped that his political passions would cool during his sojourn to the United States, allowing him to become a valuable ally. In her words, "his inherent loyalty could make him very useful when distance and time" calmed his head.[28] This statement indicates that she was primarily thinking about Hyde as a political asset and that there was considerable calculation in her letter. She may have genuinely liked him, but she also wanted to win him over, something she could do by treating him with affection. In this case she was performing a set of emotions to effect political change. If men could manipulate norms of female emotional susceptibility, as in the case of the encounter between Rémusat and Dosne, women could in turn cultivate their own emotional expressions for political purposes.

When Hyde took up his diplomatic post in the United States, Montcalm continued her attempts at reconciliation. One way she did this was through sending news to him that was designed to bring him closer to Richelieu's views. In one letter she spoke of Richelieu's latest achievements and then stated, "Your friends [i.e., the ultras], Monsieur, still want to remain estranged from a ministry which, by bringing the Church back to France and by strongly punishing conspiracies, proves definitively that it is not an enemy of the king nor of the altar."[29] Just as she used her account of events to attack the ultras and make the case for her brother's position, she also called on her access to Richelieu's emotions to convince Hyde de Neuville of her brother's high opinion of him. In the same letter she reported that Richelieu, who was Hyde's superior as minister of foreign affairs, was happy with his work. She writes, "My brother is very pleased with your letters and your reports. I continue to take a great satisfaction in hearing how highly he speaks of you."[30] Soon after, Richelieu himself wrote Hyde and praised Hyde's diplomatic achievements. This was a semi-official letter and was without Montcalm's professions of affection or warm tone. The contrast between the two letters is a further indication of how women were able to communicate in ways that men were not. Her letters were emotional and could use sentiment to create cohesion between the two men. Montcalm was also able to suggest that, as her brother's confidante, she could accurately describe Richelieu's mental state. This allowed her to build trust between these two men; not only should Hyde trust Richelieu's policies, but he should also feel positively inclined toward her brother because Richelieu appreciated his work so much. As will be discussed below, Montcalm was highly successful in her efforts, for when Hyde returned to France, he showed an eagerness to work with moderates and with Richelieu.

Many of the same uses of women in politics are apparent in Guizot's attempt to make a political comeback during the Second Republic. Examined here are his efforts after the end of the July Monarchy, but he was clearly using techniques that he had learned decades before. In May 1849, while in exile in Britain, he ran as a candidate for the Constituent Assembly of the new republic to which he was opposed. In order to win, he needed the backing of conservatives outside the doctrinaire camps and he looked to Catholics and legitimists for support, including the comte de Montalembert, Louis Veuillot, and the duc de Noailles. Here, Guizot was trying to ally himself with men who had been his opponents in the years of the July Monarchy on both the right (legitimists) and the left (the liberal Catholic Montalembert). Any animus now had to be turned into goodwill. It was his friend Mme Lenormant who made this possible and who forged this alliance. She was the adopted daughter of Mme Récamier, whose salon was a center of legitimist society during the July Monarchy. She was also married to one of Montalembert's friends and collaborators. Although Lenormant's precise politics are unknown, her letters demonstrate that she was a monarchist who abhorred the Revolution of 1848.[31]

Lenormant aided Guizot in the formation of an alliance with other conservatives in a variety of ways. She put him into contact with them, showed them his pamphlets, and reported his views to them.[32] Guizot and his newfound allies tended not to write directly to each other, but rather through Lenormant; she sent Guizot the letters she received from other conservatives about this alliance and in turn showed them the letters that he sent her. In this respect, her actions were similar to those of Montcalm over thirty years earlier. She, too, communicated between different factions, and both women used their personal correspondence with their male friends to convey political information. Similarly, as in the letters between Montcalm and Hyde de Neuville, Guizot relied on Lenormant to deploy emotions and build trust. One way he did this was by including statements in his letters to Lenormant about how much he liked and respected these other conservatives, information that Lenormant was to pass on. For instance, in a November 1848 letter, Guizot asked Lenormant to show Noailles a portion of his manuscript *De la Démocratie en France*. Then he went on to state how much he valued and trusted Noailles; in his words, "The more that I know him, the more I feel a solid esteem for him." He then reported that he thought very highly of Noailles's recent book on Mme de Maintenon.[33]

In his letters, Guizot also repeatedly mentioned that he desired more than just a temporary political alliance with these conservatives—that he actually liked them and wanted to become friends with them. For example, in a letter from February 1848, he wrote the following to Mme Lenormant about a M. de Fontette with whom he was trying to align himself: "I am happy that he has taken up my cause and am greatly touched by the zeal with which he has undertaken it. I would very much like for more than an electoral rapprochement between us to come out of this one day."[34] Here, Guizot invokes emotional terms—"happy" and "greatly touched," most notably—and indicates that he wanted to turn his political alliance with Fontette into a personal friendship. Similarly, in March 1849, Guizot wrote the following: "The *entente cordiale* with M. de Montalembert is more important to me than I can say, first for my own satisfaction, secondly so that conservatives can succeed. And I hope that when we are able to see each other more, this *entente cordiale* will become more than that."[35] The ability of Lenormant to make friends for Guizot called on the socializing power she had as a woman. In this case, though, Guizot's expressions of sentiment were functioning largely as tropes and should not be seen as the pure outpourings of his heart. His concern, after all, was with politics, not with expanding his friendship network. By using the language of affection, he could suggest that he was inclined to treat his newfound allies like friends in the political realm. In essence, he was offering promises of open communication and political—not personal—loyalty, and trying to convince Montalembert and Fontette that he had their best interests at heart. Conservative politicians also relayed their emotions and good intentions through Lenormant, although they tended to speak in terms that conveyed more distance and invoked less affection. For instance, in September 1848, Montalembert sent a letter to her that was then passed on to Guizot in which he stated the following: "Please tell M. Guizot how much I value his goodwill and respect. I have known and admired him for almost twenty years."[36] These men could not communicate directly with one another both because of the codes of emotional restraint that governed correspondence between men and because they did not know each other particularly well. But as a woman with close connections to both Guizot and his new allies, Lenormant had a unique ability to convey affection between men.

One reason that all these politicians communicated through Lenormant was that she was seen as having special access to Guizot's interiority. When Lenormant showed Montalembert some of her letters from Guizot in March 1849, he wrote her that it was so helpful to read Guizot's correspondence with Lenormant because it contained "the private outpourings of friendship."[37] In this instance, the fact that Lenormant was a private actor with a personal relationship to Guizot meant that their correspondence was especially revelatory about his true feelings. The privacy of their communications was a guarantee of the authenticity of Guizot's statements. Because she was a female friend, someone who might be understood to be Guizot's confidante, he would be entirely sincere with her. He could not and would not hide his true opinions. Thus the letters that Lenormant received from Guizot and his potential allies were both private and public, and it was their supposed privacy that made them so politically valuable. These male politicians knew that their letters were liable to be passed around, as they were writing for one another and not Lenormant. But through drawing on the codes of male/female correspondence and confidence, they could claim to be operating openly and honestly. Privacy was here not a retreat from the political but a way to facilitate it.

In the end Lenormant's efforts did bear some fruit, and, although Guizot was not elected, he did run with the support of other conservatives. This was also the first step toward a monarchical fusion, an effort that would preoccupy Guizot in his later years.[38] What Lenormant effectively did was build a chain of trust that stretched from Guizot to her and then to his new allies. Catholics and legitimists could trust her because of their own social connections to her and because they knew that she and Guizot trusted each other. Because Guizot was communicating through a female friend, they were assured of his good intentions. And indeed, it was Lenormant's gender that was crucial here. As a woman, she could facilitate contact between social and political groupings, and she could cultivate social ties between men. She could also speak to the different parties in ways that men could not in order to ensure that these politicians trusted one another.

FEMALE POWER AND FEMALE POLITICS?

If women were powerful conduits for trust and crucial political actors, this naturally leads to questions about women's power and women's politics. First, in their roles in alliance formation and emotional management, can we see some sort of female politics? In his work on salons in this period, Steven Kale describes how the salonnières of the early nineteenth century were interested in a politics of reconciliation, as they tried to overcome the divisions of the post-revolutionary era.[39] Are women's roles as mediators and forgers of alliances another version of this politics of reconciliation? In some cases the answer is a clear yes. Mme de Montcalm is the best example of this. Her diary from the early years of the Restoration records her deep distress at the factional divisions of the time. She disliked politics because it created enmity between individuals and poisoned social relations.[40] Her work on behalf of her brother thus arose in part out of a desire to heal the ideological divisions that had made high society so unpleasant. However, this should not be seen as a distinctly female politics, for the reconciliation that she effected was something that both Richelieu and prominent ultra politicians desired. Indeed it was Hyde de Neuville who first approached Montcalm. Similarly, when Rémusat reached out to Dosne in 1840 and when Guizot tried to ally himself with centrists through Gasparin that same year, it was men who initiated these negotiations. Moreover, some of the women discussed in this chapter were uninterested in reconciliation. Both Mme de La Trémoïlle and Mme de Broglie were invested in strengthening their factions and not in reaching out to other political groupings. Thus the incidents detailed here do not demonstrate so much a feminized vision of political and social reconciliation, but rather a series of functions that women were better able to undertake than men.

If we do not see a particular female politics at work here, we can still ask why women undertook these roles. What did they think they were doing and how much political change were they able to effect? In some cases, these acts of female political involvement arose out of strong ideological conviction, such as Mme de Broglie's attempt to keep Barante in France. Mme Lenormant's letters to Guizot also indicate that she was heavily invested in facilitating an alliance between Guizot and other conservatives because she hated the Revolution of 1848 and wanted to reestablish the monarchy. Uniting Catholics, legitimists and Orleanists was one way to halt the Revolution. Similarly, Mme de Montcalm provides a clear example of a woman whose actions arose from her political commitments. She was an intermediary between ultras and Richelieu because she wanted to help her brother and because it suited her politics. In her journal she spoke of herself as a royalist who was suspicious of both the far-right and the far-left. While she helped her brother work with ultras, she was opposed to their excesses. By calming the political passions of moderate ultras, she hoped to unite all monarchists and establish the regime on a more solid footing.[41] Likewise, Allart's actions as a political facilitator during the Restoration probably arose out of her commitment to liberalism. In her autobiography, she claimed that she wanted to orchestrate a meeting between Chateaubriand and Béranger because of the distinctly nonpolitical desire to bring together two literary men who admired each other.[42] But this was also a political move, for it showed the wide spectrum of opposition to the governing ministry, and in this respect the encounter between the two men bolstered the liberal cause. Hence, some of the women studied here were heavily engaged in politics and saw themselves as having clear political goals that they were in a unique position to achieve.[43]

Not all political involvement, however, arose from deep conviction, and some of these women saw themselves as having relatively limited or no political aims. Mme Récamier is an obvious example. She mediated between Chateaubriand and Mathieu de Montmorency for personal reasons, despite the fact that she was considerably more moderate than were either of them. In some cases, women made no effort to change the views of the men around them. For instance, in 1821, when Montcalm reached out to Chateaubriand so that he might gain a cabinet position, she wanted to alter how he expressed his views, and not the views themselves. The letters between Guizot and

Lenormant in 1848 and 1849 show that there was considerable disagreement between him and other conservatives over both aims and tactics. Montalembert, for instance, was unhappy with Guizot's position on Catholics and did not even think that he should run for a seat in the Constituent Assembly. Lenormant communicated these differences, but she did not try to convince Guizot that he should change his politics, nor did she state that she would try to change the views of Guizot's newfound allies on his behalf.[44] In both cases these women wanted to build working relationships between politicians despite their disagreements.

There are a few instances, however, when women did try to change the politics of the men around them, and these cases are instructive about the possibilities and limits of women's political power. Allart seems to have wanted to expose Chateaubriand to her position in 1829 and 1830; in her autobiography she writes of reading articles from Thiers's liberal journal *Le National* to him.[45] Given her own liberalism, she probably did this to expose Chateaubriand to her views. But of all the women studied here, it was Mme de Montcalm who was most invested in—and most successful at—shaping politics around personal relations, and she did manage to change Hyde de Neuville's position. This is apparent in his memoirs when he describes his political activity after his return from the United States. In his mind Montcalm had convinced him to adopt a more centrist position. For example, in an 1820 letter to her, he spoke of being "an ultra and a moderate at the same time"—that is to say, he thought of himself as having allegiances to both the far-right and the center-right. And in the same letter he indicated why he was drawn to political moderation and Richelieu's position. He wrote, "As for your brother, I am bound to him because of him, because of you."[46] By his own account his allegiance to Richelieu arose at least in part out of an allegiance to Montcalm. And indeed, Hyde backed up his words with action. This letter was written when Richelieu was trying to include ultras in a new cabinet. He and Montcalm asked Hyde to approach Villèle about joining the new government. When Hyde went to Villèle, he stated that he was not asking on Richelieu's behalf, "but on behalf of someone dear to him [i.e., Montcalm]."[47] Of course, this allowed him to reassure Villèle that he had not entirely quit the ultra camp and was not doing any favors for Richelieu. It also reflected the fact that in his mind, he was acting for Montcalm and not her brother. Thus Montcalm's estimation of Hyde's character did prove to be correct. Once she had cultivated goodwill for her brother and more importantly for herself, he was a useful ally, one who worked between ultras and moderates for her sake. To be sure, this political moderation was not too far a stretch for Hyde, for he had always held centrist views. What Montcalm did was bring his moderation to the fore while calming his impassioned hostility toward compromise. In other words, she succeeded in using the emotions to reorganize the political landscape.

During the July Monarchy, Mme de Gasparin also attempted to use her friendship with Guizot to move him to the center, but she had far less success in her endeavors. Unfortunately, we only have Guizot's side of their correspondence; at her request, he burned all her letters.[48] As a result, we cannot know her exact politics nor how she made her case to Guizot. Nevertheless, his letters make it clear that she was more moderate than he and that she wanted to move him away from his conservative stance. For example, in 1839, she argued that he should ally himself with Thiers and Odilon Barrot, which he briefly did. Barrot, in particular, was far to his left, and any long-standing alliance with him would have pulled Guizot toward a more moderate position.[49] One year later, during the crisis of 1840, Gasparin again showed her political stripes, as she backed Thiers's left-leaning cabinet, while Guizot opposed it. In May, she tried to convince him of the merits of her position. In his reply—his only flash of anger in their long correspondence—he strongly rebuked her and asserted that he was unquestionably right in his views.[50] Two months later, however, he asked her to write him about her opinions on international and domestic matters, as he saw her as a barometer of public opinion. Since he was outside of France, she could help him understand the reactions to Thiers's government.[51] In other words, he wanted to hear her views only insofar as they were useful to him. Her role was to aid him and help him achieve his goals, not to convince him to achieve hers.

Gasparin and Montcalm had many of the same desires, for both wanted to move the men around them to the center. But in Montcalm's case, her political activity gave her power, whereas Gasparin's work as a communicator deprived her of any such influence. If female political interventions did not always allow women to have a voice in politics, they did not necessarily deny this to women either. Beyond such generalizations, how can we understand the difference between Montcalm's success and Gasparin's failure? It is not that Hyde de Neuville was more open to women's political engagement than was Guizot. Both maintained that women should play no part in politics.[52] Hyde also wanted to use La Trémoïlle in many of the same ways that Guizot sought to use Gasparin.

Part of the difference may have had to do with the nature of the bonds Hyde and Guizot had with Montcalm and Gasparin, respectively. Hyde's memoirs paint him as almost besotted with Montcalm after his return from the United States. For example, he writes that their bond was "the relation that was the sweetest to me"; such intense affection made him eager to please her.[53] Guizot's tie with Gasparin was loving but appears to be have been less intense. Additionally, in 1840, the woman to whom he was closest was not Gasparin but Lieven, who heavily disliked Thiers's foreign policy.[54] But undoubtedly the most important difference was that Hyde's politics were more flexible than Guizot's. The former's ultra beliefs were tinged with moderation, whereas during the 1840s the latter's conservatism was unbending. Hyde also wanted to reach out to moderates like Richelieu, but Guizot had no interest in agreeing with Gasparin's positive assessment of Thiers's government. Indeed, had he backed the cabinet, he would have placed himself out of contention for being a viable alternative to Thiers—and therefore out of the running for forming a government himself. In other words, women could influence men when they wanted to be influenced, but they could not necessarily make them change their minds when the men had no desire to do so. In the end, it was men who would make any final decisions in the political realm. Because women accessed the world of high politics through their male friends, it was men, and not women, who held ultimate authority over this arena.

Women did not enter the political terrain on equal footing with men; they could make suggestions and open up alternatives, but they were not necessarily able to change the minds of the men around them. Despite these limitations, it is clear that women were not passive actors in the political life of the time. Certainly, the various roles that these women played within the new parliamentary system were powerful and necessary. Because women were understood as private actors who were excluded from the public sphere, they were particularly suited to work between politicians and build trust within parliamentary life in a more robust way than were men. In an era when many were concerned about high levels of anomie and suspicion, one without political parties or even necessarily clear governing majorities, female friends were invaluable in creating the trust that allowed the parliamentary system to function. They thus made the political regimes of the Restoration and July Monarchy viable. Individuals of the time may have wanted to exclude women from politics and to separate the private from the public, but they found this was impossible in practice, for in the end the social and emotional functions of female friends were too useful in political life.

EPILOGUE

In establishing a social order based on individualism and in giving birth to ideological conflict, the Revolution led the citizens of early nineteenth-century France to be fearful of a lack of social cohesion. Politics was divisive, especially for men, and public life was an arena of suspicion and anomie. As a result, trust and loyalty had to be understood as coming from the private realm. Ultimately this problem made friendship central to the political culture of the early nineteenth century. Imagined as a refuge from public life, friendship could build durable bonds of affiliation and reestablish trust, both of which were necessary to the functioning of the parliamentary system.

Discussions of the affection between friends, for instance, had a persuasive force in politics, as they could be used to secure commitments, persuade individuals to act in a particular fashion, and establish norms of interpersonal behavior. As the elites of the post-revolutionary era were learning how to practice modern politics within the framework of a representative system, they did so by relying on personal ties. The notion of a separation between public and private was a powerful norm in the period, and indeed it structured patterns of personal relations and limited women's ability to exert influence within the political system. But at the same time, the confinement of women to the private realm allowed them to play critical roles in parliamentary life as they worked between politicians to build trust. In the face of the problems of the post-revolutionary era, the ruling elites found that a strict division between a public, masculine sphere and a private, feminine one was impossible to maintain.

Looking at friendship opens up a vantage point onto the problems of early nineteenth-century French society. The revolutionary and post-revolutionary eras held out the prospect of new freedoms, such as the ability to participate in the political system (for elites, at least) and the destruction of the hierarchical and corporate social order. But both of these came with a very high price. It was difficult to imagine any cohesion among free and equals citizens. In the nineteenth century, the emerging market-based economy added to fears about what was being sacrificed in the pursuit of individual gain. Representative government also unleashed ideological hostilities into the elite strata. Political engagement meant factionalism and the poisoning of social relations. Moreover, despite the fact that the government of the Restoration was more liberal than that of the Napoleonic era—at least in terms of freedom of the press and a meaningful representative government—certain illiberal elements of the previous regime remained in place. The heavy hand of police surveillance did not disappear, nor did the state cease its efforts to control associational life. All of these forces would lead to a sense of anomie and estrangement, as well as a heightened suspicion of others.

The revolutionary and post-revolutionary eras thus left the men and women of the early nineteenth century with a series of practical problems and emotional difficulties. How could they make their way in a social climate that was perceived as being hostile? Where could they find individuals who would remain loyal to them and help them when they needed assistance? And where could they find confidantes? Friendship was one solution to these problems. Men limited their ties to other men who had the same ideological outlook. They understood that male friendship was a space of solidarity that was supposed to induce men to act for each other's benefit. Because action and not emotional expression was central to male friendship, men turned to women for the revelation of their confidences and discussions of their emotional states. Bonds with women helped them find forms of affection and connection seen as missing in an otherwise anomic society.

This is not to say that friendship was the only solution to the difficulties of the post-revolutionary era: the family was another source of solidarity and affection. But on an individual level, there were those like Béranger who were not particularly close to their families. Even Guizot, who was devoted to his children, sought extra-domestic forms of affiliation. More generally, writers, artists, and scholars needed communities of peers. Nor could politicians function if they were confined to their familial contexts. Were they to rely on their relations to serve as brokers and allies, they would be far too limited in their ability to operate within the political system. In the broadest sense, the fact that friendship was an elective tie made it especially useful, as this bond was one way to understand how citizens would voluntarily come together. Friendship could reconcile individualism and cohesion.

In certain respects, however, friendship was an old solution to a new problem. Social habits from the Old Regime remained intact in the post-revolutionary era, alongside certain understandings of how men and women operated in society. Male friends continued to be understood as allies and companions in arms. As they did in the eighteenth century, women still orchestrated elite sociability and served as political brokers. In an era of parliamentary politics, these ideas would take on a new importance and urgency. Women applied their skills with social relations to the political terrain to help men get along with one another and work with one another in the wake of ideological divisions. The notion of the friend-as-ally took on a new importance in the parliamentary systems of the Restoration and July Monarchy. Likewise, long-standing understandings of how friendship operated were applied to discussions of political life and affiliation.

The rest of the epilogue looks at both the problems and legacy of the reliance on friendship in political life. First I discuss why a political culture based on friendship was unable to prevent the Revolutions of 1830 and 1848. Indeed, the intermingling of friendship and politics led to unhealthy forms of politics. Despite this, friendship remained central to political life in the second half of the century. Between 1815 and 1848 political struggles were particularly acute and the memory of the Revolution was still fresh. But the political and social difficulties of the period of parliamentary monarchy have continued to echo throughout modern French history, as has the conflation between the political and the personal. Friends, for instance, were put to many of the same uses during the Third Republic as they had been in the era of parliamentary monarchy. Likewise, politics remained a source of division, as the men and women of France have continued to grapple with the ideological divides stemming from the Revolution.

AN IMPOSSIBLE STABILITY

Although ties of friendship restored trust within political life and thus helped the parliamentary system function, neither the Restoration nor the July Monarchy was durable in the long run. After all, both were swept away by revolutions. Why, then, was friendship unable to lead to a more permanent form of stability? If friendship could help politicians negotiate and form alliances, why was it unable to prevent revolution? One reason is that friendship ties—either those between men or those between men and women—were not good at forcing compromise. Indeed, in some cases they could reinforce the intransigence of politicians. Nor could a political culture built on friendship necessarily help facilitate the entry of new groups into parliamentary life. Instead, the centrality of friendship to politics opened up these regimes to charges of corruption, ones that would do significant damage to the July Monarchy in particular.

Insofar as they were political revolutions, the Revolutions of 1830 and 1848 both occurred because of the intransigence of the government. In neither case was this a problem that friendship could solve. The spark to the Revolution of 1830 was the July Ordinances, which restricted both the powers of the Chamber of Deputies and the freedom of the press. This came almost a year after the installation of the ultra Polignac ministry, a cabinet that closely matched Charles X's own views and shared his hostility to the very idea of a parliamentary monarchy. In this climate, women helped those who opposed the government to come together; this is what Allart did when she facilitated contact between Chateaubriand and her liberal friends. But any ability women had to span political divides and form alliances was useless to the government, for neither the king nor the ministry had any desire to compromise. Likewise, the proximate cause of the Revolution of 1848 was Guizot's inflexibility. Because he was so hostile to the expansion of the franchise, it was clear that any political reform would not happen on his watch. While he could have used some of the women in his life—such as Lieven or Gasparin—to reach out to those on his left, he saw no reason to do so. It was only after he had been deposed that he started to build bridges to his former opponents, although when he did, he turned primarily to those on his right.

Moreover, the shape of male friendship networks and assumptions about women's access to political life reinforced this intransigence. In the late 1840s, for example, all of Guizot's male friends shared his politics. He could not be friends with any man who had significant political disagreements with him. As a result, the men he trusted the most and with whom he had the most open political exchanges were not going to encourage him to be more politically flexible.[1] Indeed, the political cohesion among his male friends meant that their discussions took place in an echo chamber. Of course, this was not true for every female friend. Most notably, Gasparin's politics were more moderate than were Guizot's. Although he accepted her views and even tried to make use of them on occasion, his relationship with her contained elements of masculine presumption and an insistence that she was not a fully qualified political actor in her own right. Thus he closed himself off to political debate with one of the few individuals willing to challenge him. Female friends were able to change a politician's views only if he wanted to change them, while male friends normally had no desire to alter the opinions of the men around them.

The reliance on friendship ties was also fundamentally undemocratic, for it reaffirmed the sense that the political system was both run by and designed for the benefit of a small elite. This, too, helped undermine the July Monarchy in the 1840s. During the last years of the regime, corruption charges swirled around the government.[2] There were spectacular scandals in the late 1840s, such as the Teste-Cubières affair, in which Jean Baptiste Teste, a former minister of public works, was found guilty of accepting bribes. In the Choiseul-Praslin affair, the duc de Choiseul-Praslin, a well-connected peer, brutally murdered his wife and was then allowed to poison himself before standing trial. Other charges were more pedestrian but no less damaging to the regime, such as the accusations that the government doled out lucrative postings to deputies in exchange for their support in the Chamber. In this climate, the fact that Guizot had a habit of providing positions to those closest to him no doubt contributed to the sense that the government was run by a small clique who had their own interests at heart. From his perspective, this was being a good friend. It also helped him place men to whom he was close in important governmental positions. But from the vantage point of someone opposed to or outside the political system, this was but another illustration of the self-serving nature of the regime.

Likewise, if women's networks spanned factional divisions, they did not necessarily span social ones. This meant that women did not facilitate the entry of new social groups into politics. For instance, although Lieven had connections to politicians who ranged from the far-right to the center-left during the 1840s, her world was socially very exclusive. She was a salonnière in one of the most aristocratic neighborhoods in Paris. As Steven Kale has shown, salons were institutions that fostered elite social reproduction.[3] As a result, she had no incentive to cultivate ties with those who were not elites. Alternately, there is the case of Hortense Allart. During the July Monarchy, she had an expansive network that reached from the far-left to the far-right, and she maintained friendships with Chateaubriand, Thiers, and many on the left. Although many of her intimates were interested in social questions during this era, they were still members of the elite. As a result of the exclusivity of their networks, women could help facilitate politics between elites and between those who were already admitted into the political system. But they could not necessarily connect elites and nonelites. Thus, although ties of friendship enabled the early nineteenth-century parliamentary system to function, they did not necessarily result in a healthy and long-lasting form of politics.

FRIENDSHIP AND POLITICS IN REPUBLICAN FRANCE

Despite the problems of relying on personal ties to transact politics, friendship remained central to political life in the second half of the nineteenth century. So, too, did politics continue to be a force for division within elite society. Salons and other institutions of sociability were crucial in the formation of the opposition to the Second Empire, as well as the politics of the Third Republic. It is the Dreyfus Affair, however, that presents the clearest parallels between the political culture of the post-revolutionary era and that of the late nineteenth century. This was another battle between the "two Frances" that both ruptured social ties and formed friendships based on shared political affiliations. Here, too, women played crucial roles in orchestrating alliances between different ideological groupings.

Three new factors in the structure of politics in the second half of the century made friendship less necessary to the political system. Associational life grew considerably in strength during the mid to late nineteenth century; as clubs and organizations increasingly dotted the French landscape, men and women could find new methods of organization and cooperation.[4] The creation of official political parties in the Third Republic meant that politicians had less need of personal ties to organize political life.[5] Lastly, the rise of mass politics reshaped the political terrain. In the period of parliamentary monarchy, the centrality of social ties to political life went hand in hand with the restriction of political rights to the notables, an elite that was intermarried, interrelated, and habituated to socializing with one another. But the advent of universal manhood suffrage in 1848 and its enshrinement in the Third Republic decoupled political rights from wealth and status. High politics was no longer contained in Parisian salons and was no longer the exclusive property of an elite world.[6]

Nevertheless, remnants of the social practices of the post-revolutionary era remained. Philip Nord has shown that the burgeoning associational life of the 1860s and 1870s became imbued with a new democratic spirit. At the same time, middle-class members took over leadership positions in these organizations and challenged the domination of the notables. In turn, these men and this newly emergent civil society provided crucial support for the Third Republic.[7] Once again, social interactions and a distinct type of sociability helped to establish the basis for the political system and ensure its stability. Likewise, during the 1860s, oppositional groups—and notably republican ones—crystallized in Parisian salons, such as that of Marie d'Agoult and Juliette Adam. Two of the men who circulated in these salons were Jules Ferry and Léon Gambetta. In turn, Gambetta's friendship was crucial to Ferry's first electoral success. Gambetta had greater access to networks of republicans than did the bourgeois Ferry, and he facilitated Ferry's introduction to the electors who voted him into office in 1869.[8]

In the Third Republic, many of the problems of the post-revolutionary era reappeared, as did the same conflation between friendship and politics. The 1870s saw a revival of the politicization, social fragmentation, and bitterness that emerged in 1815. Thus, for instance, in one of his "Parisian Sketches" for the *New York Tribune* in 1876, Henry James wrote the following about politics:

> Nothing else, it is true, is talked about. The elections are all-pervasive. . . . There is, of course, an infinite amount of more or less ferocious discussion, and every man suspects a political adversary in every other. . . . The intensity of political discussions is sharper in France than it is anywhere else—which is the case, indeed, with every sort of difference of opinion. There are more camps and coteries and "sets" than among Anglo-Saxons, and the gulf which divides each group from every other is more hopelessly and fatally impassable. . . . It is simply the old story that, either in politics or in literature, Frenchmen are ignorant of the precious art of compromise. The imagination sinks helpless before the idea of a Monarchist and a Republican ever really coming to terms.[9]

James's observations could have easily been written sixty years earlier. Once again, the political divisions created during the Revolution split French society apart—in this case, the struggle was between those who supported the Republic and those who wanted to return to a monarchy. Politics overwhelmed all other preoccupations, as it made elites intensely suspicious of one another and confined individuals to mutually hostile camps of those who were like-minded. These divisions also shaped social habits and spaces. Some salons, such as that of Mme de Renneville, were centers of monarchism, while others, including Adam's, provided a space for backers of the new regime. At the same time, salons were also sites of reconciliation. Adam, for instance, sought to bring together republicans, diplomats, and military men; her aim in part was to win over the last two groups to the Republic. Likewise, the salon of the Scheurer-Kestners—a family of wealthy industrialists from Alsace—facilitated Gambetta's contact with elite circles and ensured that he had the support and financial backing of wealthy republicans.[10] And, as in the era of parliamentary monarchy, politicians' allies were often personal friends. This was the case with Gambetta, for instance, who was close to his allies Alphonse Peyrat and Eugène Spuller.[11] In some cases, too, the pre-party forms of organization transitioned into organized political parties. Founded in 1901, the Parti radical emerged from men's clubs and Masonic lodges.[12]

It was, however, the events of the Dreyfus Affair that demonstrate the clearest parallels between the politics of the Third Republic and those of the post-revolutionary era. As in 1815, French society was ripped apart along ideological lines, and once again, the divisions created during the Revolution were made manifest within society. The Affair has long been understood as a foundational moment in French political culture as well as another battle between the "two Frances"—the one that accepted the gains of the Revolution and the one that did not. Of course, the dividing lines in the 1890s were not exactly the same as they were in the 1810s. There were certainly more republicans in France during the Third Republic than there had been during the Restoration; conservatism now mingled nationalism with monarchism. But Dreyfusards and anti-Dreyfusards had profoundly different notions of what France was and should be, as did liberals and ultras during the Restoration. Anti-Dreyfusards feared that France was going into decline thanks to the Third Republic. For them, the truth of Dreyfus's guilt or innocence was less important than protecting the army, one sector of society that embodied traditional values and could regenerate the nation after its humiliation in the Franco–Prussian War. In contrast, Dreyfusards claimed individual rights, secularism, truth, and justice as their heritage from the Revolution.

Just as the Affair was the reopening of old ideological battles and the redrawing of new political lines, it also reshaped social networks. Notably, Dreyfusards and anti-Dreyfusards found that they could no longer be friends with one another. For instance, the comtesse de Martel de Janville was a noted salonnière and society writer who went by the name of "Gyp." A fierce anti-Semite, she was committed to the anti-Dreyfusard cause and broke off ties to

Dreyfusards, including Anatole France, with whom she had been friends for many years.[13] Members of the Impressionist circle also ended their friendships with one another when they found themselves in opposite camps. Edgar Degas, for instance, became a passionate anti-Dreyfusard during the Affair. As a result of his political commitments, he became estranged from Camille Pissarro and Mary Cassatt, both of whom were in the Dreyfusard camp.[14]

Shared political commitments also drew individuals together, as they had during the Restoration and July Monarchy. Alfred Dreyfus's wife Lucie's connections to other Dreyfusards sustained her during the Affair. Her relationships with Joseph Reinach, as well as Olympe and Louis Havet, were particularly important. Olympe provided Lucie with information on Dreyfus's health and the conditions on Devil's Island, where he was imprisoned. The Havets were also close to Colonel Picquart, the intelligence officer who discovered that Dreyfus had been framed. When he was imprisoned, the Havets wrote him, visited him to keep his morale up, and provided him with food that was an improvement on prison fare. Likewise, the politics of the Affair could make for relationships that had been improbable beforehand. Shared devotion to the Dreyfusard cause brought Bernard Lazare, an anarchist literary critic and journalist, together with Joseph Reinach, a committed republican.[15] Thus, when the Dreyfusard Charles Péguy reflected on the Affair in 1909, he celebrated "those friendships that one did not think were possible in the modern world."[16]

Even some of the female political roles that were so important in the early part of the century were visible once again. For instance, women remained responsible for orchestrating alliances and for keeping political figures in touch with one another. The marquise Arconati-Visconti, a prominent salonnière, brought together centrists, radicals, socialists, and academics in support of the Dreyfusard cause. Meanwhile, Gyp's network spanned the range of those in the anti-Dreyfusard camp—legitimists, military men, nationalists, and even anarchists. The salonnière Mme de Loynes also facilitated contact between the populist anti-Semite Édouard Drumont and conservatives from elite milieus.[17] Insofar as both the Dreyfusard and anti-Dreyfusard camps were coalitions, it was women who were largely responsible for forging these coalitions.

The story of the Dreyfus Affair thus demonstrates how central the Restoration and July Monarchy were in shaping French political culture, with its melding of the private and the political. The post-revolutionary era was formative in crystallizing the division between the "two Frances" and in confronting the social and political legacy of the revolutionary period. It was in this context that the political system came to rely on the personal. A recourse to private life and to friendship helped individuals find the trust and affiliation they desired, and helped the political system function in the wake of the divisive events of the Revolution.

APPENDIX A: BÉRANGER, CHATEAUBRIAND, GUIZOT, AND THEIR FRIENDS

BÉRANGER'S CIRCLE

Pierre Jean de Béranger (1780–1857) was descended from artisans and innkeepers and raised largely by his aunt, a devoted republican. During the Directory, he tried unsuccessfully to make his name as a man of letters and was saved from penury when he received patronage from Lucien Bonaparte. He started to gain prominence as a songwriter toward the end of the Empire, but it was during the Restoration that he became famous. Politicized by the events of 1815, Béranger began attacking the regime from the left and circulated in liberal salons, most notably that of the wealthy banker Jacques Laffitte. He was imprisoned in 1821 and 1828 for publishing seditious songs, and reached the height of his fame and popularity toward the end of the Restoration. During the July Monarchy, he was critical of the regime from the left although largely disengaged from political affairs. In 1848, he was elected to the Constituent Assembly but quickly stepped down. He died nine years later in poverty but surrounded by friends—much as he had lived his life.

Hortense Allart de Méritens (1801–79) was raised in a Bonapartist milieu and moved in oppositional circles during the Restoration, where she became friends with Béranger. A feminist and noted novelist, she was on the left in both the Restoration and July Monarchy, although skeptical about the desirability of democracy. In 1826 she moved to Italy; when in Rome in 1829 she began an affair with Chateaubriand, who was there as the French ambassador. Both returned to Paris later that year and continued their affair until 1830; it was she who introduced Chateaubriand and Béranger to each other, and facilitated contact between Chateaubriand and her liberal friends at the end of the Restoration. During the July Monarchy, she remained close to both Chateaubriand and Béranger.

Jacques Charles Dupont (1767–1855) was known as "Dupont de l'Eure" to distinguish himself from another politician named "Dupont." A judge during the revolutionary and Napoleonic eras, he was elected to the Council of Five Hundred in 1798 and served in the Corps législatif during the Empire and the Chamber of Deputies during the Hundred Days. He was also a member of the Chamber of Deputies from 1817 until 1848, and during the Restoration he was on the far-left with his friend Manuel. After the Revolution of 1830, he served briefly as minister of justice, but quickly came to oppose the regime. During the Revolution of 1848, he was president of the Provisional Assembly.

Jacques Antoine Manuel (1775–1827) entered into the revolutionary army in 1793 and served under Napoleon in the Italian campaign. A lawyer, he became a deputy in 1818 and was one of the foremost orators among the liberal camp. In February 1823, he was expelled from the Chamber of Deputies for a speech that appeared to condone regicide. He tried but failed to get reelected to the Chamber in 1824. He died in 1827 surrounded by his friends, including his best friend, Béranger, to whom he left a considerable legacy in his will.

Adolphe Thiers (1797–1877) was born in Marseille to a modest family. He came to Paris in 1821 and worked as a liberal journalist. Beginning in 1829, he started advocating for the overthrow of the Bourbon monarchy and the ascension of the duc d'Orleans to the throne. In the 1830s he served as a deputy and a minister in a number of different cabinets. He was leader of a center-left faction that advocated a bellicose foreign policy, and was head of a government in 1840 that almost led France to war with the rest of Europe. After this government fell, Thiers entered into the opposition.

CHATEAUBRIAND'S CIRCLE

François René de Chateaubriand (1768–1848) was an émigré during the French Revolution and returned to France in 1800. He served in the diplomatic corps during the Consulate, but resigned after the duc d'Enghien was executed. During the first decade of the nineteenth century he became famous for his literary works, and he is remembered as one of the founders of French Romanticism. With the advent of the Restoration, he served in the Chamber of Peers and in the early years of the regime was an outspoken ultra. When the ultras came to power in the 1820s, he held a number of diplomatic postings and was the ambassador to Prussia in 1821, Great Britain in 1822, and Rome in 1828. In large measure, these positions were given to him to keep him out of France, for he had difficulties getting along with other politicians both inside and outside the ultra camp. However, he was minister of foreign affairs from 1822 to 1824. When Joseph de Villèle, the head of the government and leader of the ultras, removed him from office, he began a political vendetta against Villèle. He also moved toward the political center in the mid-1820s and was leader of a center-right faction made up of former ultras who often worked with the left. After the Revolution of 1830, he refused to swear an oath of loyalty to the new regime and supported the duchesse de Berry's attempted uprising. Although a legitimist during the July Monarchy, he had some personal and political affinities with radicals and republicans. During the 1830s and 1840s, he primarily devoted himself to writing his memoirs and was increasingly withdrawn from society.

Claire Louisa Rose Bonne Lechal de Kersaint, duchesse de Duras (1777–1828) maintained one of the most prominent salons of her day. She was also an author and is best known for her novel *Ourika.* An émigré during the Revolution, she met Chateaubriand when the two were in London and was his best friend, confidante, and political adviser for many years; she was also a tireless advocate for him in politics. It is generally thought that she was in love with him but that he did not reciprocate her feelings, and their relationship was strained when he began his affair with Mme Récamier.

Jean Guillaume Hyde de Neuville (1776–1857) was a royalist conspirator during the Revolution. Exiled under Napoleon for his monarchist activities, he moved to the United States and returned to France in 1814. During the early years of the Restoration, he was an ardent ultra known for his fiery temper. Despite this, he had some moderate views and worked with Mme de Montcalm to reconcile ultras and center-right moderates. He served as ambassador to the United States and to Portugal and was also minister of the navy from 1828 to 1829. Close to Chateaubriand both personally and politically, he was opposed to the far-right Polignac government of 1829–30, but like Chateaubriand he did not support the Revolution of 1830. After the advent of the July Monarchy, he largely stayed aloof from politics.

Armande Marie Antoinette de Vignerot du Plessis de Richelieu, marquise de Montcalm-Gozon (1777–1832) was the half sister of the duc de Richelieu, who was head of the government from 1815 to 1818 and then from 1820 to 1821. A noted salonnière, she had been close to Chateaubriand during the Empire, but their relationship was deeply troubled by political differences, for she supported the moderate politics of her brother. She was, however, close to Hyde de Neuville, and their friendship was forged out of a desire for political reconciliation. Ill for much of her adult life, she died of cholera.

Juliette Récamier (1777–1849) was one of the most famous women of her day and a celebrated salonnière from the Consulate until the July Monarchy. During the Napoleonic era, she was active in the opposition. Indeed, Napoleon closed her salon and exiled her from Paris because of her friendship with Mme de Staël. When she returned to Paris at the beginning of the Restoration, she received artists, scholars, and politicians on both the left and the right. After 1830, her salon was somewhat less prominent, although it was a center for legitimism and liberal Catholicism. Récamier was known for inspiring passion in the men around her, including Benjamin Constant, Prosper de Barante, and Mathieu de Montmorency, but her only consummated affair was with Chateaubriand.

GUIZOT'S CIRCLE

François Guizot (1787–1874) was born into a bourgeois and Protestant family in Nîmes. His father was guillotined during the Terror, so he was raised largely by his mother in Geneva and came to Paris in 1805. In 1812 he married Pauline de Meulan, a noted author, and began teaching at the Sorbonne. He first held political office during the first Restoration, but he resigned during the Hundred Days and went to Ghent in an effort to win Louis XVIII over to the cause of liberalism. After Napoleon's fall, he held a number of positions within the government, and was a particularly important adviser to Élie Decazes when the latter was head of the government from 1819 to 1820. When Decazes fell from power in 1820, Guizot, too, was removed from his position on the Conseil d'État; two years later, he lost his post at the Sorbonne. During the 1820s, he was an activist on the center-left and involved in many journalistic projects. Elected to the Chamber of Deputies in 1830, he served in a number of ministries in the first decade of the July Monarchy and became a leader of the conservatives in the Chamber during this decade. From 1840 to 1848, he was minister of foreign affairs and effective head of the government. He fled to Britain in 1848, from whence he tried to make a political comeback, an effort in which he failed. Increasingly withdrawn from politics from the 1850s until his death, he devoted himself to his scholarly pursuits.

Prosper de Barante (1782–1866) was from a family of minor nobility and held a number administrative, prefectorial, and diplomatic posts under Napoleon; he was also a member of the Coppet circle during the Empire and friends with Mme de Staël and Benjamin Constant. During the Restoration, he served in the Chamber of Deputies and the Chamber of Peers from 1819 on. He was also a member of the Conseil d'État until 1820, when a more conservative government pushed him out of office. During the July Monarchy, he remained in the Chamber of Peers and was also ambassador to Piedmont–Sardinia and to Russia.

Albertine Ida Gustavine de Staël Holstein, duchesse de Broglie (1797–1838) was Mme de Staël's daughter and Victor de Broglie's wife. She had a passionate disposition and by all accounts her marriage was a mismatch. She was devoted to the doctrinaire cause and a close friend of Guizot and Barante, as well as a celebrated salonnière in the Restoration and July Monarchy. In her last years, she was increasingly depressive, and her early death devastated those around her.

Victor de Broglie (1785–1870) was from one of the great aristocratic families of France. Like Guizot, his father was guillotined in the Terror. A diplomat during the Empire, he was a republican in the early years of the Restoration, but quickly moved to the center-left position of the doctrinaires. Broglie was a member of the Chamber of Peers in both the Restoration and the July Monarchy, and he served as head of the government twice during the 1830s. Known for being somewhat of a cold fish, he was nevertheless close to both Barante and Guizot from the 1810s to his death.

Dorothée de Courlande, duchesse de Dino (1793–1862) was a member of the Baltic German aristocracy. In 1809 she married one of Talleyrand's nephews; the marriage was unhappy but she eventually became Talleyrand's mistress and companion. She maintained a salon in Paris and assiduously cultivated allies on behalf of her uncle-in-law. After Talleyrand's death in 1838, she spent more and more time outside of France, although she maintained close connections to her French friends, including Guizot and Barante.

Gabrielle Henriette Catherine Laure de Daunant de Gasparin (1790–1864) was from a family of Protestant aristocrats from Nîmes and was the sister of Guizot's childhood friend Achille de Daunant. She was married to Auguste de Gasparin, a politician during the July Monarchy. From the mid-1830s to her death she was a close friend and confidante of Guizot, although consistently to his left in political terms.

Princesse Dorothea von Lieven, née Benckendorff (1785–1857) was born into the Baltic German aristocracy and raised at the Russian court. Her husband was the Russian ambassador to Berlin and then to London from 1812 to 1834, although it was widely understood that she was the real diplomat of the two and she achieved considerable influence over foreign policy in her years in Britain. In 1834, she and her husband were recalled to Russia, but after her two youngest sons died of scarlet fever, she fled to Paris against the wishes of her husband and the tsar. In Paris, she opened a salon that attracted politicians, diplomats, and foreigners, and at a dinner party in 1837 she and Guizot fell in love. Their liaison would last until her death, and she served as an important diplomatic adviser to Guizot in the 1840s.

Charles de Rémusat (1797–1875) was born into a family that served the Empire and the Restoration successively. Introduced into the doctrinaire circle by Barante, he quickly became very close to Guizot and his first wife during the 1820s. He served as Guizot's deputy on a number of journalistic projects during the Restoration. In 1830 he was elected to the Chamber of Deputies, and during that decade he balanced an attachment to the doctrinaires with one to Thiers and the men of the center-left. In 1840, after he was minister of the interior in a left-leaning cabinet led by Thiers, he broke off relations with Guizot and entered into the opposition.

APPENDIX B: DETAILED SOCIAL NETWORKS IN THE 1820S AND 1840S

This appendix provides more details about the social networks discussed in chapter 4.

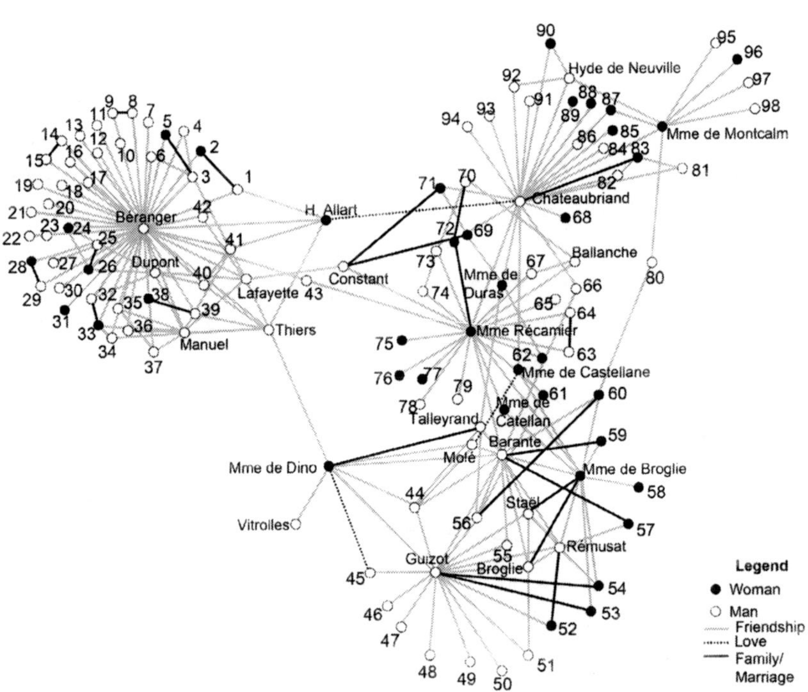

FIGURE 5 Detailed social networks, 1825–29

Legend for figures 5 and 6

1. Étienne de Jouy
2. Mme Boudonville
3. Pierre Lebrun
4. Benjamin Antier
5. Mme Lebrun
6. Bosquillon Wilhem
7. Montandon
8. Charles Louis Cadet de Gassicourt
9. Félix Cadet de Gassicourt
10. René Théophile Chatelain
11. Casimir Delavigne
12. Félix Barthe
13. Rouget de Lisle
14. Berville
15. Andrieux
16. Louis Bro
17. Guernu
18. Vaissière

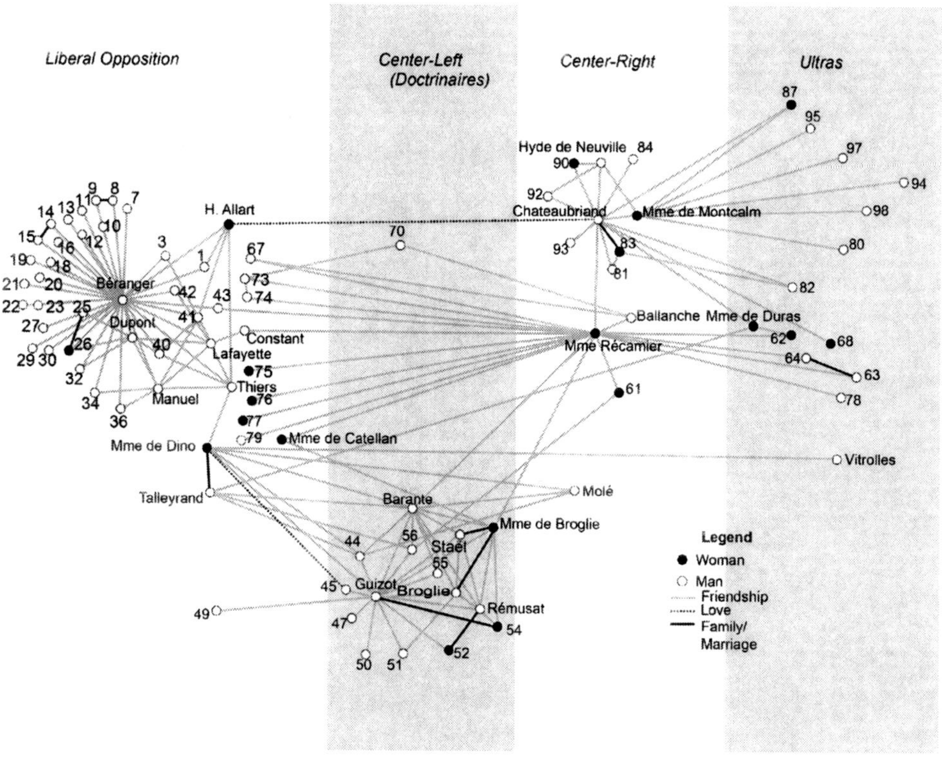

FIGURE 6 Detailed social networks and political affiliations, 1825–29

19. Prosper Mérimée
20. Lucien Arnault
21. Coulmann
22. Horace Sébastiani
23. André Dupin
24. Mme Brissot-Thivars
25. Louis François Auguste Cauchois-Lemaire
26. Judith Cauchois-Lemaire
27. Charles Augustin Sainte-Beuve
28. Anaïs Bernard
29. Joseph Bernard
30. Béjot
31. Juliette Quenescourt
32. Auguste Simon Louis Bérard
33. Mme Heurtaux
34. Charles Guillaume Étienne
35. Thomas
36. Pierre François Tissot
37. Bastide
38. Mme Firmin
39. Firmin
40. Jacques Laffitte
41. François Mignet
42. Ary Scheffer
43. Comte de Kératry
44. Pierre Paul Royer-Collard
45. Théobald Piscatory
46. Édouard Verdier de Flaux
47. Pellegrino Rossi
48. Henry Hallam
49. Joseph Madier de Montjau
50. Achille de Daunant
51. Abel François Villemain
52. Mme de Rémusat
53. Mme Guizot (Guizot's mother)
54. Pauline Guizot (Guizot's first wife)
55. Élie Decazes
56. Comte de Sainte-Aulaire
57. Mme de Barante
58. Mlle Pomaret
59. Mme Anisson du Perron

60. Mme de Sainte-Aulaire
61. Mme de Boigne
62. Mme Swetchine
63. Adrien de Laval-Montmorency
64. Mathieu de Montmorency
65. Paul David
66. Comte de Montlosier
67. Joseph Marie de Gérando
68. Mme de Custine
69. Rosalie de Constant
70. Charles Lenormant
71. Mme de Cottens
72. Mme Lenormant
73. Jean Jacques Ampère
74. Étienne Delécluze
75. Caroline Murat
76. Mme Salvage
77. Hortense Bonaparte
78. Duc de Doudeauville
79. Comte de Montbel
80. Alphonse de Lamartine
81. Clausel de Coussergues
82. Duc de Lévis
83. Mme de Chateaubriand
84. Louis François Bertin
85. Mme de Pierreclau
86. Arnaud Joubert
87. Mme d'Orglandes
88. Mlle de Villeneuve
89. Mme de Pisieux
90. Mme de Vichet
91. John Fraser Frisell
92. Comte de La Ferronnays
93. François Marie Agier
94. François Régis de La Bourdonnaye
95. Gontaut
96. Lady Elliot
97. Marquis de Caraman
98. Alexis de Noailles

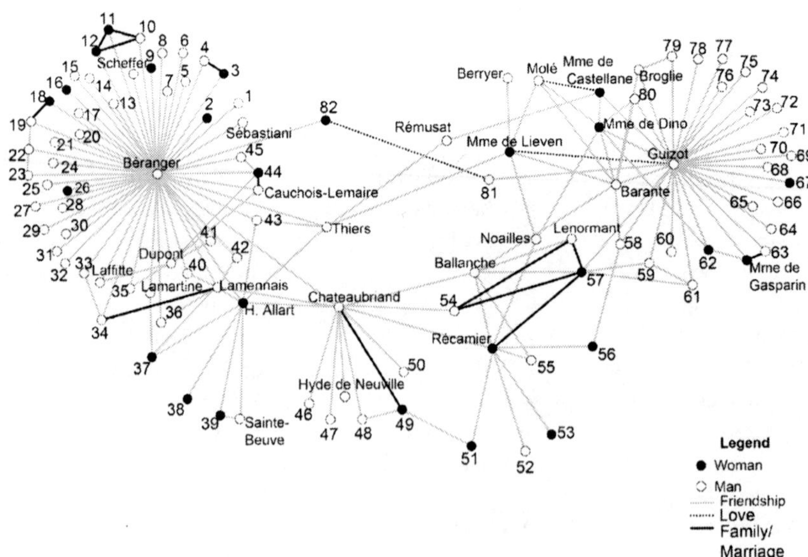

FIGURE 7 Detailed social networks, 1843–47

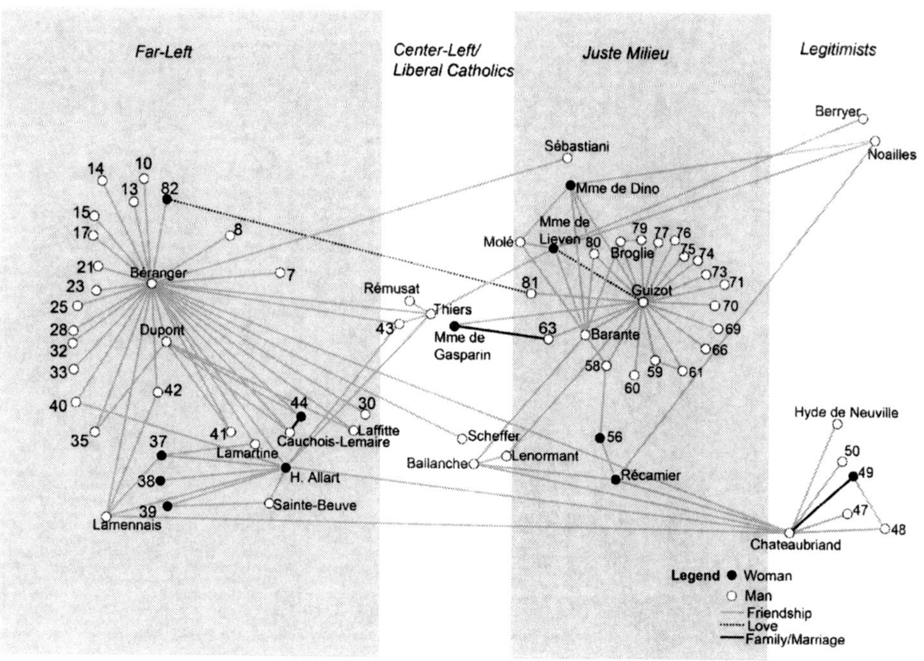

FIGURE 8 Detailed social networks and political affiliations, 1843–47

Legend for figures 7 and 8

1. Eugène Haag
2. Mme Scribe
3. Mme Firmin
4. Firmin
5. Béjot
6. Édouard Charton
7. Napoléon Peyrat
8. Jean Reynaud
9. Mme Brissot-Thivars
10. Joseph Bernard
11. Anaïs Bernard
12. Mme Bernard
13. Savinien Lapointe
14. Michel Roly
15. Jules Michelet
16. Mme Valchere
17. Henri Martin
18. Mme Lebrun
19. Pierre Lebrun
20. Génin
21. Charles Thomas
22. Benjamin Antier
23. Gilhard
24. Brissot
25. Louis Blanc
26. Mme Frank
27. Prosper Mérimée
28. Henri de Latouche
29. Étienne de Jouy
30. Comte des Fossez
31. Bertrand
32. Adrien Benoît-Champy
33. Bastide
34. Ange Blaize
35. Ulysse Trélat
36. Bretonneau
37. Marie d'Agoult
38. Pauline Roland
39. George Sand
40. Pierre Leroux
41. Auguste Simon Louis Bérard
42. Hippolyte Fortoul
43. François Mignet
44. Judith Cauchois-Lemaire
45. Charles Perrotin
46. John Fraser Frisell
47. Jean Baptiste Julien Mandaroux-Vertamy

48. Clausel de Coussergues
49. Mme de Chateaubriand
50. Duc de Lévis
51. Mme Auguste de Caffarelli
52. Alexander von Humboldt
53. Mme Salvage
54. Louis de Loménie
55. Jean Jacques Ampère
56. Mme de Boigne
57. Mme Lenormant
58. Comte de Sainte-Aulaire
59. Charles Tanneguy Duchâtel
60. Élie Decazes
61. Ludovic Vitet
62. Mme Mollien
63. Achille de Daunant
64. Henry Hallam
65. John Wilson Croker
66. Théobald Piscatory
67. Sarah Austin
68. Édouard Verdier de Flaux
69. Félix de La Farelle
70. Pellegrino Rossi
71. Ernest de Chabaud-Latour
72. Earl of Aberdeen
73. Comte de Ségur
74. Laurent Cunin-Gridaine
75. Pierre Sylvain Dumon
76. Louis de Guizard
77. Augustin Thierry
78. Madier de Montjau
79. Abel François Villemain
80. Pierre Paul Royer-Collard
81. Victor Cousin
82. Mme Colet

NOTES

INTRODUCTION

1. On the politics of funerary practices, see Fureix, *France des larmes*. On Manuel dying in Béranger's arms, see Béranger, *Ma Biographie*, 197n2. For the song about Manuel using "tu," see Bonnal, *Manuel et son temps*, 416. On the tradition of friends sharing a tomb, see Bray, *The Friend*.

2. See, for instance, Baudouin, *Dictionnaire des gens du monde*, 11; Lemaire, *Conseils d'un père*, 94–96; and *Honnête homme à la cour et dans le monde*, 53–55.

3. Mme de Barante to François Guizot, 7 January 1867, in Archives nationales de France (hereafter AN), Archives privées, Fonds Guizot, 42 AP 200, no. 175; Broglie, *Guizot*, plates; Witt, *Monsieur Guizot dans sa famille*, 339; Guizot, *Lettres à sa fille Henriette*, 980. Unless otherwise noted, all translations are the author's own.

4. Recent works discussing the family as producing social cohesion include Desan, *Family on Trial*; Rosanvallon, *Demands of Liberty*; and Surkis, *Sexing the Citizen*.

5. One example of the political uses of family ties can be found in chapter 6, where the marquise de Montcalm served as a crucial intermediary for her brother, the duc de Richelieu.

6. See, for instance, Allgor, *Parlor Politics*; and Charmley, *Princess and the Politicians*.

7. Recent works on the politics and political culture of the Restoration and July Monarchy include Alexander, *Re-writing the French Revolutionary Tradition*; Broglie, *Monarchie de Juillet*; Démier, *France de la Restauration*; Fureix, *France des larmes*; Gunn, *When the French Tried to Be British*; Kroen, *Politics and Theater*; Margadant, "Gender, Vice, and the Political Imaginary"; Price, *Perilous Crown*; Rosanvallon, *Moment Guizot*; Rosanvallon, *Monarchie impossible*; Skuy, *Assassination, Politics, and Miracles*; Waresquiel, *Histoire à rebrousse-poil*; and Waresquiel and Yvert, *Histoire de la Restauration*.

8. Rosanvallon, *Monarchie impossible*, 9. Other works that examine the Restoration as France's education in constitutional government and parliamentary life include Alexander, *Re-writing the French Revolutionary Tradition*; Bertier de Sauvigny, *Bourbon Restoration*; Kroen, *Politics and Theater*; Price, *Perilous Crown*; and Waresquiel and Yvert, *Histoire de la Restauration*.

9. Waresquiel and Yvert, *Histoire de la Restauration*, 479.

10. Works on separate sphere include Hunt, *Family Romance*; and Landes, *Women and the Public Sphere*. For the British case, see Davidoff and Hall, *Family Fortunes*. On male rationality and the privatization and feminization of emotion, see Goldstein, *Post-Revolutionary Self*; Reddy, *Navigation of Feeling*; and Vincent-Buffault, *History of Tears*.

11. One example is in Guizot to princesse de Lieven, 7 July 1837, AN, Archives privées, Fonds Guizot, 42 AP 100, no. 24.

12. Adams, *Poverty, Charity, and Motherhood*; Davidson, *France after Revolution*; Hesse, *Other Enlightenment*; Rogers, *From the Salon to the Schoolroom*. Margadant, *New Biography*, studies the public personae of notable women in the nineteenth century.

13. On political sociability, see Kale, *French Salons*.

14. Hoffmann, "Civility, Male Friendship, and Masonic Sociability"; Linton, "Fatal Friendships"; Loiselle, "Nouveau mais vrais amis."

15. Three foundational texts in this tradition are Faderman, *Surpassing the Love of Men*; Sedgwick, *Between Men*; and Smith-Rosenberg, "Female World of Love and Ritual." More recently, see Bray, *The Friend*; Marcus, *Between Women*; Martin, *Napoleonic Friendship*; and Merrick, "Male Friendship in Prerevolutionary France."

16. See, however, Colwill, "Epistolary Passions."

17. Two early—and formative works—in sociology are Granovetter, "Strength of Weak Ties"; and Wellman and Berkowitz, *Social Structures*.

18. Hardin, *Trust and Trustworthiness*, xix.

19. Baier, *Moral Prejudices*, 99.

20. On this issue and on definitions of trust more generally, see McLeod, "Trust."

21. Putnam, *Making Democracy Work*; and Putnam, *Bowling Alone*. This is not to say that Putnam's claims are uncontroversial. See, for instance, Fischer, "*Bowling Alone*." Fischer suggests that the changing nature of interpersonal connections, including the rise of individualism and the privatization of social ties, can better account for the decline of trust in contemporary America that Putnam notes in *Bowling Alone*. In this respect, *Friendship and Politics in Post-Revolutionary France* follows Fischer's model more closely than it follows Putnam's.

22. Works discussing an endemic lack of trust within French society include Algan and Cahuc, *Société de défiance*; and Rosanvallon, *Counter-Democracy*.

23. *Dictionnaire de L'Académie française*, 6th ed. (1832–35), s.v. "amitié" and "ami, ie."

24. For instance, in a letter to Aberdeen written after the death of his mistress princesse de Lieven, Guizot spoke of his relationship with Lieven as being an "amitié." Guizot to Aberdeen, Val-Richer, 25 February 1857, AN, Archives privées, Fonds Guizot, 42 AP 211, 145.188. Likewise, the correspondence guide *Modèles de lettres* uses the term "amitié" to describe a relationship between siblings.

25. Sue, *Mystères de Paris*, 1248.

26. In this book, I refer to women by their last name or the names by which they were referred in their lifetime, with the exception of the first reference to women whose lives or relationships I substantively discuss. In this case, I provide their full names as well as their maiden names in instances where the maiden name is available but not part of their full married name (as it was for Montcalm and Broglie). Thus Armande Marie Antoinette de Vignerot du Plessis de Richelieu, marquise de Montcalm-Gozon, is generally referred to as "Mme de Montcalm" or "Montcalm." Perhaps because of her bourgeois background or her status as an unconventional woman of letters, Allart is typically referred to as "Hortense Allart," as opposed to "Madame Allart," a convention that I follow here. For women who are only mentioned, I use the naming conventions of the nineteenth century and do not provide their full names.

27. The memoirs of these men and their friends can be found in Allart, *Enchantements de prudence*; Béranger, *Ma Biographie*; Broglie, *Souvenirs*; Chateaubriand, *Mémoires*; Guizot, *Mémoires*; Hyde de Neuville, *Mémoires*; and Rémusat, *Mémoires*. The diary of Mme de Montcalm, one of Chateaubriand's friends, can be found in Montcalm, *Mon Journal*. Béranger's letters can be found in Béranger, *Correspondance de Béranger*; Béranger, *Lettres inédites à P. Lebrun et à Mme Lebrun*; Béranger, *Lettres inédites de Béranger à Dupont de l'Eure*; and Psichari, "Béranger." Chateaubriand's letters are in Chateaubriand, *Correspondance générale*. Guizot's personal papers are located in AN, Archives privées, Fonds Guizot, 42 AP. Some of Guizot's correspondence has also been published in Guizot and Lieven, *Lettres de François Guizot et de la princesse de Lieven*; Guizot, *Lettres à sa fille Henriette*; Guizot, *François Guizot et Madame Laure de Gasparin*; Guizot, *Années de retraite*; Guizot, *Lettres de M. Guizot à sa famille*. Letters of Guizot's friends can be found in Barante, *Souvenirs*; and Broglie, *Lettres de la duchesse de Broglie*. Letters of Chateaubriand's companion Récamier can be found in Lenormant, *Madame Récamier, les amis de sa jeunesse, et sa correspondance intime*; and Lenormant, *Souvenirs et correspondance*. Some of Montcalm's letters are available in Montcalm, *Salon politique*. Letters from Chateaubriand's friend the duchesse de Duras are in Pailhès, *Duchesse de Duras et Chateaubriand*. Some letters of Hortense Allart, friend to both Chateaubriand and Béranger, can be found in Allart, *Lettres inédites à Sainte-Beuve*; and Séché, *Hortense Allart*. Biographies also provide a great deal of information on these men and their personal ties. Touchard, *Gloire de Béranger*, is particularly good on Béranger's friendship network, as are Broglie, *Guizot*; and Theis, *François Guizot* for Guizot. One relatively recent biography of Chateaubriand with information on his friendships is Diesbach, *Chateaubriand*.

28. On the elite neighborhoods of Paris, see Martin-Fugier, *Vie élégante*, 100–112. On the notables as the ruling class during this period, see Jardin and Tudesq, *France des notables*.

29. Noël, *Souvenirs de Béranger*, 80.

30. Béranger, *Ma Biographie*, 77.

31. Clément, *Chateaubriand*, 381.

32. On songs and political protest, see Darriulat, *Muse du peuple*.

33. Works that take Guizot and the doctrinaires as representative of the age include Gunn, *When the French Tried to Be British*; Jaume, *Individu effacé*; Reddy, *Navigation of Feeling*; and Rosanvallon, *Moment Guizot*.

34. Reddy, *Navigation of Feeling*, 129. On the history of the emotions, see also Rosenwein, *Emotional Communities*; and Stearns and Stearns, "Emotionology."

35. For instance, there is the relationship between Mme de Broglie and Mme Récamier, two women who called each other friends but never really liked each other, as discussed in chapter 4.

36. See, for example, Rémusat, *Mémoires*, 1:439, 444.

37. Montcalm, *Mon Journal*, 122.

CHAPTER 1

1. Smith, "No More Language Games," 1431.

2. Herman, "Language of Fidelity," 9.

3. Quoted in ibid., 22–23.

4. There has been considerable debate among historians as to how to understand these utterances of affection. Some scholars have described this language as a reflection of actual feeling, while others describe this rhetoric as a mask for relations of domination and subordination. For the debate, see Beik, *Absolutism and Society*; Herman, "Language of Fidelity"; Kettering, "Friendship and Clientage"; Mousnier, "Concepts de 'ordres,' d'états, de fidélité, et de 'monarchie absolue'"; and Smith, "No More Language Games."

5. Rentet, "Network Mapping."

6. Beik, *Social and Cultural History of Early Modern France*, 158.

7. Ibid., 160.

8. Kettering, "Friendship and Clientage."

9. Kettering, *Patrons, Brokers, and Clients*, 94; Rentet, "Network Mapping," 116.

10. Kettering, "Patronage Power of Early Modern French Noblewomen"; Stephenson, *Patronage Power of Marguerite de Navarre*. On male brokerage, see Kettering, *Patrons, Brokers, and Clients*. On men connecting regional and royal networks, see Rentet, "Network Mapping."

11. Le Roy Ladurie, *Saint-Simon*, 122–49.

12. Smith, *Culture of Merit*.

13. Elias, *Court Society*, 110–11.

14. Reddy, *Navigation of Feeling*, 164; Silver, "Friendship in Commercial Society," 1482. See also Linton, "Fatal Friendships," 56.

15. Hunt, *Inventing Human Rights*, 39.

16. On sentimentalism as an oppositional political movement, see Denby, *Sentimental Narrative*; Hunt, *Family Romance*, 15–22; Maza, *Myth of the French Bourgeoisie*, 61–67; Maza, *Private Lives and Public Affairs*; Reddy, *Navigation of Feeling*, 141–72.

17. Kaiser, "Louis *le Bien-Aimé*," 137.

18. See Halévi, *Loges maçonniques*, where the phrase "democratic sociability" appears in the subtitle. On Masonry, see also Jacob, *Living the Enlightenment*; and Loiselle, "New but True Friends." On salons, see Goodman, *Republic of Letters*. For a view that salon practices were tied to hierarchical aristocratic norms, see Lilti, *Monde des salons*.

19. Sennett, *Fall of Public Man*.

20. Garrioch, "From Christian Friendship to Secular Sentimentality," 204; Loiselle, "New but True Friends."

21. Goodman, *Republic of Letters*, 83.

22. Rousseau, *Julie*, 401.

23. On the issue of epistolarity and transparency, see Altman, *Epistolarity*, 68–81.

24. On emotions and friendship in particular during the Revolution, see Linton, *Choosing Terror*. Unfortunately, *Choosing Terror* was published after this book went to press.

25. Higonnet, "Terror, Trauma, and the 'Young Marx,'" 154.

26. Quoted in Shapiro, *Traumatic Politics*, 23.

27. Quoted in Tackett, *Becoming a Revolutionary*, 156.

28. Hunt and Jacob, "Affective Revolution," 497.

29. Shapiro, *Traumatic Politics*.

30. Quoted in Tackett, *Becoming a Revolutionary*, 150.

31. Ibid.

32. Quoted in ibid., 174–75.

33. Kale, *French Salons*, 47, 53.

34. Quoted in Tackett, *Becoming a Revolutionary*, 256.

35. Quoted in ibid.

36. Quoted in David, *Fraternité*, 74.

37. On the distinction between friendship and fraternity, see Linton, "Fatal Friendships," 56.

38. Furet, *Interpreting the French Revolution*, 53–58; Tackett, "Conspiracy Obsession," 713; Tackett, *When the King Took Flight*. See also Wahnich, *Liberté ou la mort*.

39. Higonnet, "Terror, Trauma, and 'Young Marx,'" 152, 154.

40. Adams, *Poverty, Charity, and Motherhood*, 45. The earliest manifestation of this anti-associational tendency was the Le Chapelier Law of 1791.

41. Rosanvallon, *Demands of Liberty*, 16–21.

42. David, *Fraternité*, 127, 137.

43. Saint-Just, "Institutions républicaines," 1102–3.

44. Quoted in David, *Fraternité*, 125.

45. Ibid., 124.

46. Quoted in Reddy, *Navigation of Feeling*, 195.

47. Darnton, *Kiss of Lamourette*, xii–xiv. See also Vincent-Buffault, *History of Tears*, 85–87.

48. Quoted in Reddy, *Navigation of Feeling*, 191.

49. Linton, "Fatal Friendships," 62, 69–75.

50. Quoted in ibid., 63–64.

51. Ibid., 51–60.

52. Ibid.

53. Lucas, "Theory and Practice of Denunciation," 20.

54. Hunt, *Politics, Culture, and Class*, 13.

55. Quoted in Higonnet, *Goodness beyond Virtue*, 187.

56. Reddy, *Navigation of Feeling*, 197.

57. Ibid., 200–202. However, even after Thermidor, some continued to see a political role for sentiment. See Vincent, *Benjamin Constant*.

58. Quoted in Desan, "Reconstituting the Social," 109.

59. Quoted in Steinberg, "Afterlives of the Terror," 166.

60. Ibid., 167.

61. Ibid., 162–209; Desan, "Reconstituting the Social."

62. Guizot, *Mémoires*, 1:113. The word "pacification" was also used in the nineteenth century in colonial contexts to describe French attempts to end resistance, including in Algeria; as a politician of the July Monarchy, Guizot supported this effort. "Pacification" thus had connotations of ending political resistance, including through force if need be.

63. Lentz, *France et l'Europe de Napoléon*, 600–613; Woloch, *Napoleon and His Collaborators*, 55–56.

64. Woloch, *Napoleon and His Collaborators*, 177.

65. Lentz, *France et l'Europe de Napoléon*, 119.

66. Quoted in Thiers, *Histoire de la révolution française*, 582.

67. Kale, *French Salons*, 77.

68. Lentz, *France et l'Europe de Napoléon,* 224–38. Surveillance of associations during the Napoleonic era can be found in AN, F7 8779, objets généraux.

69. Kale, *French Salons,* 77–104; Rémusat, *Mémoires,* 1:66–67.

70. Quoted in Marcou, *Napoléon and les femmes,* 87–88.

71. Branda, *Napoléon et ses hommes,* 314.

72. Lilti, *Monde des salons,* 393; Malandain, "Mouches de la police"; Ravel, *Contested Parterre,* 133–60.

73. Merriman, *Police Stories,* 17.

74. Aulard, *Paris sous le Consulat,* 1:78, 263, 285; d'Hauterive, *Police secrète,* 25; Kale, *French Salons,* 87; Lentz, *France et l'Europe de Napoléon,* 325.

75. Couchery, *Moniteur secret,* 92.

76. Fouché, *Mémoires,* 45. Although there is some debate as to whether Fouché actually wrote his *Mémoires,* the consensus is that he contributed to them and was involved in their writing, even if others did much of the work. See Zanone, *Écrire son temps,* 355.

77. Martin, *Napoleonic Friendship,* 19–100.

78. On the problem of social dissolution, see Andrews, *Socialism's Muse*; and Rosanvallon, *Demands of Liberty,* 94–106.

79. "Individualisme," 48–49.

80. "*L'individualisme* . . . rapporte au seul *moi* humain non seulement les affections, mais les pensées, les habitudes et la croyance." Ibid., 48.

81. On the origins of the term "individualism," see Lukes, *Individualism,* 3–4. For Chateaubriand's statement, see Chateaubriand, *Mémoires,* 2:921. For de Maistre's, see Maistre, *Oeuvres complètes,* 286.

82. Lukes, *Individualism,* 3–16; Rosanvallon, *Demands of Liberty,* 96–97.

83. Royer-Collard, *Vie politique,* 2:130–31. See also Rosanvallon, *Moment Guizot,* 75–82.

84. See, for instance, Tocqueville, *Democracy in America,* 506–8; and Tocqueville, *Old Regime and the French Revolution,* xiii.

85. Leroux, "Aux Philosophes," 78.

86. Lukes, "Meaning of Individualism."

87. Rosanvallon, *Demands of Liberty,* 98–99.

CHAPTER 2

1. Maistre, *Oeuvres complètes,* 286.

2. On the divides within France, see Owre, "United in Division." Other works that stress the factionalism and divisions of the Restoration include Alexander, *Bonapartism and Revolutionary Tradition*; Resnick, *White Terror*; Price, *Perilous Crown*; and Waresquiel and Yvert, *Histoire de la Restauration.*

3. Eymery, *Dictionnaire des girouettes*; Serna, *République des girouettes*; Spitzer, "Malicious Memories."

4. Chateaubriand, *Mémoires,* 1:1423–24.

5. On the male honor code of the nineteenth century, see Nye, *Masculinity and Male Codes of Honor*; and Reddy, *Invisible Code.*

6. Serna, *République des girouettes*, 240. See also Waresquiel, *Cent jours*, 58–63.

7. Quoted in Waresquiel and Yvert, *Histoire de la Restauration*, 181. See also Démier, *France de la Restauration*, 109.

8. Pilbeam, *Constitutional Monarchy*, 7; Rémond, *Right Wing in France*, 61; Resnick, *White Terror*.

9. Waresquiel and Yvert, *Histoire de la Restauration*, 182.

10. Quoted in ibid.

11. Béranger, *Ma Biographie*, 161.

12. Alexander, *Re-writing the French Revolutionary Tradition*, 17–18.

13. Furet, *Interpreting the French Revolution*, 28–61.

14. Skuy, *Assassination, Politics, and Miracles*, 86.

15. Rémond, *Right Wing in France*, 33.

16. The heterogeneity of the liberal opposition is a theme of Alexander, *Re-writing the French Revolutionary Tradition*.

17. Ibid.; Price, *Perilous Crown*, 83–84; Resnick, *White Terror*.

18. Salvandy, *Vues politiques*, 77, 79. On civility and sociability as essential elements of French national character in the Old Regime, see Gordon, *Citizens without Sovereignty*.

19. Montcalm, *Mon Journal*, 89. See also pp. 26, 121, where she repeats this theme.

20. Other authors of the time, including Guizot, his fellow doctrinaire Auguste de Staël, Mme de Staël's son, and the philosopher Maine de Biran, all spoke of the hatred that ran rampant throughout French society in the aftermath of the upheaval of 1815. See Guizot, *Mémoires*, 1:113; Maine de Biran, *Journal intime*, 1:195; Waresquiel and Yvert, *Histoire de la Restauration*, 278. See also Kale, *French Salons*, 105–64.

21. Lesur, *La France et les français en 1817*, 159–60.

22. Ibid., 159. See also Genlis, *Dictionnaire*, 1:218.

23. Béranger, *Ma Biographie*, 151, 143; Béranger, *Correspondance de Béranger*, 2:151n1.

24. Molé, *Le Comte Molé*, 2:7; Neely, *Lafayette and the Liberal Ideal*, 37.

25. Theis, *François Guizot*, 115.

26. Montcalm, *Mon Journal*, 258.

27. Ibid., 122.

28. Dupaty, *Délateurs*, 11.

29. Genlis, *Dictionnaire*, 1:185.

30. A sampling of anonymous denunciations can be found in AN, F7 6632, notes de police, from May 1816.

31. One example of a personally motivated denunciation can be found in AN, F7 6915, police politique, dossier 8285, letter to the director of the departmental administration of the police, Paris, 10 December 1821.

32. "Dame Roger, née Bringuet: Ses révélations," AN, F7 6854, police politique, dossier 4316.

33. Dupaty, *Délateurs*, 10, 13.

34. Salvandy, *Vues politiques*, 76.

35. On the politicization of the police in the Restoration, see Merriman, *Police Stories*.

36. For the surveillance of Napoleonic officers, see Martin, *Napoleonic Friendship*, 149. AN, F7 6632, notes de police, May 1816, details the surveillance of an ultra gathering.

37. Daudet, *Police politique*, 263, 269, 272, 285; Vaillé, *Cabinet noir*, 365.

38. Daudet, *Police politique*, 290–91.

39. AN, F7 6718, députés, dossier 9; AN, F7 6719, députés, dossier 8; AN, F7 6720, députés; AN, F7 6720, députés, dossier 8371.

40. AN, F7 3796, police générale, Minister of the Interior, Office of the Police, Bulletin, 26 July 1825, no. 64 and AN, F7 3796, police générale, Minister of the Interior, Office of the Police, Bulletin, 20 August 1825, no. 70; AN, F7 6961, police politique, Minister of the Interior, Office of the Police, to the Prefect of the Bas-Rhin, Paris, 13 April 1827.

41. For instance, the information the police obtained about Auguste de Staël clearly came from his servants. AN, F7 6952, police politique, folio 11558, Prefect of the Police to Minister of the Interior, Paris, 17 January 1824.

42. Thus, in two instances, the police mentioned not being able to listen at doors or windows. One involved Horace Vernet and the other involved Lafayette. AN, F7 6923, police politique, folio 8953, Prefect of the Police to the Minister of the Interior, Paris, 16 July 1823; AN, F7 6720, députés, dossier 8371, Prefect of the Police to the Minister of the Interior, Paris, 1 October 1822. On using ruses, see Année, *Livre noir*, 2:389.

43. Galtier-Boissière, *Mysteries of the French Secret Police*, 169.

44. Caillot, *Mémoires*, 2:296–97; Froment, *Police dévoilée*, 3:311–14.

45. Karila-Cohen, "Les Fonds secrets."

46. Jouy, *Morale appliquée*, 346. See also Morgan, *France*, 1:229–30.

47. Nourrisson, *Histoire de la liberté*, 215–16.

48. See AN, F7 6699, affaires politiques, dossier 27, on the Cercle de l'Union; and AN F7 6960, affaires politiques, dossier 12024, on the Société de la morale chrétienne.

49. AN, F7 6700, affaires politiques, folio 29.

50. Agulhon, *Cercle dans la France bourgeoise*; Harrison, *Bourgeois Citizen*. However, Duprat, *Usage et pratiques*, describes the strength of early nineteenth-century philanthropic organizations.

51. Recent works that discuss the problem of social cohesion in the July Monarchy include Andrews, *Socialism's Muse*; Bouton, "Reconciliation, Hope, Trust, and Instability"; and Broglie, *Monarchie de Juillet*, 256–91.

52. Rémusat, *Mémoires*, 3:373–77.

53. Agulhon, *Cercle dans la France bourgeoise*, 26–27; Broglie, *Monarchie de Juillet*, 122; Hoffman, "Democracy and Associations."

54. Backouche, *Monarchie parlementaire*, 244; Bastid, *Institutions politiques*, 297.

55. Touchard, *Gloire de Béranger*, 1:446.

56. Béranger to Virlet d'Aoust, 5 November 1834, in Béranger, *Correspondance de Béranger*, 2:257; Béranger to Antier, Tours, 4 October 1837, in Béranger, *Correspondance de Béranger*, 3:58.

57. Béranger to Gilhard, Passy, 9 January 1843, in Béranger, *Correspondance de Béranger*, 3:269–70. See also Béranger to Thiers, Passy, 18 February 1833, Papiers Adolphe Thiers, Correspondance, 1830–34, Bibliothèque nationale de France, NAF 20601, no. 169, where Béranger reassures Thiers of his continuing friendship, suggesting that Thiers was concerned about the state of their relationship.

58. See Rémusat, *Mémoires*, 1:439.

59. Guizot to Dorothea Lieven, Val-Richer, 14 July 1837, in Guizot and Lieven, *Lettres de François Guizot et de la princesse de Lieven*, 1:24.

60. On the necessity of alliances between factions, see Price, *Perilous Crown*, 195.

61. See, for example, Maza, *Myth of the French Bourgeoisie*; Reddy, *Invisible Code*; and Thompson, *Virtuous Marketplace*, 15–51.

62. Fortescue, "Morality and Monarchy"; Margadant, "Gender, Vice, and the Political Imaginary."

63. Ancelot, *Salon de Paris*, xiv, 150.

64. Balzac, "Z. Marcas," 755.

65. Ibid., 748.

66. Ibid., 738–39.

67. Ibid., 755.

68. Ibid., 750.

69. Ibid., 758.

70. Ibid., 761.

71. The literature on Balzac and the market is large. See, for example, Thesen, *Function of Gift Exchange*.

72. On the privatization of friendship in the early nineteenth century, see Houbre, *Discipline de l'amour*, 102; Reddy, *Navigation of Feeling*, 242; and Vincent-Buffault, *Exercice de l'amitié*, 51–52.

73. Balzac, *Illusions perdues*, 844.

74. Ibid., 741.

75. Ibid., 749.

76. Ibid., 765.

77. Ibid., 735.

78. Ibid., 736.

79. Ibid., 656.

80. On Balzac and male friendship, see Lucey, *Misfit of the Family*, 124–70; and Martin, *Napoleonic Friendship*, 145–228.

81. Balzac, *Illusions perdues*, 656.

82. Ibid., 651.

83. Ibid., 656.

84. Ibid., 655.

85. Ibid., 661.

86. Thesen, *Function of Gift Exchange*, 197–98.

87. Balzac, *Illusions perdues*, 654.

CHAPTER 3

1. Guizot to Victor de Broglie, Paris, 26 September 1832, AN, Archives privées, Fonds Guizot, 42 AP 14, no. 214.

2. On this issue, see the essays in part 2 of Johnson and Sabean, *Sibling Relations*.

3. The literature on epistolarity is large. Crucial works include Altman, *Epistolarity*; Dauphin, Lebrun-Pézerat, and Poublan, *Ces Bonnes lettres*; Goodman, *Becoming a Woman*; and Redford, *Converse of the Pen*.

4. *Honnête homme à la cour et dans le monde*, 54.

5. Souza, *Charles et Marie*, 173.

6. On the practice of keeping a journal with or for friends, see Vincent-Buffault, *Exercice de l'amitié*, 60–61.

7. See, for example, *Politesse et les usages du monde*, 52; Bouilly, *Conseils à ma fille*, 225–26. See also a letter from Rémusat to Alexis de Tocqueville quoted in Arlet, *Rémusat*, 212, which uses the word "épancher."

8. Sue, *Mystères de Paris*, 1247.

9. Ibid., 1253.

10. Mme de Dino to Barante, Rochecotte, 9 February 1841, in Barante, *Souvenirs*, 6:573.

11. Barante to Guizot, Thiers, 19 June 1827, AN, Archives privées, Fonds Guizot, 42 AP 200, no. 6; Molé to Barante, Saint-Sauveur, 12 July 1817, in Barante, *Souvenirs*, 2:287.

12. See, for instance, Barante to Guizot, Thiers, 8 October 1827, AN, Archives privées, Fonds Guizot, 42 AP 200, no. 12; and Barante to Guizot, 21 September 1828, AN, Archives privées, Fonds Guizot, 42 AP 200, no. 14.

13. Guizot to Barante, Paris, 26 October 1833, AN, Archives privées, Fonds Guizot, 42 AP 200, no. 243.

14. Barante to Guizot, 26 July 1834, AN, Archives privées, Fonds Guizot, 42 AP 200, no. 37.

15. See, for example, Guizot to Lenormant, Brompton, 11 January 1849, in Guizot, *Années de retraite*, 25, for the use of "mille amitiés." See Guizot to Théobald Piscatory, Val-Richer, 10 October 1838, in Guizot, *Lettres de M. Guizot à sa famille*, 178, for the use of "tout à vous."

16. Charles de Rémusat to Guizot, Grenoble, 9 June 1826, in AN, Archives privées, Fonds Guizot, 42 AP 204, no. 29.

17. On the sovereignty of reason, see Craiutu, *Liberalism under Siege*, 123–53.

18. Rémusat, *Mémoires*, 3:70. Rémusat also repeats this anecdote in Rémusat, *Mémoires*, 1:439. For the importance of this relationship for Guizot, see Guizot, *Mémoires*, 6:4–6.

19. On men and the sentimental culture of mourning in the post-revolutionary era, see Fureix, *France des larmes*.

20. Guizot to Prosper de Barante, Château de Broglie, 27 September 1827, AN, Archives privées, Fonds Guizot, 42 AP 200, no. 224.

21. Charles de Rémusat to Guizot, Paris, 23 July 1827, AN, Archives privées, Fonds Guizot, 42 AP 204, no. 92, premier cahier, 18.

22. On Rémusat's marital history, see Arlet, *Rémusat*, 47–52, 80–88.

23. Vitet, *Comte Duchâtel*, 24–25.

24. Cicero, *Laelius de Amicitia*, vi.20.

25. Ibid., xxv.92.

26. Frame, *Montaigne in France*, 16–27. References to this essay can be found in Guizot, *M. de Barante*, 9; and Mme de Dino to Barante, Marseille, 7 November 1825, in Barante, *Souvenirs*, 3:291.

27. Montaigne, "Of Friendship," 139.

28. Ibid.

29. Foucault, *History of Sexuality*; Muhlstein, *Taste for Freedom*; Sibalis, "Regulation of Male Homosexuality."

30. Thompson, "Creating Boundaries," 103. See also Hunt and Jacob, "Affective Revolution." On gender fluidity in the eighteenth century, see Kates, *Monsieur d'Eon Is a Woman.*

31. Smith-Rosenberg, "Female World," 8.

32. Quoted in Muhlstein, *Taste for Freedom*, xx. See also Lucey, *Misfit of the Family*, 124–70.

33. Martin, *Napoleonic Friendship*, 1.

34. The classic study of male homosocial desire is Sedgwick, *Between Men.*

35. Rémusat to Barante, Paris, 28 October 1831, in Barante, *Souvenirs*, 4:370.

36. Molé to Barante, Paris, 10 November 1833, in ibid., 5:91.

37. On emotions as a spur to action, see Reddy, *Navigation of Feeling*, 211–56.

38. Lemaire, *Conseils d'un père à ses enfants*, 96.

39. Hyde de Neuville to Chateaubriand, 19 October 1820, in Chateaubriand, *Chateaubriand et Hyde de Neuville*, 24–25.

40. Touchard, *Gloire de Béranger*, 2:167–68.

41. Ibid., 1:380, 455.

42. See Béranger, *Lettres inédites à P. Lebrun et à Mme Lebrun.*

43. Touchard, *Gloire de Béranger*, 1:380.

44. Thies, *François Guizot*, 129, 134. On the patronage economy, see Reddy, *Invisible Code.*

45. Barante to Guizot, 26 July 1834, AN, Archives privées, Fonds Guizot, 42 AP 200, no. 37; Barante to Guizot, 5 June 1834, AN, Archives privées, Fonds Guizot, 42 AP 200, no. 36.

46. Barante to Guizot, 10 August 1837, AN, Archives privées, Fonds Guizot, 42 AP 200, no. 45; Barante to Guizot, St. Petersburg, 1 July 1839, AN, Archives privées, Fonds Guizot, 42 AP 200, no. 47.

47. Barante to Guizot, 27 September 1834, AN, Archives privées, Fonds Guizot, 42 AP 200, no. 39.

48. Barante to Guizot, St. Petersburg, 1 July 1839, AN, Archives privées, Fonds Guizot, 42 AP 200, no. 47; Mme de Barante to Guizot, St. Petersburg, 1 July 1839, AN, Archives privées, Fonds Guizot, 42 AP 200, no. 47 bis.

49. Barante to Guizot, St. Petersburg, 16 March 1841, AN, Archives privées, Fonds Guizot, 42 AP 200, no. 51.

50. Barante, *Communes et de l'aristocratie*, 65–66.

51. Guizot to Sarah Austin, Paris, 18 April 1852, AN, Archives privées, Fonds Guizot, 42 AP 180, no. 130. For Chateaubriand's statement, see Chateaubriand, *Mémoires*, 1:1435.

52. On the impact of Romanticism on notions of personal relations, see Houbre, *Discipline de l'amour.*

53. Éméric, *Nouveau guide de la politesse*, 80.

54. This is true in the correspondence between Guizot and Mme Mollien and Guizot and Mme Lenormant. For the Mollien/Guizot letters, see AN, Archives privées, Fonds Guizot, 42 AP 210. For the Lenormant/Guizot letters, see AN, Archives privées, Fonds Guizot, 42 AP 199. However, Guizot used "chère amie" with both Mme de Gasparin and Mme de Broglie.

55. Allart to Sainte-Beuve, Herblay, 10 October 1845, in Allart, *Lettres inédites à Sainte-Beuve*, 130.

56. Béranger to Mme de Cauchois Lemaire, 16 August 1834, in Béranger, *Correspondance de Béranger*, 2:185–86.

57. Theis, *François Guizot*, 201; Guizot to Mme de Broglie, 20 August 1835, AN, Archives privées, Fonds Guizot, 42 AP 214, no. 221.

58. Guizot to Mme de Broglie, 20 August 1835, in AN, Archives privées, Fonds Guizot, 42 AP 214, no. 221.

59. Ibid.

60. Mme de Broglie to Guizot, Coppet, 17 July 1837, in Broglie, *Lettres de la duchesse de Broglie*, 269.

61. Mme de Broglie to Barante, Broglie, 6 October 1828, in Barante, *Souvenirs*, 3:466.

62. See, for instance, Mme de Broglie to Mme de Castellane, Cauterets, 29 August 1820, in Broglie, *Lettres de la duchesse de Broglie*, 67–68.

63. On the importance of brother/sister relationships in the early nineteenth century, see Johnson, "Siblinghood and the Emotional Dimensions"; and Sabean, "Kinship and Issues of the Self," both in Johnson and Sabean, *Sibling Relations and the Transformation of European Kinship*

64. For statements of affection between female friends in the doctrinaire circle, see Mme de Broglie to Mme Anisson du Perron, Eaux-Bonnes, 21 July 1820, in Broglie, *Lettres de la duchesse de Broglie*, 54; and Mme de Broglie to Mme Anisson du Perron, Coppet, 16 September 1822, in Broglie, *Lettres de la duchesse de Broglie*, 102. On the emotional intensity of female friendships, see Marcus, *Between Women*, 23–108; and Smith-Rosenberg, "Female World of Love and Ritual."

65. See, for instance, Chateaubriand to Castellane, Paris, 31 January to 4 February 1826, in Chateaubriand, *Correspondance*, 7:131; and Chateaubriand to Mme de Duras, 21 August 1815, in Chateaubriand, *Correspondance*, 3:51.

66. Mme de Broglie to Guizot, 13 July 1836, AN, Archives privées, Fonds Guizot, 42 AP 214, no. 179.

67. Guizot to Gasparin, Val-Richer, 29 August 1845, in Guizot, *François Guizot et Madame Laure de Gasparin*, 264–65.

68. Chateaubriand to Mme de Castellane, Paris, 30 October 1825, in Chateaubriand, *Correspondance*, 7:93.

69. Chateaubriand to Mme de Castellane, Paris, 14–17 January 1826, in ibid., 7:125.

70. Broglie, *Guizot*, 209–10.

71. Berchet, *Chateaubriand*, 909.

72. Hyde de Neuville, *Mémoires*, 2:302.

73. Chateaubriand to Mme de Duras, 13 February 1812, in Chateaubriand, *Correspondance*, 2:150; Chateaubriand to Mme de Duras, 27 July 1812, in Chateaubriand, *Correspondance*, 2:169.

74. See, for example, Chateaubriand to Mme de Duras, 10 May 1822, in Chateaubriand, *Correspondance*, 5:98.

75. See, for example, Mme de Broglie to Mme Anisson du Perron, 12 January 1820, in Broglie, *Lettres de la duchesse de Broglie*, 33, for an example of a letter between women that contains society gossip; as well as Mme de Broglie to Mme Anisson du Perron, Coppet, 18 July 1818, in Broglie, *Lettres de la duchesse de Broglie*, 12, where Mme de Broglie requests that her friend send her political news.

76. See, for instance, the letters reproduced in Hyde de Neuville, *Mémoires*, 2:297–305, 353–57.

77. Mme de Broglie to Prosper de Barante, Paris, January 1824, in Barante, *Souvenirs*, 3:166–67.

78. See, for example, Guizot to Gasparin, London, 24 April 1840, in Guizot, *Guizot et Madame Laure de Gasparin*, 190–92; or Guizot to Gasparin, 24 September 1841, in Guizot, *Guizot et Madame Laure de Gasparin*, 216–17.

79. See, for instance, Mme de Broglie to Guizot, Coppet, 8 November 1826, AN, Archives privées, Fonds Guizot, 42 AP 214, no. 158; and Mme de Broglie to Guizot, Broglie, 2 July 1827, AN, Archives privées, Fonds Guizot, 42 AP 214, no. 161.

80. Prosper de Barante to Guizot, Turin, 24 August 1838, AN, Archives privées, Fonds Guizot, 42 AP 200, no. 38; Barante to Guizot, 6 September 1842, AN, Archives privées, Fonds Guizot, 42 AP 200, no. 60.

81. Mme de Dino to Guizot, Rochecotte, 30 July 1828, AN, Archives privées, Fonds Guizot, 42 AP 250, no. 4; Mme de Dino to Guizot, Valençay, 2 October 1828, AN, Archives privées, Fonds Guizot, 42 AP 250, no. 7; Mme de Dino to Guizot, Valençay, 9 September 1836, AN, Archives privées, Fonds Guizot, 42 AP 250, no. 33.

82. Madame de Broglie to Guizot, Broglie, 4 August 1828, AN, Archives privées, Fonds Guizot, 42 AP 214, no. 170.

83. Guizot, *Mémoires*, 3:42.

84. Séché, *Hortense Allart*, 122.

85. See, for instance, ibid., 296.

86. Goldstein, Post-*Revolutionary Self*.

CHAPTER 4

1. On this idea—and on social network analysis as one of a number of methodologies that could revive social history—see Ruggiu, "A Way out of the Crisis"; and Thompson, "Working within the Crisis." Two relatively early uses of network analysis can be found in Padgett and Ansell, "Robust Action"; and Spitzer, *French Generation of 1820*.

2. Béranger's network has been derived from Béranger, *Ma Biographie*; Béranger, *Lettres inédites de Béranger à Dupont de l'Eure*; Béranger, *Correspondance de Béranger*; Béranger, *Lettres inédites à P. Lebrun et à Mme Lebrun*; Boiteau d'Ambly, *Vie de Béranger*; Psichari, "Béranger"; and Touchard, *Gloire de Béranger*. Data on some of his friends are drawn from Bonnal, *Manuel et son temps*; Kramer, *Lafayette in Two Worlds*; and Lafayette, *Mémoires, correspondance, et manuscrits*. For Guizot, I have relied on his personal papers in AN, Archives privées, Fonds Guizot, 42 AP, as well as the following works: Barante, *Souvenirs*; Broglie, *Guizot*; Rémusat, *Mémoires*; Theis, *François Guizot*. The following have been used for Chateaubriand's network: Berchet, *Chateaubriand*; Chateaubriand, *Correspondance générale*; Chateaubriand, *Mémoires*; Mme de Chateaubriand, *Un Complément*; Mme de Chateaubriand, *Lettres inédites à M. Clausel de Coussergues*; Diesbach, *Chateaubriand*; Hyde de Neuville, *Mémoires*; Clément, *Chateaubriand*; and Pailhès, *Duchesse de Duras et Chateaubriand*. Information on some individuals' politics are drawn from Assemblé nationale, "Base de données des députés"; Desplaces, Michaud, and Michaud, *Biographie universelle*; Kolb, *Ary Scheffer*; and Plessix Gray, *Rage and Fire*.

3. It should be said that not all of these women were part of these men's networks in both the 1820s and 1840s. Broglie, Duras, and Montcalm all died before the 1840s, while

Castellane and Lieven were not close to Guizot in the 1820s. These women's networks are studied only in the periods when they were close to these men.

4. Two biographies of Dino that provide information on her social ties are Dupuy, *Duchesse de Dino*; and Ziegler, *Duchess of Dino*. For Hortense Allart, see Allart, *Enchantements de prudence*; Allart, *Lettres inédites à Sainte-Beuve*; Hansen, *Hortense Allart*; Séché, *Hortense Allart*; and Walton, *Eve's Proud Descendants*. For Mme de Montcalm, see Montcalm, *Salon politique*. For Mme de Broglie, see Broglie, *Lettres de la duchesse de Broglie*. On Récamier, see Bruyère and Paccoud, "Cercles de Juliette Récamier"; Herriot, *Madame Récamier et ses amis*; Lenormant, *Madame Récamier, les amis de sa jeunesse, et sa correspondance intime*; Lenormant, *Souvenirs et correspondance*; and Wagener, *Madame Récamier*. Information on Duras's network can be found in Bardoux, *Duchesse de Duras*; and Pailhès, *Duchesse de Duras et Chateaubriand*. Daudet, *Vie d'ambassadrice*, contains information on Lieven's network. Information on Castellane's can be found in Rémusat, *Mémoires*, vol. 3; and Theis, *François Guizot*.

5. On the social calendar of Parisian elites, see Martin-Fugier, *Vie élégante*, 117.

6. On the importance of this salutation for Guizot, see Theis, *François Guizot*, 109. In Guizot's case, those who were mere political allies merited the salutation "mon honorable ami," the same term used to refer to allies in the Chamber of Deputies. See, for example, *Moniteur universel*, 2 March 1842, 345; and 2 April 1846, 833. Guizot's use of the salutation "mon honorable ami" appears throughout his correspondence with his political allies in the 1830s and 1840s, as in a letter from Vigier to François Guizot, 15 September 1843, in AN, Archives privées, Fonds Guizot, 42 AP 128, where Vigier used the salutation "Monsieur et honorable ami." Béranger used the terms "mon cher ami" interchangeably with the salutation "mon cher" followed by the name of his correspondent. Thus Dupont de l'Eure was often "mon cher Dupont." For his part, Chateaubriand used a variety of salutations for his male friends, such as "mon cher ami," "mon fidèle et bon ami," or "mon excellent ami." He also used "mon honorable ami" with his friends, whereas for Guizot this did not indicate any personal tie. See, for example, Chateaubriand to Hyde de Neuville, 21 February 1826, in Chateaubriand, *Chateaubriand et Hyde de Neuville*, 46. In a few instances, however, men who were friends—and in some cases quite close ones—did not use these salutations. Notably, when Chateaubriand and Béranger began their friendship in the July Monarchy, they often used the highly formal salutation "monsieur" with each other. For the Béranger/Chateaubriand letters, see Béranger, *Correspondance de Béranger*, vol. 3. For Chateaubriand's description of their friendship, see Chateaubriand, *Mémoires*, 2:2380. See also Touchard, *Gloire de Béranger*, 2:165–79.

7. See, for instance, the letters from Mme de Broglie to Guizot in Broglie, *Lettres de la duchesse de Broglie*.

8. Although it is much easier to find this type of personal news in letters between men and women or those between women, male friends still included personal information in their letters to one another, but to a lesser extent.

9. In cases where there is a lack of certainty about whether a friendship existed, I have gone with the preponderance of evidence. If memoirs and biographies suggest that two individuals were close, I count them as such even if their patterns of correspondence do not always display the hallmarks of friendship.

10. In some cases, we have the correspondence or memoirs of these individuals; this is particularly true in the circle around Guizot. See Rémusat, *Mémoires*; and Barante, *Souvenirs*. The correspondence, memoirs, and biographies of our three principals also provide additional information. For instance, the fact that Dupont and Manuel were friends is largely clear through the Béranger/Dupont correspondence.

11. For example, I count Mme Récamier as a friend as opposed to a lover here, despite the complications of their relationship as discussed in chapter 3. This is the category that their biographers use to describe their bond in the late 1820s, as the two had ceased their physical relationship. See Berchet, *Chateaubriand*, 721.

12. For instance, in his autobiography, Béranger stated that he never really trusted Lafayette. Béranger, *Ma Biographie*, 250. Béranger may have wanted to distance himself from this man because of Lafayette's role in ushering in the July Monarchy, a regime of which Béranger was critical. Lafayette had given Louis-Philippe's reign a very public blessing in 1830, one that assured that the king would have the support of the left. Béranger's discussion of his deep-seated suspicion of Lafayette may have had more to do with the nature of the latter's actions in 1830 than the state of his feelings in the 1820s.

13. For instance, Mme de Gasparin asked Guizot to burn her letters. See Broglie, *Guizot*, 210. His daughter Henriette was guilty of destroying one set of correspondence; she disliked Mme de Dino so much that she destroyed all of Dino's letters after 1857, the year in which Dino and her father became close. See Broglie, *Guizot*, 434.

14. Guizot, *Mélanges biographiques*, 111.

15. Ibid., 144.

16. Mme de Broglie to Prosper de Barante, Paris, 4 February 1824, in Barante, *Souvenirs*, 3:181. Emphasis in original.

17. Montalembert to Guizot, Maîche, 23 August 1868, AN, Archives privées, Fonds Guizot, 42 AP 265, no. 15

18. See, for instance, Chateaubriand to Jean Baptiste Le Moine, Lausanne, 14 June 1826, in Chateaubriand, *Correspondance*, 7:194, where he refers to Le Moine as "mon vieil ami."

19. One example is the relations between Benjamin Constant and Béranger discussed in chapter 5.

20. Wagener, *Madame Récamier*, 279.

21. Dino's letters to Guizot can be found in AN, Archives privées, Fonds Guizot, 42 AP 250.

22. All visualizations were created with the Sci^2 program using the GUESS algorithm and the GEM algorithm. Sci^2 Team, *Science of Science (Sci^2) Tool* (Bloomington: Indiana University and SciTech Strategies, 2009), available at http://sci2.cns.iu.edu.

23. Kale, *French Salons*, 141–44. For instance, Lieven's salon attracted politicians, diplomats, and foreign visitors, particularly from Britain (where she had lived for many years) and Russia (her native country) during the years of the July Monarchy, Second Republic, and Second Empire. A list of the visitors to her salon in the 1850s can be found in the British Library, Additional Manuscripts 47392–94, Lieven Papers.

24. On this issue, see Agulhon, *Cercle dans la France bourgeoise*; Goodman, *Republic of Letters*; and Vincent-Buffault, *Exercice de l'amitié*, 185–247.

25. This idea is particularly evident in Agulhon, *Cercle dans la France bourgeoise*, where he posits an opposition between the mixed sociability of aristocratic salons and the all-male sociability of bourgeois men's clubs. See also Kale, *French Salons*, where he describes the persistence of salons and aristocratic sociability as an example of the legacy of the Old Regime. In contrast, Mona Ozouf has suggested that gender mixing is characteristic of French sociability. See Ozouf, *Women's Words*.

26. Included in this faction are Hortense Bonaparte and Caroline Murat (two friends of Récamier). They are included in the liberal opposition because they belonged to the Bonaparte family, although both lived in exile and were not necessarily politically active during this time.

27. The politics of the doctrinaires during the Restoration are explored in Craiutu, *Liberalism under Siege*; and Rosanvallon, *Moment Guizot*. Also included in this faction is Achille de Daunant, a lifelong friend of Guizot. Although he was not active in doctrinaire circles during the 1820s, Guizot indicated that the two men had the same political beliefs. See Guizot, *Mélanges biographiques*, 371–96. On Guizot's first wife's politics, see Bates, "Madame Guizot and Monsieur Guizot."

28. On the politics of the Defection, see Mitchell, "Chateaubriand and Hyde de Neuville"; and Watel, *Jean-Guillaume Hyde de Neuville*, 192–202. On the placement of this faction in the center-right, see Alexander, *Re-writing the French Revolutionary Tradition*, 190.

29. However, within these factions, individuals are not situated according to their politics. For instance, Royer-Collard was more conservative than was Guizot, but their placement within the doctrinaire camp is not an indication of their relative political positions. On the difference between their politics, see Theis, *François Guizot*, 95.

30. Lenormant, *Souvenirs et correspondance*, 1:284.

31. Ampère, *Ballanche*, 225.

32. Pouthas, *Guizot pendant la Restauration*, 109; Theis, *François Guizot*, 132.

33. Béranger, *Ma Biographie*, 197; Touchard, *Gloire de Béranger*, 1:311.

34. On political and social networks among liberals in this period, see Goblot, *Jeune France libérale*; Kramer, *Lafayette in Two Worlds*; and Spitzer, *French Generation of 1820*. On party formation among members of the liberal opposition, see Alexander, *Re-writing the French Revolutionary Tradition*.

35. On Talleyrand's politics at this phase in the Restoration, see Waresquiel, *Talleyrand*, 561. On Dino's politics as being the same as his, see Ziegler, *Duchess of Dino*, 186–89.

36. Ziegler, *Duchess of Dino*, 163. Their letters can be found in Dino, "La duchesse de Dino et le baron de Vitrolles."

37. Pailhès, *Duchesse de Duras et Chateaubriand*, 394.

38. Récamier was particularly insistent that her salon be a "neutral space," in her words. See Herriot, *Madame Récamier et ses amis*, 2:195. Yet in 1816, she tried to pull Benjamin Constant to the right. See Constant to Récamier, November 1816, in Constant, *Lettres de Benjamin Constant à Madame Récamier*, 304–12.

39. Mme de Dino to baron de Vitrolles, Rochecotte, 23 July 1829, in Dino, "La duchesse de Dino et le baron de Vitrolles," 44.

40. Included in this camp are Lieven and Récamier, both of whom claimed to be neutral. Lieven was not particularly interested in domestic politics, although she did pull

Guizot into a more conservative direction. See Guizot, *Mélanges biographiques*, 207–8; and Theis, *François Guizot*, 160–63. Little is known about Récamier's politics in this era, although she was horrified by the Revolution of 1848. See Lenormant, *Madame Récamier*, 345.

41. Touchard, *Gloire de Béranger*, 2:118.

42. Lamennais was also close to the baron de Vitrolles, a legitimist. See Lamennais and Vitrolles, *Correspondance inédite*.

43. Atkin and Tallett, *Right in France*, 63.

44. Quoted in Berchet, *Chateaubriand*, 823.

45. Chateaubriand, *Mémoires*, 2:2380.

46. Touchard, *Gloire de Béranger*, 2:209.

47. The one exception is Charles Lenormant, who had affinities with liberal Catholics. However, Lenormant was not a politician but a scholar, and Guizot was in any case closer to his wife than to Lenormant.

48. On the importance of ideological similarity for Guizot's friendships, see Pouthas, *Jeunesse de François Guizot*, 390; and Theis, *François Guizot*, 106–15.

49. See, for example, Sédouy, *Comte Molé*, 180, where Castellane helped Molé and Guizot reconcile with each other in 1836.

50. Mme de Dino to Barante, Sagan, 6 December 1848, in Barante, *Souvenirs*, 7:397.

51. On Lieven's influence on Guizot's foreign policy, see Theis, *François Guizot*, 160–63.

52. See, for example, Guizot to Gasparin, London, 10 September 1840, in Guizot, *Guizot et Madame Laure de Gasparin*, 205–7.

53. Guizot to Lieven, Val-Richer, 14 July 1837, in *Lettres de François Guizot et de la Princesse de Lieven*, 1:24.

CHAPTER 5

1. Thiers to Guizot, February 1836, AN, Archives privées, Fonds Guizot, 42 AP 246, no. 11.

2. Guizot to Thiers, AN, Archives privées, Fonds Guizot, 42 AP 246, no. 11 bis. On Guizot's use of "mon cher ami," see Theis, *François Guizot*, 109.

3. This is not to say that there were no differences between the political culture of the Restoration and that of the July Monarchy. As the electorate expanded after 1830, politics became less exclusively aristocratic; newspapers also became more important after 1830. On the composition of the Chamber of Deputies in the July Monarchy, see Higonnet and Higonnet, "Class, Corruption, and Politics." On the press, see Popkin, *Press, Revolution, and Social Identities*.

4. In the Restoration, at least, the ministry did not need a majority, and as a result there were times when the government was at odds with the Chamber of Deputies. One occurred at the beginning of the Restoration when the ultra *Chambre introuvable* opposed the moderate Richelieu ministry. Another occurred at the end of the regime when liberals dominated the Chamber but the head of the government was the archconservative prince de Polignac. Nevertheless, there were still some in the Chambers who backed these ministries.

5. In principle, the composition of the cabinet was up to the king. See Bastid, *Institutions politiques*, 299. But in practice, the composition of any ministry relied on input from the Chambers and on negotiations among politicians.

6. Ibid., 296–98; Neely, *Lafayette and the Liberal Ideal*, 94. Gunn, *When the French Tried to Be British*, discusses the problems of imagining factional unity.

7. Backouche, *Monarchie parlementaire*, 244.

8. Price, *Perilous Crown*, 195.

9. Agulhon, *Cercle dans la France bourgeoise*, 65–72.

10. Kale, *French Salons*.

11. Hercule de Serre to Mme de Serre, Paris, 22 December 1818, in de Serre, *Correspondance*, 375. On ultra salons, see ibid., 121–23. On the importance of reunions, see also Démier, *France de la Restauration*, 168–69.

12. Comte de Villèle to Mme de Villèle, Paris, 3 January 1817, in Villèle, *Mémoires et correspondance*, 155.

13. The way in which Old Regime salon culture was reappropriated to fit the needs of the post-revolutionary era is a central theme of Kale, *French Salons*.

14. *Moniteur universel*, 2 March 1842, 345; and 2 April 1846, 833. See also Vigier to Guizot, 15 September 1843, in AN, Archives privées, Fonds Guizot, 42 AP 128, where Vigier used the salutation "monsieur et honorable ami."

15. See, for instance, the speeches in Goodrich, *Select British Eloquence*.

16. Manuel to Dupont de l'Eure, Maisons, 7 August 1824, in Béranger, *Lettres inédites de Béranger à Dupont de l'Eure*, 37.

17. For these maneuvers, see Waresquiel and Yvert, *Histoire de la Restauration*, 409, 434.

18. On Montbel as mayor of Toulouse, see ibid., 434.

19. Thiers to Guizot, 2 March 1840, AN, Archives privées, Fonds Guizot, 42 AP 246, no. 12.

20. Rémusat, *Mémoires*, 3:304–5.

21. Johnson, *Guizot*, 162.

22. Broglie, *Guizot*, 200–201.

23. Waresquiel and Yvert, "Duc de Richelieu et le comte Decazes."

24. Quoted in Waresquiel, *Duc de Richelieu*, 368n. The dispute between them is described on pp. 356–68.

25. Collingham and Alexander, *July Monarchy*, 290; Koepke, "Failure of Parliamentary Government," 440.

26. Soult to Guizot, Soult-Berg, 30 September 1847, AN, Archives privées, Fonds Guizot, 42 AP 256, no. 48.

27. Alexander, "Benjamin Constant," 154–55.

28. Béranger, *Ma Biographie*, 230–31.

29. Constant to Béranger, 29 January 1829, in Béranger, *Correspondance*, 1:355.

30. Ibid.

31. Ibid., 1:354–55.

32. Ibid., 1:356.

33. Waresquiel, *Talleyrand*, 569.

34. Ibid., 575.

35. Ibid.

36. Dupuy, *Duchesse de Dino*, 262.

37. Talleyrand to Molé, London, 8 October 1830, in Talleyrand-Périgord, *Mémoires*, 777.

38. Thus Chateaubriand served as ambassador to Rome in 1829 because of his personal and political affiliation with the comte de La Ferronnays, who was minister of foreign affairs. See Chateaubriand to Mme Récamier, Rome, 20 January 1829, in Chateaubriand, *Correspondance*, 8:218.

39. Chateaubriand to Mathieu de Montmorency, London, 9 April 1822, in Chateaubriand, *Correspondance*, 5:135.

40. See, for example, Mathieu de Montmorency to Chateaubriand, Paris, 13 May 1822, in ibid., 5:431–33.

CHAPTER 6

1. Montcalm, *Mon Journal*, 144.

2. François Guizot, *Moniteur universel*, August 19, 1842, 1812.

3. On this issue, see Gunn, *When the French Tried to Be British*.

4. See, for example, Hyde de Neuville, *Mémoires*, 2:283–86.

5. Mme de Broglie to François Guizot, Coppet, 8 November 1826, AN, Archives privées, Fonds Guizot, 42 AP 214, no. 158; and Mme de Broglie to François Guizot, Broglie, 2 July 1827, AN, Archives privées, Fonds Guizot, 42 AP 214, no. 161.

6. Kale, *French Salons*, 121.

7. Hyde de Neuville to princesse de La Trémoïlle, 13 October 1816, in Hyde de Neuville, *Mémoires*, 2:231.

8. For instance, Mme de Montcalm called her "the queen of the ultras." See Montcalm, *Mon Journal*, 224.

9. Denis, *Amable-Guillaume-Prosper Brugière*, 309.

10. Mme de Broglie to Barante, Cauterets, 21 July 1820, in Barante, *Souvenirs*, 2:449.

11. Denis, *Amable-Guillaume-Prosper Brugière*, 306.

12. Chateaubriand to Mme de Pisieux, 16 January 1821, in Chateaubriand, *Correspondance*, 4:38.

13. Diesbach, *Chateaubriand*, 348, 382. See, for example, Chateaubriand to Mme Récamier, Berlin, 20 January 1821, in Chateaubriand, *Correspondance*, 4:43.

14. Sédouy, *Comte Molé*, 180.

15. In his classic work on the right-wing in France, René Rémond suggests that while ultras and moderates both feared revolution, the ultras were characterized by their "immoderate excesses and verbal violence" and thus by the tone of their politics. See Rémond, *Right Wing in France*, 33.

16. Montcalm to Chateaubriand, 21 July 1821, quoted in Rousseau, "Observateur secret," 1182.

17. Rémusat, *Mémoires*, 3:304.

18. In his words, "I exaggerated my concerns to her about the remarks that were being launched at me." Ibid.

19. Ibid., 5:252.

20. Price, *Perilous Crown*, 195.

21. Touchard, *Gloire de Béranger*, 1:471–83; Allart, *Enchantements de prudence*, 169–72.

22. Guizot to Gasparin, London, 3 March 1840, in Guizot, *François Guizot et Madame Laure de Gasparin*, 185.

23. Thureau-Dangin, *Histoire de la Monarchie de Juillet*, 442.

24. On this issue of temperament, see Mitchell, "Chateaubriand and Hyde de Neuville," 114.

25. Montcalm, *Mon Journal*, 142.

26. Ibid., 144.

27. Hyde de Neuville, *Mémoires*, 2:180.

28. Montcalm, *Mon Journal*, 145.

29. Montcalm to Hyde de Neuville, 3 August 1817, in Hyde de Neuville, *Mémoires*, 2:298.

30. Ibid., 2:302.

31. Mme Lenormant's letters to Guizot can be found in AN, Archives privées, Fonds Guizot, 42 AP 199.

32. Guizot to Mme Lenormant, Brompton, 27 November 1848, in Guizot, *Années de retraite*, 16.

33. Ibid., 16.

34. Guizot to Mme Lenormant, Brighton, 9 February 1849, in ibid., 27.

35. Guizot to Mme Lenormant, Brompton, 27 March 1849, in ibid., 32. "Entente cordiale" is underlined in the original.

36. Comte de Montalembert to Mme Lenormant, 18 September 1848, AN, Archives privées, Fonds Guizot, 42 AP 199, no. 32 bis.

37. Comte de Montalembert to Mme Lenormant, 14 March 1849, AN, Archives privées, Fonds Guizot, 42 AP 199, no. 70.

38. On Guizot and the monarchical fusion, see Johnson, *Guizot*, 45.

39. Kale, *French Salons*, 108–9.

40. See, for example, Montcalm, *Mon Journal*, 89.

41. In ibid., 214, she speaks of her royalism and her dislike of both the far-left and the far-right.

42. Allart, *Enchantements*, 171–72.

43. In contrast, Kale sees salonnières as far less engaged and as facilitators who were often without their own political goals.

44. Comte de Montalembert to Mme Lenormant, 14 March 1849, AN, Archives privées, Fonds Guizot, 42 AP 199, no. 70.

45. Allart, *Enchantements*, 170.

46. Hyde de Neuville to Montcalm, quoted in Hyde de Neuville, *Mémoires*, 2:470–71.

47. Ibid., 2:459.

48. Broglie, *Guizot*, 210.

49. See Guizot, *François Guizot et Madame Laure de Gasparin*, 161. On this alliance, see Broglie, *Monarchie de Juillet*, 344–45.

50. Guizot to Gasparin, London, 30 May 1840, in Guizot, *François Guizot et Madame Laure de Gasparin*, 193.

51. Guizot to Gasparin, London, 27 July 1840, in ibid., 201. See also Guizot to Gasparin, London, 10 September 1840, in ibid., 206.

52. For Hyde's views on women's political involvement, see Montcalm, *Mon Journal*, 144.

53. Hyde de Neuville, *Mémoires*, 2:469.

54. Lieven, *Lieven-Palmerston Correspondence*, 181–99.

EPILOGUE

1. As Rémusat stated about Guizot in the 1840s, "I have enough pride to believe that he would not have done certain things if our intimacy had survived." Rémusat, *Mémoires*, 4:40.

2. Fortescue, "Morality and Monarchy."

3. Kale, *French Salons*.

4. Nord, *Republican Moment*.

5. On the shift away from salons to political parties, see ibid., 165–99.

6. Various historians have dated the end of the reign of the notables differently. André Jardin and André-Jean Tudesq end their *La France des notables* in 1848, whereas Daniel Halévy dates the transition to the 1870s, and Philip Nord dates the shift to the 1860s and 1870s. See Jardin and Tudesq, *France des notables*; Halévy, *End of the Notables*; Nord, *Republican Moment*. Thus the shift away from a politics based around the notables should be seen as gradually occurring over the course of the mid-nineteenth century.

7. Nord, *Republican Moment*.

8. Martin-Fugier, *Salons de la IIIe République*, 25–35.

9. See ibid., 44; James, *Parisian Sketches*, 54–56.

10. Martin-Fugier, *Salons de la IIIe République*, 58.

11. Duclert and Prochasson, "L'Amitié," 92. More generally, they describe friendship as a key republican value.

12. On the establishment of political parties in France, see Kreuzer, *Institutions and Innovation*, 23–51.

13. Harris, *Dreyfus*, 293. My discussion of the Dreyfus Affair is heavily indebted to Harris's work.

14. Ibid., 285; Nord, *Impressionists and Politics*, 100–107.

15. Harris, *Dreyfus*, 250–54.

16. Quoted in Duclert and Prochasson, "L'Amitié," 88.

17. Harris, *Dreyfus*, 274, 286, 293.

BIBLIOGRAPHY

PRIMARY SOURCES

Archival Sources

Archives nationales de France

Archives privées. Fonds Guizot, 42 AP.
F7 3796. Police générale: Bulletins de police.
F7 6632. Notes de police: Arrestations et perquisitions.
F7 6699–6700, 6960. Affaires politiques.
F7 6718–20. Députés.
F7 6854, 6915, 6923, 6952, 6961. Police politique.
F7 8779. Objets généraux: Associations.

Bibliothèque nationale de France, Département des manuscripts

Nouvelle acquisitions françaises 20601. Fonds Thiers: Correspondance d'Adolphe Thiers.

British Library

Additional Manuscripts 47392–94. Lieven Papers.

Printed Sources

Allart, Hortense. *Les Enchantements de prudence.* 2nd ed. Paris: Calmann Lévy, 1877.

———. *Lettres inédites à Sainte-Beuve, 1841–1848.* Edited by Léon Séché. Paris: Société du Mercure de France, 1908.

Ancelot, Madame. *Un Salon de Paris, 1824 à 1864.* Paris: E. Dentu, 1866.

Année, Antoine. *Le Livre Noir de messieurs Delavau et Franchet; ou, Répertoire alphabétique de la police politique sous le minstère déplorable.* 4 vols. 2nd ed. Paris: Moutardier, 1829.

Aulard, A., ed. *Paris sous le Consulat: Recueil de documents pour l'histoire de l'esprit public à Paris.* Vol. 1. Paris: Librairie Leopold Cérf, Librairie Noblet, Maison Quantin, 1903.

Balzac, Honoré de. *Les Illusions perdues.* In *La Comédie humaine.* Vol. 4. Paris: Gallimard, 1952.

———. "Z. Marcas." In *La Comédie humaine.* Vol. 8. Paris: Gallimard, 1977.

Barante, Prosper de. *Des communes et de l'aristocratie.* Paris: Ladvocat, 1821.

———. *Souvenirs de baron de Barante de l'Académie française, 1782–1866.* 8 vols. Edited by Claude de Barante. Paris: Calmann Lévy, 1890.

Baudouin, Alexandre. *Dictionnaire des gens du monde; ou, Petit cours de morale à l'usage de la cour et de la ville, par un jeune hermite.* Paris: Chez Alexis Eymery, Libraire, 1818.

Béranger, Pierre Jean de. *Correspondance de Béranger.* Edited by Paul Boiteau d'Ambly. 4 vols. Paris: Garnier, 1860.

———. *Lettres inédites à P. Lebrun et à Mme Lebrun.* Edited by Paul Bonnefon. Paris: Éditions de la Revue politique et littéraire et de la Revue scientifique, 1913.

———. *Lettres inédites de Béranger à Dupont de l'Eure (correspondance intime et politique), 1820–1854.* Paris: P. Douville, 1908.

———. *Ma Biographie.* Paris: Garnier Frères, 1875.

Bouilly, J. N. *Conseils à ma fille.* Vol. 2. 3rd ed. Paris: Chez Rosa, 1813.

Broglie, Achille-Charles-Léonce-Victor de. *Souvenirs, 1785–1870, du feu duc de Broglie.* 4 vols. Paris: Calmann Lévy, 1886.

Broglie, duchesse de. *Lettres de la duchesse de Broglie, 1814–1838, publiées par son fils le duc de Broglie.* Paris: Calmann Lévy, 1896.

Caillot, Antoine. *Mémoires pour servir à l'histoire des moeurs et usages des français . . .* 2 vols. Paris: Chez Dauvin, 1827.

Chateaubriand, François René de. *Chateaubriand et Hyde de Neuville; ou, Trente ans d'amitié: Correspondance inédite.* Edited by M. J. Durry. Paris: Le Divan, 1929.

———. *Correspondance générale.* 7 vols. Paris: Gallimard, 1977–2010.

———. *Mémoires d'outre-tombe.* 2 vols. Paris: Gallimard, 1997.

Chateaubriand, Mme de. *Un Complément aux "Mémoires d'outre-tombe": Mémoires et lettres de Madame de Chateaubriand.* Paris: H. Jonquières, 1929.

———. *Lettres inédites à M. Clausel de Coussergues.* Edited by G. Pailhès. Paris: Feret et Fils Champion, 1888.

Cicero. *Laelius de Amicitia.* In *De Senectute, De Amicitia, De Divinatione.* Translated by W. A. Falconer. Cambridge: Harvard University Press, 1934.

Constant, Benjamin. *Lettres de Benjamin Constant à Madame Récamier, 1807–1830.* Edited by Amélie Cyvoct Lenormant and Louis de Loménie. 2nd ed. Paris: Calmann Lévy, 1882.

Couchery, Jean Baptiste Claude François. *Le Moniteur secret; ou, Tableau de la cour de Napoléon, de son caractère, et de celui de ses agens.* Vol. 1. London: Imprimerie de Schulze et Dean and Paris, 1814.

de Serre, Hercule. *Correspondance du comte de Serre, 1796–1824.* 6 vols. Paris: Auguste Vaton, 1876.

d'Hauterive, Ernest, ed. *La Police secrète du premier empire: Bulletins quotidiens adressés par Fouché à l'Empereur.* Vol. 4. Paris, Librairie Historique R. Clavreuil, 1963.

Dino, duchesse de. "La duchesse de Dino et le baron de Vitrolles, lettres inédits." *Bulletin de la Société d'études des Hautes-Alpes* (1937): 1–49.

Dupaty, Emmanuel Mercier. *Les Délateurs; ou, Trois années du dix-neuvième siècle.* Paris: Didot, 1819.

Éméric, Louis-Damien. *Nouveau guide de la politesse.* 2nd ed. Paris: Roret et Roussel, Eymery, Blanchard, Raynal, 1821.

Eymery, Alexis. *Dictionnaire des girouettes; ou, Nos contemporains peints d'après eux-mêmes . . .* 3rd ed. Paris: A. Eymery, 1815.

Fouché, Joseph. *Mémoires de Joseph Fouché, duc d'Otrante, ministre de la police générale.* Vol. 2. Brussels: P. J. de Mat, 1825.

Froment. *La Police dévoilée depuis la Restauration, et notamment sous messieurs Franchet et Delavau.* 4 vols. Paris: Garnier, 1829.

Genlis, Stéphanie Félicité Ducrest de Saint-Aubin, comtesse de. *Dictionnaire critique et raisonné des étiquettes de la cour, des usages du monde, des amusemens, des modes, des moeurs, etc., des françois, depuis la mort de Louis XIII jusqu'a nos jours.* 2 vols. Paris: P. Mongie, 1818.

Goodrich, Chauncey Allen. *Select British Eloquence: Embracing the Best Speeches Entire, of the Most Eminent Orators of Great Britain for the Last Two Centuries.* New York: Harper and Brothers, Publishers, 1852.

Guizot, François. *Les Années de retraite de M. Guizot: Lettres à M. et Mme Charles Lenormant.* Paris: Hachette et Cie, 1902.

———. *François Guizot et Madame Laure de Gasparin, documents inédits, 1830–1864.* Edited by André Gayot. Paris: Editions Bernard Grasset, 1934.

———. *Lettres à sa fille Henriette, 1836–1874.* Edited by Laurent Theis. Paris: Perrin, 2002.

———. *Lettres de M. Guizot à sa famille et à ses amis.* Paris: Hachette, 1884.

———. *M. de Barante, extrait de la Revue des deux mondes.* Paris: Imprimerie de J. Claye, 1867.

———. *Mélanges biographiques et littéraires.* 2nd ed. Paris: Michel Lévy frères, 1868.

———. *Mémoires pour servir à l'histoire de mon temps.* 8 vols. 2nd ed. Paris: Michel Lévy frères, 1858.

Guizot, François, and Dorothea Lieven. *Lettres de François Guizot et de la princesse de Lieven.* Edited by Jacques Naville. 3 vols. Paris: Mercure de France, 1963.

L'Honnête homme à la cour et dans le monde. Lyon: Chez Rusand, 1816.

Hyde de Neuville, Jean Guillaume. *Mémoires et souvenirs du baron Hyde de Neuville.* 3 vols. Paris: Librairie Plon, 1890.

"De l'individualisme, considéré par rapport à la religion et la morale." *Le Mémorial catholique* 4 (1825): 48–49.

James, Henry. *Parisian Sketches: Letters to the "New York Tribune," 1875–1876.* Edited by Leon Edel and Ilse Dusoir Lind. New York: New York University Press, 1957.

Jouy, Étienne de. *La Morale appliquée à la politique.* In *Oeuvres complètes d'Étienne Jouy.* Vol. 22. Paris: Imprimerie de Jules Didot, 1832.

Lafayette, Marie Joseph Paul Yves Roch Gilbert Du Motier. *Mémoires, correspondance, et manuscrits du général Lafayette.* Edited by Georges Washington Louis Gilbert du Motier Lafayette. Vol. 6. Paris: H. Fournier, 1837.

Lamennais, Robert de, and Eugène François Auguste d'Arnaud Vitrolles. *Correspondance inédite entre Lamennais et le Baron de Vitrolles.* Paris: G. Charpentier et Cie, 1886.

Lemaire, Henri. *Conseils d'un père à ses enfants.* 2nd ed. Paris: Le Prieur, 1818.

Lenormant, Amélie Cyvoct. *Madame Récamier, les amis de sa jeunesse, et sa correspondance intime.* 2nd ed. Paris: Michel Lévy frères, 1874.

———. *Souvenirs et correspondance tirés des papiers de Madame Récamier.* 2 vols. 2nd ed. Paris: M. Lévy frères, 1860.

Leroux, Pierre. "Aux Philosophes." In *Aux Philosophes, aux artistes, aux politiques: Trois discours et autres texts*, edited by Jean-Pierre Lacassagne, 75–133. Paris: Éditions Payot and Rivages, 1994.

Lesur, Charles Louis. *La France et les français en 1817: Tableau moral et politique, precedé d'un coup d'oeil sur la révolution.* 2nd ed. Paris: H. Nicolle and Delaunay, 1818.

Lieven, Dorothea. *The Lieven-Palmerston Correspondence, 1828–1856.* Translated and edited by Lord Sudley. London: J. Murray, 1943.

Maine de Biran, Pierre. *Journal intime de Maine de Biran.* Vol. 1. Paris: Plon, 1927.

Maistre, Joseph de. *Oeuvres complètes de Joseph de Maistre.* Vol. 14. 2nd ed. Lyon: Librairie générale catholique et classique, 1886.

Modèles de lettres sur toutes sortes de sujets, contenant lettres familières, protocoles pour les personnes en place . . . Lyon: Mme Ve Buynand née Bruyset, 1813.

Molé, Mathieu, comte. *Le Comte Molé, 1781–1855: Sa vie, ses mémoires.* Edited by the marquis de Noailles. 2 vols. Paris: E. Champion, 1923.

Moniteur universel. 1830–48. Bibliothèque historique de la ville de Paris.

Montaigne, Michel de. "Of Friendship." In *The Complete Essays of Montaigne.* Translated by Donald M. Frame. Stanford: Stanford University Press, 1976.

Montcalm, marquise de. *Mon Journal pendant le premier ministère de mon frère.* Paris: Éditions Bernard Grasset, 1936.

———. *Un Salon politique sous la Restauration: Correspondance de la marquise de Montcalm.* Edited by Emmanuel de Lévis-Mirepoix. Paris: Éditions du grand siècle, 1949.

Morgan, Lady Sydney. *France.* 2 vols. London: Henry Colburn, 1817.

Noël, Eugène. *Souvenirs de Béranger.* Paris: Pagnerre, 1857.

La Politesse et les usages du monde, expliqués a la jeunesse, à l'usage des pensions et des maison d'éducation. 2nd ed. Mans: Ch. Richelet, 1839.

Psichari, Jean. "Béranger: Lettres à Ary Scheffer." *Grande revue* (1 January 1901): 253–76.

Rémusat, Charles de. *Mémoires de ma vie.* 5 vols. Edited by Charles Pouthas. Paris: Plon, 1958.

Rousseau, François. "Un Observateur secret de Chateaubriand." *Le Correspondant* (25 March 1912): 1159–85.

Rousseau, Jean-Jacques. *Julie; or, The New Heloise.* Translated by Philip Stewart and Jean Vaché. Hanover: University Press of New England, 1997.

Royer-Collard, Pierre Paul. *La Vie politique de M. Royer-Collard: Ses discours et ses écrits.* 2 vols. 2nd ed. Edited by Prosper de Barante. Paris: Didier et Cie, 1863.

Saint-Just, Louis-Antoine de. "Institutions républicaines." In *Oeuvres complètes*, edited by Anne Kupiec and Miguel Absensour, 1085–1147. Paris: Gallimard, 2004.

Salvandy, Narcisse Achille de. *Vues politiques.* Paris: Chez Poulet, Imprimeur-Libraire, 1819.

Souza, Mme de. *Charles et Marie.* In *Oeuvres de Mme de Souza.* Paris: Garnier, 1865.

Sue, Eugène. *Les Mystères de Paris.* Paris: Robert Lafont, 1989.

Talleyrand-Périgord, Charles Maurice de. *Mémoires du prince de Talleyrand: Suivis de 135 lettres inédites du prince de Talleyrand à la duchesse de Bauffremont, 1808–1838.* Edited by Emmanuel de Waresquiel. Paris: R. Laffont, 2007.

Thiers, Adolphe. *Histoire de la révolution française.* 8th ed. Vol. 2. Brussels: Adolphe Wahlen, 1836.

Tocqueville, Alexis de. *Democracy in America.* Translated by George Lawrence. New York: HarperCollins, 2000.

———. *The Old Regime and the French Revolution.* Translated by Stuart Gilbert. Garden City, N.Y.: Doubleday, 1955.

Villèle, Comte de. *Mémoires et correspondance du comte de Villèle.* Vol. 3. Paris: Perrin et Cie, 1888–90.

Vitet, Ludovic. *Le Comte Duchâtel.* Paris: Michel Lévy frères, 1875.

Witt, Henriette de. *Monsieur Guizot dans sa famille: Et avec ses amis, 1787–1874.* Paris: Librairie Hachette et Cie, 1880.

SECONDARY SOURCES

Adams, Christine. *Poverty, Charity, and Motherhood: Maternal Societies in Nineteenth-Century France.* Urbana: University of Illinois Press, 2010.

Agulhon, Maurice. *Le Cercle dans la France bourgeoise, 1810–1848: Étude d'une mutation de sociabilité.* Paris: Librarie Armand Collin, 1977.

Alexander, R. S. "Benjamin Constant as a Second Restoration Politician." In *The Cambridge Companion to Constant*, edited by Helena Rosenblatt, 146–70. Cambridge: Cambridge University Press, 2009.

———. *Bonapartism and Revolutionary Tradition in France: The Fédérés of 1815.* Cambridge: Cambridge University Press, 1991.

———. *Re-writing the French Revolutionary Tradition.* Cambridge: Cambridge University Press, 2003.

Algan, Yann, and Pierre Cahuc. *La Société de défiance: Comment le modèle social français s'autodétruit.* Paris: Éditions rue l'Ulm, 2007.

Allgor, Catherine. *Parlor Politics: In Which the Ladies of Washington Help Build a City and a Government.* Charlottesville: University Press of Virginia, 2000.

Altman, Janet Gurkin. *Epistolarity: Approaches to a Form.* Columbus: Ohio State University Press, 1982.

Ampère, J. J. *Ballanche.* Paris: A. René et Cie, 1849.

Andrews, Naomi. *Socialism's Muse: Gender in the Intellectual Landscape of French Romantic Socialism.* Lanham, Md.: Lexington Books, 2006.

Arlet, Jacques. *Rémusat: Mémorialiste, grand témoin du XIXe siècle.* Paris: Remi Perrin, 2003.

Assemblé nationale. "Base de données des députés français depuis 1789." Available at http://www.assemblee-nationale.fr/sycomore/index.asp.

Atkin, Nicholas, and Frank Tallett. *The Right in France: From Revolution to Le Pen.* London: I. B. Tauris, 2003.

Backouche, Isabelle. *La Monarchie parlementaire, 1815–1848, de Louis XVIII à Louis-Phillipe.* Paris: Pygmalion, 2000.

Baier, Annette. *Moral Prejudices: Essays on Ethics.* Cambridge: Harvard University Press, 1994.

Bardoux, A. *La Duchesse de Duras.* Paris: C. Lévy, 1898.

Bastid, Paul. *Les Institutions politiques de la monarchie parlementaire française, 1814–1848.* Paris: Recueil Sirey, 1954.

Bates, Robin. "Madame Guizot and Monsieur Guizot: Domestic Pedagogy and the Post-Revolutionary Order in France, 1807–1830." *Modern Intellectual History* 8, no. 1 (2011): 31–59.

Beik, William. *Absolutism and Society in Seventeenth-Century France: State Power and Provincial Aristocracy in Languedoc*. Cambridge: Cambridge University Press, 1985.

———. *A Social and Cultural History of Early Modern France*. Cambridge: Cambridge University Press, 2009.

Berchet, Jean Claude. *Chateaubriand*. Paris: Gallimard, 2012.

Bertier de Sauvigny, Guillaume de. *The Bourbon Restoration*. Philadelphia: University of Pennsylvania Press, 1967.

Boiteau d'Ambly, Paul. *Vie de Béranger, 1780–1857*. Paris: Perrotin, 1861.

Bonnal, Edmond. *Manuel et son temps: Étude sur l'opposition parlementaire sous la Restauration*. Paris: Dentu, 1877.

Bouton, Cynthia. "Reconciliation, Hope, Trust, and Instability in July Monarchy France." *French Historical Studies* 35, no. 3 (2012): 541–75.

Branda, Pierre. *Napoléon et ses hommes: La Maison de l'Empereur*. Paris: Fayard, 2011.

Bray, Alan. *The Friend*. Chicago: University of Chicago Press, 2003.

Broglie, Gabriel de. *Guizot*. Paris: Perrin, 1990.

———. *La Monarchie de Juillet, 1830–1848*. Paris: Fayard, 2011.

Bruyère, Gérard, and Stéphane Paccoud. "Les Cercles de Juliette Récamier." In *Juliette Récamier: Muse et mécène*, edited by Stéphane Paccoud, 104–9. Paris: Hazan, 2009.

Charmley, John. *The Princess and the Politicians: Sex, Intrigue, and Diplomacy, 1812–1840*. London: Viking, 2005.

Clément, Jean-Paul. *Chateaubriand: Biographie morale et intellectuelle*. Paris: Flammarion, 1998.

Collingham, H. A. C., and R. S. Alexander. *The July Monarchy: A Political History of France, 1830–1848*. New York: Longman, 1988.

Colwill, Elizabeth. "Epistolary Passions: Friendship and the Literary Public of Constance de Salm, 1767–1845." *Journal of Women's History* 12, no. 3 (2000): 39–68.

Craiutu, Aurelian. *Liberalism under Siege: The Political Thought of the French Doctrinaires*. Lanham, Md.: Lexington Books, 2003.

Darnton, Robert. *The Kiss of Lamourette: Reflections in Cultural History*. New York: Norton, 1989.

Darriulat, Philippe. *La Muse du peuple: Chansons politiques et sociales en France, 1815–1871*. Rennes: Presses universitaires de Rennes, 2011.

Daudet, Ernest. *La Police politique: Chronique des temps de la Restauration, d'après les rapports des agents secrets et les papiers du Cabinet noir, 1815–1820*. Paris: Plon-Nourrit, 1912.

———. *Une Vie d'ambassadrice au siècle dernier: La Princesse de Lieven*. 2nd ed. Paris: Librairie Plon, 1933.

Dauphin, Cécile, Pierrette Lebrun-Pézerat, and Danièle Poublan. *Ces Bonnes lettres: Une Correspondance familiale au XIXe siècle*. Paris: Albin Michel, 1995.

David, Marcel. *Fraternité et Révolution française, 1789–1799*. Paris: Aubier, 1987.

Davidoff, Leonore, and Catherine Hall. *Family Fortunes: Men and Women of the English Middle Class, 1780–1850*. Chicago: University of Chicago Press, 1987.

Davidson, Denise Z. *France after Revolution: Urban Life, Gender, and the New Social Order.* Cambridge: Harvard University Press, 2007.

Démier, Francis. *La France de la Restauration, 1814–1830: L'impossible retour du passé.* Paris: Gallimard, 2012.

Denby, David. *Sentimental Narrative and the Social Order in France, 1760–1820.* Cambridge: Cambridge University Press, 1994.

Denis, Antoine. *Amable-Guillaume-Prosper Brugière, baron de Barante, 1782–1866: Homme politique, diplomate, et historien.* Paris: Honoré Champion, 2000.

Desan, Suzanne. *The Family on Trial in Revolutionary France.* Berkeley: University of California Press, 2004.

———. "Reconstituting the Social after the Terror: Family, Property, and the Law in Popular Politics." *Past and Present* 164 (August 1999): 81–121.

Desplaces, Eugène Ernest, Joseph Fr. Michaud, and Louis Gabriel Michaud, eds. *Biographie universelle ancienne et moderne . . .* 45 vols. Paris: Madame C. Desplaces, 1854.

Diesbach, Ghislain de. *Chateaubriand.* Paris: Perrin, 1995.

Duclert, Vincent, and Christophe Prochasson. "L'Amitié." In *Dictionnaire critique de la République*, edited by Vincent Duclert and Christophe Prochasson, 87–94. Paris: Flammarion, 2002.

Duprat, Catherine. *Usage et pratiques de la philanthropie: Pauvreté, action sociale, et lien social, à Paris, au cours du premier XIXe siècle.* 2 vols. Paris: Association pour l'étude de l'histoire de la sécurité sociale, 1996.

Dupuy, Micheline. *La Duchesse de Dino: Princesse de Courlande, égérie de Talleyrand, 1793–1862.* Paris: Perrin, 2002.

Elias, Norbert. *The Court Society.* Translated by Edmund Jephcott. Oxford: Blackwell, 1983.

Faderman, Lillian. *Surpassing the Love of Men: Romantic Friendship and Love between Women, from the Renaissance to the Present.* New York: Morrow, 1981.

Fischer, Claude. "*Bowling Alone*: What's the Score?" *Social Networks* 27, no. 2 (2005): 155–67.

Fortescue, William. "Morality and Monarchy: Corruption and the Fall of the Regime of Louis-Philippe in 1848." *French History* 16, no. 1 (2002): 83–100.

Foucault, Michel. *The History of Sexuality.* Vol. 1. Translated by Robert Hurley. New York: Vintage Books, 1990.

Frame, Donald. *Montaigne in France, 1812–1852.* New York: Columbia University Press, 1940.

Fureix, Emmanuel. *La France des larmes: Deuils politiques à l'âge romantique, 1814–1840.* Seyssel: Champ Vallon, 2009.

Furet, François. *Interpreting the French Revolution.* Translated by Elborg Forster. Cambridge: Cambridge University Press, 1981.

Galtier-Boissière, Jean. *Mysteries of the French Secret Police.* Translated by Ronald Leslie-Melville. London: S. Paul, 1938.

Garrioch, David. "From Christian Friendship to Secular Sentimentality: Enlightenment Re-evaluations." In *Friendship: A History*, edited by Barbara Caine, 165–214. London: Equinox, 2008.

Goblot, Jean-Jacques. *La Jeune France libérale: "Le Globe" et son groupe littéraire, 1824–1830.* Paris: Plon, 1995.

Goldstein, Jan. *The Post-Revolutionary Self: Politics and Psyche in France, 1750–1850.* Cambridge: Harvard University Press, 2005.

Goodman, Dena. *Becoming a Woman in the Age of Letters.* Ithaca: Cornell University Press, 2009.

———. *The Republic of Letters: A Cultural History of the French Enlightenment.* Ithaca: Cornell University Press, 1994.

Gordon, Daniel. *Citizens without Sovereignty: Equality and Sociability in French Thought, 1670–1789.* Princeton: Princeton University Press, 1994.

Granovetter, Mark S. "The Strength of Weak Ties." *American Journal of Sociology* 78, no. 6 (1973): 1360–80.

Gunn, J. A. W. *When the French Tried to Be British: Party, Opposition, and the Quest for Civil Disagreement, 1814–1848.* Montreal: McGill-Queen's University Press, 2009.

Halévi, Ran. *Les Loges maçonniques dans la France d'Ancien Régime: Aux origines de la sociabilité démocratique.* Paris: A. Colin, 1984.

Halévy, Daniel. *The End of the Notables.* Translated by Alain Silvera and June Guicharnaud. Middletown: Wesleyan University Press, 1974.

Hansen, Helynne. *Hortense Allart: The Woman and the Novelist.* Lanham, Md.: University Press of America, 1998.

Hardin, Russell. *Trust and Trustworthiness.* New York: Russell Sage Foundation, 2002.

Harris, Ruth. *Dreyfus: Politics, Emotion, and the Scandal of the Century.* New York: Metropolitan Books, 2010.

Harrison, Carol. *The Bourgeois Citizen in Nineteenth-Century France: Gender, Sociability, and the Uses of Emulation.* Oxford: Oxford University Press, 1999.

Herman, Arthur L., Jr. "The Language of Fidelity in Early Modern France." *Journal of Modern History* 67, no. 1 (1995): 1–24.

Herriot, Édouard. *Madame Récamier et ses amis.* 2 vols. 2nd ed. Paris: Librairie Plon, 1905.

Hesse, Carla. *The Other Enlightenment: How French Women Became Modern.* Princeton: Princeton University Press, 2001.

Higonnet, Patrice. *Goodness beyond Virtue: The Jacobins during the French Revolution.* Cambridge: Harvard University Press, 1998.

———. "Terror, Trauma, and the 'Young Marx' Explanation of Jacobin Politics." *Past and Present* 191, no. 1 (2006): 121–64.

Higonnet, Patrice, and Trevor B. Higonnet. "Class, Corruption, and Politics in the French Chamber of Deputies, 1846–1848." *French Historical Studies* 5, no. 2 (1967): 204–24.

Hoffmann, Stefan-Ludwig. "Civility, Male Friendship, and Masonic Sociability in Nineteenth-Century Germany." *Gender and History* 13, no. 2 (2001): 224–48.

———. "Democracy and Associations in the Long Nineteenth Century: Toward a Transnational Perspective." *Journal of Modern History* 75, no. 2 (2003): 269–99.

Houbre, Gabrielle. *La Discipline de l'amour: L'éducation sentimentale des filles et des garçons à l'âge du romantisme.* Paris: Plon, 1997.

Hunt, Lynn. *The Family Romance of the French Revolution.* Berkeley: University of California Press, 1992.

———. *Inventing Human Rights: A History.* New York: Norton, 2007.

———. *Politics, Culture, and Class in the French Revolution.* Berkeley: University of California Press, 1984.

Hunt, Lynn, and Margaret Jacob. "The Affective Revolution in 1790s Britain." *Eighteenth-Century Studies* 34, no. 4 (2001): 491–521.

Jacob, Margaret C. *Living the Enlightenment: Freemasonry and Politics in Eighteenth-Century Europe.* Oxford: Oxford University Press, 1991.

Jardin, André, and André-Jean Tudesq. *La France des notables, 1815–1848.* 2 vols. Paris: Éditions du Seuil, 1988.

Jaume, Lucien. *L'Individu effacé; ou, Le Paradoxe du libéralisme français.* Paris: Fayard, 1997.

Johnson, Christopher, and David Sabean, eds. *Sibling Relations and the Transformation of European Kinship, 1300–1900.* New York: Berghahn Books, 2011.

Johnson, Douglas W. J. *Guizot: Aspects of French History, 1787–1874.* London: Routledge and K. Paul, 1963.

Kaiser, Thomas. "Louis *le Bien-Aimé* and the Rhetoric of the Royal Body." In *From the Royal to the Republican Body: Incorporating the Political in Seventeenth- and Eighteenth-Century France*, edited by Sara Melzer and Kathryn Norberg, 131–61. Berkeley: University of California Press, 1998.

Kale, Steven. *French Salons: High Society and Political Sociability from the Old Regime to the Revolution of 1848.* Baltimore: Johns Hopkins University Press, 2004.

Karila-Cohen, Pierre. "Les Fonds secrets; ou, La Méfiance légitime: L'Invention paradoxale d'une 'tradition républicaine' sous la Restauration et la Monarchie de Juillet." *Revue historique* 636 (October 2005): 731–66.

Kates, Gary. *Monsieur d'Eon Is a Woman: A Tale of Political Intrigue and Sexual Masquerade.* New York: Basic Books, 1995.

Kettering, Sharon. "Friendship and Clientage in Early Modern France." *French History* 6, no. 2 (1992): 139–58.

———. "The Patronage Power of Early Modern French Noblewomen." *Historical Journal* 32, no. 4 (1989): 817–41.

———. *Patrons, Brokers, and Clients in Seventeenth-Century France.* Oxford: Oxford University Press, 1986.

Koepke, Robert. "The Failure of Parliamentary Government in France, 1840–1848." *European Studies Review* 9, no. 4 (1979): 433–55.

Kolb, Marthe. *Ary Scheffer et son temps, 1795–1858.* Paris: Boivin, 1937.

Kramer, Lloyd. *Lafayette in Two Worlds: Public Cultures and Personal Identities in an Age of Revolutions.* Chapel Hill: University of North Carolina Press, 1996.

Kreuzer, Marcus. *Institutions and Innovation: Voters, Parties, and Interest Groups in the Consolidation of Democracy: France and Germany, 1870–1939.* Ann Arbor: University of Michigan Press, 2001.

Kroen, Sheryl. *Politics and Theater: The Crisis of Legitimacy in Restoration France, 1815–1830.* Berkeley: University of California Press, 2000.

Landes, Joan. *Women and the Public Sphere in the Age of the French Revolution.* Ithaca: Cornell University Press, 1988.

Lentz, Thierry. *La France et l'Europe de Napoléon, 1804–1814.* Paris: Fayard, 2007.

Le Roy Ladurie, Emmanuel. *Saint-Simon and the Court of Louis XIV.* Translated by Arthur Goldhammer. Chicago: Chicago University Press, 2001.

Lilti, Antoine. *Le Monde des salons: Sociabilité et mondanité à Paris au XVIIIe siècle.* Paris: Fayard, 2005.

Linton, Marisa. *Choosing Terror: Virtue, Friendship, and Authenticity in the French Revolution.* Oxford: Oxford University Press, 2013.

———. "Fatal Friendships: The Politics of Jacobin Friendship." *French Historical Studies* 31, no. 1 (2008): 51–76.

Loiselle, Kenneth. "'New but True Friends': Freemasonry and the Culture of Male Friendship in Eighteenth-Century France." Ph.D. diss., Yale University, 2007.

———. "'Nouveau mais vrais amis': La Franc-Maçonnerie et les rites de l'amitié aux dix-huitième siècle." *Dix-Huitième Siècle* 39, no. 1 (2007): 303–18.

Lucas, Colin. "The Theory and Practice of Denunciation in the French Revolution." In *Accusatory Practices: Denunciation in Modern European History, 1789–1989*, edited by Sheila Fitzpatrick and Robert Gellately, 22–39. Chicago: University of Chicago Press, 1997.

Lucey, Michael. *The Misfit of the Family: Balzac and the Social Forms of Sexuality.* Durham: Duke University Press, 2003.

Lukes, Steven. *Individualism.* Oxford: Blackwell, 1973.

———. "The Meaning of Individualism." *Journal of the History of Ideas* 32, no. 1 (1971): 45–66.

Malandain, Gilles. "Les Mouches de la police et le vol des mots: Les gazetins de la police secrète et la surveillance de l'expression publique à Paris au deuxième quart du XVIIIe siècle." *Revue d'histoire moderne et contemporaine* 42–43 (July/September 1995): 376–404.

Marcou, Lilly. *Napoléon and les femmes.* Paris: La Martinière, 2008.

Marcus, Sharon. *Between Women: Friendship, Desire, and Marriage in Victorian England.* Princeton: Princeton University Press, 2007.

Margadant, Jo Burr. "Gender, Vice, and the Political Imaginary in Postrevolutionary France: Reinterpreting the Failure of the July Monarchy, 1830–1848." *American Historical Review* 104, no. 4 (2000): 1461–96.

———, ed. *The New Biography: Performing Femininity in Nineteenth-Century France.* Berkeley: University of California Press, 2000.

Martin, Brian. *Napoleonic Friendship: Military Fraternity, Intimacy, and Sexuality in Nineteenth-Century France.* Durham: University of New Hampshire Press, 2011.

Martin-Fugier, Anne. *Les Salons de la IIIe République: Art, littérature, politique.* Paris: Perrin, 2003.

———. *La Vie élégante; ou, La Formation du Tout-Paris, 1815–1848.* Paris: Librairie Arthème Fayard, 1990.

Maza, Sarah. *The Myth of the French Bourgeoisie: An Essay on the Social Imaginary, 1750–1850.* Cambridge: Harvard University Press, 2003.

———. *Private Lives and Public Affairs: The Causes Célèbres of Prerevolutionary France.* Berkeley: University of California Press, 1993.

McLeod, Carolyn. "Trust." In *The Stanford Encyclopedia of Philosophy*. Stanford University, 1997–. Article published 20 February 2006, revised 7 February 2011. http://plato.stanford.edu/archives/spr2011/entries/trust/.

Merrick, Jeffrey. "Male Friendship in Prerevolutionary France." *GLQ: A Journal of Lesbian and Gay Studies* 10, no. 3 (2004): 407–32.

Merriman, John M. *Police Stories: Building the French State, 1815–1851.* New York: Oxford University Press, 2006.

Mitchell, Marilyn. "Chateaubriand and Hyde de Neuville: The Loyal Opposition." Ph.D. diss., University of Kansas, 1972.

Mousnier, Roland. "Les Concepts de 'ordres,' d'états, de fidélité, et de 'monarchie absolue' en France de la fin du XV siècle à la fin du XVIIe." *Revue historique* 247, no. 2 (1972): 289–312.

Muhlstein, Anka. *A Taste for Freedom: The Life of Astolphe de Custine.* New York: Helen Marx Books, 1999.

Neely, Sylvia. *Lafayette and the Liberal Ideal, 1814–1824: Politics and Conspiracy in an Age of Reaction.* Carbondale: Southern Illinois University Press, 1991.

Nord, Philip. *Impressionists and Politics: Art and Democracy in the Nineteenth Century.* London: Routledge, 2000.

———. *The Republican Moment: Struggles for Democracy in Nineteenth-Century France.* Cambridge: Harvard University Press, 1995.

Nourrisson, Paul. *Histoire de la liberté d'association en France depuis 1789.* Vol. 1. Paris: L. Tenin, 1920.

Nye, Robert A. *Masculinity and Male Codes of Honor in Modern France.* New York: Oxford University Press, 1993.

Owre, Maximilian. "United in Division: The Polarized French Nation, 1814–1830." Ph.D. diss., University of North Carolina, 2008.

Ozouf, Mona. *Women's Words: Essay on French Singularity.* Chicago: University of Chicago Press, 1997.

Padgett, John, and Christopher Ansell. "Robust Action and the Rise of the Medici, 1400–1434." *American Journal of Sociology* 98, no. 6 (1993): 1259–1319.

Pailhès, G. *La Duchesse de Duras et Chateaubriand d'après des documents inédits.* Paris: Perin, 1910.

Pilbeam, Pamela M. *The Constitutional Monarchy in France, 1814–48.* Harlow, UK: Longman, 2000.

Plessix Gray, Francine du. *Rage and Fire: A Life of Louise Colet, Pioneer Feminist, Literary Star, Flaubert's Muse.* New York: Simon and Schuster, 1994.

Popkin, Jeremy. *Press, Revolution, and Social Identities in France, 1830–1835.* University Park: Pennsylvania State University Press, 2002.

Pouthas, Charles-H. *Guizot pendant la Restauration, préparation de l'homme d'état, 1814–1830.* Paris: Librairie Plon, 1923.

———. *La Jeunesse de François Guizot, 1787–1814.* Paris: F. Alcan, 1936.

Price, Munro. *The Perilous Crown: France between Revolutions.* London: Pan, 2008.

Putnam, Robert. *Bowling Alone: The Collapse and Revival of American Community.* New York: Simon and Schuster, 2000.

———. *Making Democracy Work: Civic Traditions in Modern Italy.* Princeton: Princeton University Press, 1993.

Ravel, Jeffrey. *The Contested Parterre: Public Theater and French Political Culture, 1680–1791.* Ithaca: Cornell University Press, 1999.

Reddy, William M. *The Invisible Code: Honor and Sentiment in Postrevolutionary France, 1814–1848.* Berkeley: University of California Press, 1997.

———. *The Navigation of Feeling: A Framework for the History of Emotions.* Cambridge: Cambridge University Press, 2001.

Redford, Bruce. *The Converse of the Pen: Acts of Intimacy in the Eighteenth-Century Familiar Letter.* Chicago: University of Chicago Press, 1986.

Rémond, René. *The Right Wing in France from 1815 to De Gaulle.* Translated by James M. Lau. 2nd ed. Philadelphia: University of Pennsylvania Press, 1969.

Rentet, Thierry. "Network Mapping: Ties of Fidelity and Dependency among the Major Domestic Officers of Anne de Montmorency." *French History* 17, no. 2 (2003): 109–26.

Resnick, Daniel. *The White Terror and the Political Reaction after Waterloo.* Cambridge: Harvard University Press, 1966.

Rogers, Rebecca. *From the Salon to the Schoolroom: Educating Bourgeois Girls in Nineteenth-Century France.* University Park: Pennsylvania State University Press, 2005.

Rosanvallon, Pierre. *Counter-Democracy: Politics in an Age of Distrust.* Translated by Arthur Goldhammer. Cambridge: Cambridge University Press, 2008.

———. *The Demands of Liberty: Civil Society in France since the Revolution.* Translated by Arthur Goldhammer. Cambridge: Harvard University Press, 2007.

———. *Le Moment Guizot.* Paris: Gallimard, 1985.

———. *La Monarchie impossible: Les Chartes de 1814 et 1830.* Paris: Fayard, 1994.

Rosenwein, Barbara. *Emotional Communities in the Early Middle Ages.* Ithaca: Cornell University Press, 2006.

Ruggiu, François-Joseph. "A Way out of the Crisis: Methodologies of Early Modern Social History in France." *Cultural and Social History* 6, no. 1 (2009): 65–85.

Séché, Léon. *Hortense Allart de Méritens: Dans ses rapports avec Chateaubriand, Béranger, Lamennais, Sainte-Beuve, G. Sand, Mme d'Agoult.* Paris: Mercure de France, 1908.

Sedgwick, Eve Kosofsky. *Between Men: English Literature and Male Homosocial Desire.* New York: Columbia University Press, 1985.

Sédouy, Jacques-Alain de. *Le Comte Molé; ou, La Séduction du pouvoir.* Paris: Perrin, 1994.

Sennett, Richard. *The Fall of Public Man.* New York: Knopf, 1977.

Serna, Pierre. *La République des girouettes, 1789–1815, et au-delà: Une anomalie politique, la France de l'extrême centre.* Paris: Champ Vallon, 2005.

Shapiro, Barry M. *Traumatic Politics: The Deputies and the King in the Early French Revolution.* University Park: Pennsylvania State University Press, 2009.

Sibalis, Michael. "The Regulation of Male Homosexuality in Revolutionary and Napoleonic France, 1789–1815." In *Homosexuality in Modern France*, edited by Jeffrey Merrick and Bryant Ragan, Jr., 80–101 Oxford: Oxford University Press, 1996.

Silver, Allan. "Friendship in Commercial Society: Eighteenth-Century Social Theory and Modern Sociology." *American Journal of Sociology* 95, no. 6 (1990): 1474–1504.

Skuy, David. *Assassination, Politics, and Miracles: France and the Royalist Reaction of 1820.* Montreal: McGill-Queen's University Press, 2003.

Smith, Jay. *The Culture of Merit: Nobility, Royal Service, and the Making of Absolute Monarchy in France, 1600–1789.* Ann Arbor: University of Michigan Press, 1996.

———. "No More Language Games: Words, Beliefs, and the Political Culture of Early Modern France." *American Historical Review* 102, no. 5 (December 1997): 1413–40.

Smith-Rosenberg, Carroll. "The Female World of Love and Ritual: Relations between Women in Nineteenth-Century America." *Signs* 1, no. 1 (1975): 1–29.

Spitzer, Alan B. *The French Generation of 1820.* Princeton: Princeton University Press, 1987.

———. "Malicious Memories: Restoration Politics and a Prosopography of Turncoats." *French Historical Studies* 24, no. 1 (2001): 37–61.

Stearns, Peter N., and Carol Z. Stearns. "Emotionology: Clarifying the History of Emotions and Emotional Standards." *American Historical Review* 90, no. 4 (1985): 813–36.

Steinberg, Ronen. "The Afterlives of the Terror: Dealing with the Legacy of Violence in Post-Revolutionary France, 1794–1830s." Ph.D. diss., University of Chicago, 2010.

Stephenson, Barbara. *The Patronage Power of Marguerite de Navarre.* Aldershot, UK: Ashgate, 2004.

Surkis, Judith. *Sexing the Citizen: Morality and Masculinity in France, 1870–1920.* Ithaca: Cornell University Press, 2006.

Tackett, Timothy. *Becoming a Revolutionary: The Deputies of the French National Assembly and the Emergence of a Revolutionary Culture, 1789–1790.* Princeton: Princeton University Press, 1996.

———. "Conspiracy Obsession in a Time of Revolution: French Elites and the Origins of the Terror, 1789–1792." *American Historical Review* 105, no. 3 (2000): 691–713.

———. *When the King Took Flight.* Cambridge: Harvard University Press, 2003.

Theis, Laurent. *François Guizot.* Paris: Fayard, 2008.

Thesen, Doreen. *The Function of Gift Exchange in Stendhal and Balzac.* New York: Peter Lang, 2000.

Thompson, Victoria. "Creating Boundaries: Homosexuality and the Changing Social Order in France, 1830–1870." In *Homosexuality in Modern France*, edited by Jeffrey Merrick and Bryant Ragan, Jr., 102–27. Oxford: Oxford University Press, 1996.

———. *The Virtuous Marketplace: Women and Men, Money and Politics in Paris, 1830–1870.* Baltimore: Johns Hopkins University Press, 2000.

———. "Working within the Crisis: Meditations on the Edge of a Cliff." *Cultural and Social History* 6, no. 1 (2009): 87–95.

Thureau-Dangin, Paul. *Histoire de la Monarchie de Juillet.* Vol. 5. Paris: E. Plon, Nourrit et Cie, 1890.

Touchard, Jean. *La Gloire de Béranger.* 2 vols. Paris: A. Colin, 1968.

Vaillé, Eugène. *Le Cabinet noir.* Paris: Presses universitaires de France, 1950.

Vincent, K. Steven. *Benjamin Constant and the Birth of French Liberalism.* New York: Palgrave Macmillan, 2011.

Vincent-Buffault, Anne. *L'Exercice de l'amitié: Pour une histoire des pratiques amicales aux XVIIIe et XIXe siècles.* Paris: Editions du Seuil, 1995.

———. *The History of Tears: Sensibility and Sentimentality in France.* Hampshire, UK: Macmillan, 1991.

Wagener, Françoise. *Madame Récamier, 1777–1849.* Paris: J. C. Lattès, 1986.

Wahnich, Sophie. *La Liberté ou la mort: Essai sur la terreur et le terrorisme*. Paris: La Fabrique editions, 2003.

Walton, Whitney. *Eve's Proud Descendants: Four Women Writers and Republican Politics in Nineteenth-Century France*. Stanford: Stanford University Press, 2000.

Waresquiel, Emmanuel de. *Cent jours: La Tentation de l'impossible, mars–juillet 1815*. Paris: Fayard, 2008.

———. *Le Duc de Richelieu, 1766–1822: Un Sentimental en politique*. Paris: Perrin, 1990.

———. *L'Histoire à rebrousse-poil: Les Élites, la Restauration, la Révolution*. Paris: Fayard, 2005.

———. *Talleyrand: Le Prince immobile*. Paris: Fayard, 2003.

Waresquiel, Emmanuel de, and Benoît Yvert. "Le duc de Richelieu et le comte Decazes d'après leur correspondance inédite pendant le congrès d'Aix-la-Chapelle." *Revue de la Société d'histoire de la Restauration et la Monarchie de Juillet* 2 (1988): 79–107.

———. *Histoire de la Restauration, 1814–1830: Naissance de la France moderne*. Paris: Perrin, 1996.

Watel, Françoise. *Jean-Guillaume Hyde de Neuville, 1776–1857: Conspirateur et diplomate*. Paris: Direction des archives et de la documentation, Ministère des Affaires étrangéres, 1997.

Wellman, Barry, and Stephen D. Berkowitz. *Social Structures: A Network Approach*. Cambridge: Cambridge University Press, 1988.

Woloch, Isser. *Napoleon and His Collaborators: The Making of a Dictatorship*. New York: Norton, 2001.

Zanone, Damien. *Écrire son temps: Les Mémoires en France de 1815–1848*. Lyon: Presses Universitaires de Lyon, 2006.

Ziegler, Philip. *The Duchess of Dino*. London: Collins, 1962.

INDEX

Page numbers in italics refer to figures; those followed by n refer to notes, with note number.

Acte additionnel, 43
Adam, Juliette, 160, 161
Adams, Christine, 31
Adélaïde, Mme, 128
Agoult, Marie d', 106, 160
Aide toi, le ciel t'aidera, 52
Allart de Méritens, Hortense
  and Béranger, 83, 89
  biography, 164
  as Chateaubriand's mistress, 86–87, 89, 104, 142, 143, 164
  friendship network, 98, *99*, *101*, 102–3, 105, *106*, 106–7, *107*; limitation of to elites, 158; sources on, 92
  personal life, documentation of, 12
  political activity of, 133–34, 142, 150, 151, 157
  politics of, 11, *101*, 102–3, 103–4
  and Sainte-Beuve, 82–83, 87, 93
alliances, formation of, women's role in, 142–49
"ami" and "amitié," definitions of, 10
Ampère, Jean Jacques, 99, 101, 102
Ancelot, Virginie, 57
Anisson du Perron, Mme, 84
Anne de Montmorency, 23
anomie, post-Revolution, 41–48, 60, 64. *See also* factionalism; social cohesion
  and Balzac's *Illusions perdues*: on friendship, as positive form of individualism, 60, 64; on friendship as solution to problem of atomizing self-interest, 60, 63–64; on impossibility of friendship in public competitive world, 61, 64
  echoes of through French history, 156
  French concern about, 39–40
  ideological divide of Restoration and, 42, 44–48, 114, 181n20
  and parliamentary government, necessity of trust in, 115, 116, 142
  political uses of friendship as remedy for, 131–32, 154–56
  Restoration police state and, 48–53
  and trust, lack of, 3–4, 9, 22, 33–34, 154
  variety of political beliefs and, 41
anthropological approach to political practice, 6
Arconati-Visconti, marquise, 162
associational life. *See also* anomie, post-Revolution; salons; social cohesion
  efforts to control: Napoleon era, 36–38; Restoration era, 49, 52–53
  18th-century, and rise of democratic sensibility, 27
  increase in, in late 19th century, 159
  in July Monarchy, 54
  post-Revolution: and friendship, reshaping of, 29; government shutdown of, 31, 34–35
  in second half of 19th century, 159–60

Baier, Annette, 8–9
Ballanche, Pierre Simon de
  friendship network, 99, *99*, *101*, 102, 106, *106*, *107*
  politics of, 100, 101, *101*
Balzac, Honoré de, 2, 42, 57–59, 78. *See also* *Illusions perdues* (Balzac)
Barante, Prosper de
  biography of, 168
  and Broglie, Mme de, 84, 88, 96, 136–38, 150

Barante, Prosper de (*continued*)
correspondence, homoerotic overtones in, 76–77
and Dino, Mme de, 69
on friendship, 2
friendship network, 88, 99, *99*, *101*, 102, *106*, *107*, 109
friends of, exchange of favors among, 79–80
and Guizot: correspondence, 70–71, 72–73; friendship with, 79–80, 118
and Molé, correspondence, 76–77
political career of, 2
politics of, *101*
and Récamier, 167
and Rémusat, 76–77
sister of as confidante, 84
women's political activities and, 136–38, 150
Barère, Bertrand, 31
Barrot, Odilon, 56, 152
Barthe, Félix, 54–55
Bellaguet, Louis François, 79–80
Béranger, Pierre Jean de
and Allart, 83, 89
biography, 164
and Cauchois-Lemaire, 83
character and personality of, 12–13
and Chateaubriand: friendship with, 12, 13, 17, 108, 164; political dealings with, 142, 150
and Constant, alliance between, 125–27
and Dupont, 118
family of, 155
female correspondents, 83
friendship network, 118, 164–65; characteristic salutation in letters of, 93, 188n6; 1825–1829, 98, *99*, 101, *101*, 102, 104, *170*, *171*; 1843–1847, 105, 106, *106*, *107*, 107–8, 110, *172*, *173*; maintenance of by female friends, 89; politics as influence on, 91, 101, *101*, 102, 104–5, 107, *107*; sources on, 94–95, 105
friends of: among elites, 12; exchange of favors among, 78; factionalism of July Monarchy and, 54–55; factionalism of Restoration and, 47; financial assistance interchanged with, 17, 78; importance to Béranger, 13; women as, 81, 100
and Lafayette, 189n12
and Lamartine, 12, 107
and Lebrun, 78
and Manuel, friendship with, 1, 94; closeness of, 97; as political act, 1, 2, 102, 118; possible erotic component of, 1, 75
political career, 14, 125, 164
politics of, 1, 11, 12, 101, *101*, 104
representativeness of, 13–14
on Restoration, foreign military support of, 45
social class of, 12
as songwriter, 1, 13–14
sources on, 133–34
tomb of, 1
Bérard, Louis, 78
Berry, duc de, 51
Berry, duchess de, 165
Berryer, *106*, *107*, 109
Biran, Maine de, 181n20
Boigne, comtesse de, 96
Bonaparte, Lucien, 164
Bonaparte, Napoleon. *See also* Hundred Days
on atomization of French society, 36
and homosexuality, 75–76
return to France in 1815, and political factionalism, 4
Bonaparte family, friendship network, 99, 102
Brissot, Jacques Pierre, 32
Broglie, Albertine Ida Gustavine de Staël Holstein, duchesse de
and Barante, correspondence, 84, 88, 96, 136–38, 150
biography of, 168
female correspondents, 84
friendship network, 94, 98, 99, *99*, *101*, 103; sources on, 92
and Guizot: correspondence with, 17, 83–84, 85, 135; friendship with, 97
and husband's friendship network, maintenance of, 88–89
personal life, documentation of, 12
political activity of, 135, 136–38, 149, 150
politics of, 11, *101*
and Récamier, friendship of, 97
as salonnière, 116
as source, 105

Broglie, Victor de
and Barante, friendship with, 118
biography of, 168
character and personality of, 89
on friendship, 2
friendship network, *99*, *101*, 102, *106*, *107*; maintenance of by wife, 88–89
and Guizot: correspondence, 72; friendship with, 65, 69, 118, 121, 140
political career of, 2, 111
and political instability, suffering due to, 65
politics of, *101*
and Rémusat, political support for, 121, 140
Brune, Marshal, 44
Bulwer-Lytton, Henry, 83

cabinet
negotiations over members of: and friends as stand-ins for friends, 119–21; and political tensions, relief of, 122–23
in parliamentary system, selection of, 115, 116
cafés, and democratic sensibility, rise of, 27
Cassatt, Mary, 162
Castellane, Cordélia Greffulhe, comtesse de
and Broglie, Mme de, 84
Chateaubriand and, 83, 85, 86, 105
friendship network, 98, *99*, *101*, 105, *106*, *107*, 109; sources on, 92
political activity of, 139
politics of, *101*, 109
Catellan, Mme de, 98, *99*, *101*
Catholics, on individualism after Revolution, 39
Cauchois-Lemaire, Judith, 83, *106*, *107*
Caveau (songwriters and authors group), 47
center-left, friendship networks of, 106, *107*
Cercle de l'Union, 52
Charles et Marie (Souza), 68
Charles X (king of France), 100, 157
Chateaubriand, François René de
and Allart, as mistress, 86–87, 89, 104, 142, 143, 150, 164
and Béranger: friendship with, 12, 13, 17, 108, 164; political dealings with, 142, 150
biography of, 165–66
and Castellane, 83, 85, 86, 105
character and personality, 13, 95, 108
correspondence, salutations used in, 188n6
and duchesse de Berry affair, 14
and Duras, 86, 87
ex-mistresses, continued friendship with, 86–87
and factionalism of Restoration, 48
as faction leader, 115
friendship network: and definition of friend, 96–97; 1825–1829, 98, *99*, *101*, 101–2, 103, *170*, *171*; 1843–1847, 105, 106, *106*, 107, *107*, 107–8, 110, *172*, *173*; maintenance of by female friends, 89; members of, 165–67; politics as influence on, 91, *101*, 101–2, 103, 104–5, *107*, 118; sources on, 94–95, 105
on friendships with women, 81
friends of: financial assistance and, 17, 78; women as, 81, 100
on Hundred Days, disgust created by, 43
and Hyde de Neuville, 118, 166
on individualism after Revolution, 39
and Martignac cabinet, negotiations surrounding, 119–20, 121
and Montcalm, 167
police surveillance of, 51
political career of, 103, 131, 138, 139, 193n38
politics of, 11, 12, 101–2, 108, 143–44
and Récamier: love affair with, 51, 87, 166, 167; politics of, 100
representativeness of, 13
sister of as confidante, 84
social class of, 12
sources on, 133
women correspondents, 83, 86
women's political activism and, 138–41, 142, 150, 151, 157
Chevreuse, duchesse de, 96
Choiseul-Praslin, duc de, 158
Choiseul-Praslin affair, 158
cholera epidemic (1832), 65
Church, sentimentalism as challenge to, 26
Cicero, 74
Clausel de Coussergues, 118
clubs
18th-century, and democratic sensibility, rise of, 27
increase in, in late 19th century, 159
in July Monarchy, 54

clubs (*continued*)
of Napoleonic era, surveillance of, 36–37, 37–38
post-Revolution: and friendship, reshaping of, 29; government shutdown of, 31, 34–35
Restoration era, 53
Colbert, Jean Baptiste, 23
Coleridge, Samuel Taylor, 29
Comédie humaine (Balzac), 49
compromise, political uses of friendship and, 157
conservatives
on Hundred Days, disgust created by, 43
on individualism after Revolution, 39
Constant, Benjamin
and *Acte additionnel*, 43
and Barante, 168
and Béranger, alliance between, 125–27
friendship network, 99, *99*, *101*, 102
police surveillance of, 51
politics of, 46, *101*
and Récamier, 100, 167
Constitution of Year III, 34
cooperation among politicians, women's role in facilitation of, 133, 135, 138–41
Corbière, 139
Corps législatif, Napoleon's ban on debate in, 36
correspondence
importance to elite friendships, 93
markers of deference in, 131
salutations as indication of friendship, 93, 112, 188n6
as source, reliability of, 67, 94–95
of women, characteristic salutation in, 93
Couchery, Jean Baptiste, 38
Cousin, Victor, 90, 96
Le Cousin Pons (Balzac), 78
Couthon, Georges, 32
Custine, Astolphe de, 76
Custine, Delphine de (née Sabran), 86–87

Danton, Georges, 33, 34
Daunant, Achille de, 169
De Amicitia (Cicero), 74
Decazes, Élie, 51, 123–24, 167
Defection faction, 100, 115, 119
Degas, Edgar, 162
De la Démocratie en France (Guizot), 147
Les Délateurs (Dupaty), 49
"De l'Esprit de conquête et de l'usurpation" (Constant), 43
democracy
government by friendship networks and, 158
Tocqueville on atomism of, 39
Democracy in America (Tocqueville), 39
democratic sensibility
sentimentalism and, 26–27
socializing in clubs and cafés and, 27
denunciations
and culture of fear, 33, 34, 50
as duty, during Revolution of 1789, 33
frequency of, 49
motives of, 49
in Restoration period, 41, 48–50
and social cohesion, destruction of, 35, 41
Deputies
emotions experienced by, 28–29
and political friendships, 30
Désaugiers, Marc Antoine, 47
Desmoulins, Camille, 33
Dictionnaire de l'Académie française (1835), on "ami" and "amitié," 10
Diderot, Denis, 26
Dino, Dorothée de Courlande, duchesse de
and Barante, friendship with, 69
biography of, 168–69
friendship network, 98, *99*, *101*, 102, 105, *106*, *107*, 109; sources on, 92, 94
and Guizot, 88, 97
politics of, *101*, 102, 103, 109
as salonnière, 98
Directory period, self interest as focus of, 34
distrust among citizens. *See also* anomie, post-Revolution; social cohesion; trust
Napoleon's police surveillance and, 22, 35, 37–38
political denunciations and, 33, 34, 50
political side-switching of Hundred Days and, 43–45
political side-switching of Restoration and, 50
the Terror and, 33–34

doctrinaires, 2
  correspondence and support among, 70
  friendship network, 98, 100, *101*
  ideology, 100
  leadership of, 115
  surveillance of during Restoration, 52
Dosne, Eurydice Sophie Matheron, 116, 140–41, 149
Dreyfus, Alfred, 162
Dreyfus Affair, and late 19th century parallels with post-Revolutionary era, 159, 161–62
droit d'aubaine, abolishment of, 30
Drumont, Édouard, 162
Duchâtel, Charles Tanneguy, 74, 75
Dupaty, Emmanuel, 49
Dupin, André, 54–55
Dupleix de Mézy, M., 51
Dupont de l'Eure, Jacques Charles
  biography, 165
  friendship network, 94, *99*, *101*, 102, *106*, *107*, 118
  and Manuel, friendship with, 118–19
  politics of, *101*
Duras, Claire Louisa Rose Bonne Lechal de Kersaint, duchess de
  biography of, 166
  and Chateaubriand: affair with, 51, 87; correspondence, 85, 86, 87; friendship between, 87, 103
  friendship network, 98, *99*, *101*, 103
  political activity by, 138
  politics of, *101*

early modern France, and expressions of love as political tool, 22–23
Éméric, Louis Damien, 81–82
emotionalism, in novels of 18th century, 26
emotions
  control of, as value in Old Regime, 25, 26
  feminization of in early 19th century, 89–90
  functional (empty) expressions of: identification of, 15, 16; as marker of political loyalty, post-Revolution, 10–11, 16, 111–19, 121–22, 122–25, 130, 147–48; as political tool in Old Regime, 21, 22–25
  historical mediation of, 14
  of long-dead individuals, difficulty of investigating, 1, 9, 14–16, 75
  male: calming of, as role of women, 139–41; discussion of, in friendships with women, 13, 17, 81–87, 137, 141, 146, 148, 155
  sincerity of expressions of, as issue, 11, 15, 16, 67
Estates General, opening of, as emotional event, 28

factionalism. *See also* anomie, post-Revolution; social cohesion
  causes of, 42, 44–48, 181n20
  and denunciations, 49
  and friendship: important political function of, 3–5, 114; in July Monarchy, 55–56; shaping of, 6
  in July Monarchy, 4, 41, 53, 54, 55–56, 104, 110
  political consequences of, 157–58
  in Restoration, 3–4; Balzac on, 42, 59–61; and political alliances, difficulty of forming, 143
  return of, in second half of 19th century, 160–62
  women's bridging of, 4, 5, 91, 98–100, *101*, 102–4, 105, 109–10, 133, 149
factions, functioning of as political parties, 115–17
family
  as political force in 19th century, 3
  as source of connection and affection, 155
far left, friendship networks of, 106, *107*
favors, exchange of
  as expectation among friends, 78–80
  and self-interest, overcoming of, 79–80
fear
  denunciations and, 33, 34, 50
  in Napoleonic era, 22, 35, 37–38
  police surveillance and, 52
  politics as brutal arena and, 4, 48, 50, 53, 55–56, 58–59
  Revolution of 1789 and, 29; and failure of *fraternité*, 28, 30–31
  White Terror and, 43–44, 143
Ferry, Jules, 160
Fiévée, Joseph, 38, 75–76

financial assistance, as norm of male-to-male friendship, 17, 63, 78–79
Fischer, Claude, 176n21
Fontette, M. de, 147, 148
Fouché, Joseph, 32, 37, 38, 51
France, Anatole, 162
François I (king of France), court politics under, and personal ties as political tool, 23–24
fraternité
as duty, under *étatiste* model, 31–32
efforts to unite post-revolutionary France through, 28, 30–35, 40
vs. friendship, differences between, 30
as product of sentimentalism, 30
replacement of with *étatiste* model, 31
Freemasonry
and democratic sensibility, rise of, 27
in Napoleonic era, 36
Restoration government concerns about, 52–53
friend(s)
use of term among elites, 95–97
political, distinction between personal friends and, 96, 97
as political allies, 118
as stand-in (proxy) for friends, in political transactions, 4–5, 113, 117–22
friendship
Balzac's *Illusions perdues* on: impossibility of, in public competitive world, 61, 64; loyalty and assistance as expressions of, 62–63, 77, 78; as positive form of individualism, 60, 64; as solution to problem of atomizing self-interest, 60, 63–64; true nature of, 62–63
centralization of, under *étatiste* model, 31–32
clubs and salons and, 29
cultural importance in early 19th century, 2, 15–16
definition of, 9–10
denunciations of Restoration period and, 50
as elective tie, 155–56
and factionalism: in July Monarchy, 55–56; political functions of friendship within, 3–5; shaping influence of, 6
and fear of betrayal, 33–34 (*See also* fear)
female-to-female, expressions of affection in, 85
female-to-male, 80–88; as bridge to private inner life, 72–73, 81, 90; confidences and secrets in, 83–84; erotic overtones in, 86–88; expressions of affection in, 85–86; and friendship networks, maintenance of, 88–90, 98–100; normative expectations for, 66; normative texts on, 81–82; play of formality and intimacy in, 82–83; psychological relief as function of, 69, 81, 82, 84–85; self-exploration as function of, 84; self-revelation (*épanchement*) as expectation in, 13, 17, 81–87, 137, 141, 146, 148, 155; as understudied subject, 8; unreciprocated love in, 87–88
as focus of official concern, 32–33
vs. fraternité, 30
in friendship network analysis, 93–94, 95–98
functional (empty) expressions of (*see also* friendship, political uses of): identification of, 15, 16; as marker of political loyalty, post-Revolution, 10–11, 16, 111–19, 121–22, 122–25, 130, 147–48; as political tool in Old Regime, 21, 22–25
as highly gendered, 66, 69, 90
impossibility of in public competitive world, 61, 64, 66, 69
male-to-male, 69–80; circumscribed range of, 132; emotional expressions and, 69–72; expression of through loyalty, 66, 77–80, 121; expression of through support and patronage, 17, 62–63, 77–80, 82, 90; homoerotic overtones in, 70, 73–74, 75–77, 82; normative expectations for, 66–68, 69, 78; similarity and union as expectation of, 69, 74–75, 77, 102, 104, 108, 111, 113; as solution to anomic society, 69
and Napoleonic era, culture of fear in, 37
normative texts on, 74–75, 78; confluence with individual's expectations, 66–67; on female-male friendships, nature of, 81–82; focus on male friendships in, 81;

on male-male friendships, nature of, 81–82
in novels of 18th century, 27
political uses of: in early transition to parliamentary government, 113–14, 115, 154; friends as stand-ins (proxies), in political transactions, 4–5, 113, 117–22; limited effectiveness of, 132–33; as marker of political loyalty, 10–11, 16, 21, 22–25, 111–19, 121–22, 122–25, 130, 147–48; in reduction of political tensions, 125–31; as remedy for post-Revolution anomie, 3–5, 7, 131–32, 154–56; as repetition of Old Regime practices, 117, 122, 156; in second half of 19th century, 159–63; as subject of scholarly interest, 7–8; as substitute for political parties, 102, 113, 115–17; in Third Republic, 156; as undemocratic, 158; as unhealthy form of politics, 156–58
reality of: as issue for friends themselves, 16–17; as issue for modern researchers, 11, 15–16, 17–18, 67
reshaping of, post-Revolution, 29–30, 47–48
rise of as paradigm, sentimentalism and, 27
and romantic love, blurred boundary between, 2, 9–10, 65, 76, 86, 87–88, 94
self-exploration as function of, 65, 66, 68
self-revelation (*épanchement*) as expectation in, 17, 67–69, 77; male-to-female friendships and, 13, 17, 81–87, 137, 141, 146, 148, 155
as solution to problem of atomized self-interest, 60, 63–64, 67, 73, 77, 79–80
as statement of political affiliation, 2–3
trust as basis of, 74, 80; Balzac on, 60, 62, 64; Guizot on, 65; in male-female relationships, 81; and male loyalty, expectations for, 66; normative expectations on, 66, 67–68, 69, 80; normative texts on, 66
friendship network analysis, 8, 91–92. *See also* friendship networks
friendship networks
coalescing of political groups around, 28, 32
and differences of men's and women's ties, 91
1825–1829, *17*, 98–104, *99*, *101*, *170*, *171*
1843–1847, 104–10, *106*, *107*, *172*, *173*
and friends as stand-in (proxy) for friends, 4–5, 113, 117–22
male: constraints on, consequences of, 108–9, 157–58. 101–102; influence of politics on, 100–102, *101*, 104, 105, *107*, 108–10; as substitute for political parties, 102, 113, 115–17
social relations illuminated by, 92
sources on, 92–98; and definition of friendship, 93–94, 95–98; as incomplete record, 92–93, 94–95; reliability of, 94–95
of women, as bridge across political factions, 4, 5, 91, 98–100, *101*, 102–4, 105, 109–10, 133, 149
women's role in maintenance of, 88–90

Gambetta, Léon, 160, 161
Gasparin, Auguste de, 169
Gasparin, Gabrielle Henriette Catherine Laure de Daunant de
biography of, 169
friendship network of, *106*, *107*
and Guizot: correspondence, 83, 85–86, 88; friendship with, 83, 85–86, 109, 143, 152–53, 157–58
political activity of, 143, 149, 152
Gaultier de Biauzat, Jean François, 28
Genlis, Madame de, 38, 49
Girondins, friendship networks among, 32, 33
girouettes, 43–48
Guérin, Pierre Narcisse, 47
Guizot, Elisa (née Dillon), 84
Guizot, François
and Barante: correspondence, 70–71, 72–73; friendship with, 79–80, 118
biography of, 167–68
and Broglie, Mme de: correspondence with, 17, 83–84, 85, 135; friendship with, 97
and Broglie, Victor de: correspondence with, 72; friendship with, 65, 69, 118, 121, 140
character and personality, 13
circle of friends, correspondence of, 67

Guizot, François (*continued*)
- correspondence: characteristic salutation between friends in, 93, 112, 188n6; political, 111–12
- and corruption of July Monarchy, 158
- death of first wife, emotional correspondence occasioned by, 72–73
- and Dino, 88, 97
- and factionalism of Restoration, 48
- as faction leader, 115
- family of, 155
- female correspondents, 83–84; expressions of affection toward, 85–86
- on friendship, 2
- friendship network, 112, 118, 167–69; characteristic salutation in letters of, 93, 112, 188n6l 1825–1829, 98, *99*, 101, *101*, 102, 104, *170*, *171*; 1843–1847, 105, *106*, *107*, 108–10, *172*, *173;* maintenance of by female friends, 88; politics as influence on, 91, 101, *101*, 102, 104, 105, *107*, 108–10; sources on, 92, 94, 95, 105
- friendships of: exchange of favors and, 78–80; Guizot's pride in, 13; male, freedom from emotion, 70; with women, 81, 100
- on friendships with women, 81
- and Gasparin: correspondence, 83, 85–86, 88; friendship with, 109, 152, 153, 157–58
- and Lieven, 55, 109–10, 157
- *Mélanges biographiques et littéraires*, 96
- and Mollien, correspondence with, 83
- and Montalembert, 96, 147–48
- on Napoleonic era, 35
- personal life, documentation of, 12
- political career, 2, 11, 120, 146–47
- political education, 115
- and political instability, suffering due to, 65
- politics of, 11, 12, 101, *101*, 109
- on politics of July Monarchy, 55–56
- and public-private distinction, 7
- on Récamier, friends of, 96
- and Rémusat: correspondence, 71, 73; friendship with, 16–17, 55, 71–72, 73, 109, 120–21, 132, 169
- on Restoration, factionalism in, 181n20
- and Revolution of 1848, 157–58
- Royer-Collard and, 71
- secrets shared with friends, 17
- social class of, 12
- and Soult, political alliance with, 124–25
- sources on, 133
- and Thiers: correspondence, 111–13; political alliance with, 121–22, 143, 152, 169; rivalry with, 54, 55–56
- and Thiers' cabinet, negotiations over, 120–22, 123
- on women, role of, 7, 134, 152
- women's political activity and, 134, 139, 142–43, 146–49, 150–51, 152–53

Guizot, Guillaume, 17, 83

Guizot, Pauline (née de Meulan), 72, 73, 167–68

Halévi, Ran, 27

Hardin, Russell, 8–9

Havet, Olympe and Louis, 162

Henri II (king of France), 23

Higonnet, Patrice, 31

homoerotic overtones in male-to-male friendship, 70, 73–74, 75–77, 82

homosexual relationships
- language of friendship used to describe, 76
- of long-dead persons, difficulty of evaluating, 1, 9, 75
- perception of in 19th century, 75–76
- perception of in Old Regime, 75–76
- scholars of, on political functions of friendship, 8

honor, importance of for men of 19th century, 79–80

Hume, David, 26

Hundred Days
- appeal of Napoleon during, 43
- and ideological divisions, reigniting of, 42–46
- political side-switching in, and post-Revolution anomie, 43–45
- Restoration concerns about loyalty following, 51

Hunt, Lynn, 26, 29

Hyde de Neuville, Jean Guillaume de
- biography of, 166
- and Chateaubriand, friendship with, 13, 17, 78, 118, 166

friendship network, *99*, *101*, *106*, *107*
and La Trémoïlle, correspondence with, 88, 135–36
and Montcalm: correspondence, 87, 88; friendship with, 143–46, 151–53, 166, 167
political career, 119–20
politics of, *101*
women's political activity and, 143–46, 149, 151–52
on women's role, 152

Illusions perdues (Balzac), 59–64
on corrosive effects of factionalism and self-interest, 42, 59–61
on friendship: impossibility of in public competitive world, 61, 64; loyalty and assistance as expressions of, 62–63, 77, 78; as positive form of individualism, 60, 64; as solution to problem of atomizing self-interest, 60, 63–64; true nature of, 62–63
friendships in, as exclusively male, 81
plot of, 60
Impressionists, Dreyfus Affair and, 162
individualism. *See also* self-interest
desire for autonomy, in novels of 18th century, 26
friendship as positive form of, 155–56; in Balzac's *Illusions perdues*, 60, 64
of post-revolutionary era (*see also* anomie, post-Revolution): Directory period, 34; French concern about, 39–40, 154, 155; and friendship, role of, 3–5, 154; Napoleon's efforts to counter, 35–38; as specifically French problem, 40; the Terror and, 34–35; Thermidorian period, 34
"Institutions républicaines" (Saint-Just), 31

Jacob, Margaret, 29
Jacobins
on *fraternité* as duty, 30–32
on friendship, 32–33
James, Henry, 160
Jaubert, Hippolyte François, 120
Josephine, Empress, 37
Jouy, Étienne de, 52
Julie; ou, La Nouvelle Héloïse (Rousseau), 26, 27
July Monarchy
associational life in, 54
electorate, size of, 116
elite reconciliation in, 53, 104
and factional hostilities, decline of, 41, 53, 54, 104, 110
and men's personal ties, effect of politics on, 91
ministry-Chamber disputes in, 191n4
and police state, 37, 53, 54
political culture of, 162–63, 191n3
political instability, causes of, 156–58
politics in: alliances in, 56; as brutal arena, 4, 55–56, 58–59; and factional hostilities, 4; organization of around patronage networks, 54; problem of self-interest in, 53, 56–59; scholarly interest in, 5; uses of friendship in, 115
July Ordinances, 157
juste milieu
friendship networks of, 105, *107*
politics of, 105

Kale, Steven, 149–50, 158
king, love for, sentimentalist views on, 26–27

La Boétie, Étienne de, 75
La Bourdonnaye, François Régis de, 44–45
Lafayette, Marquis de
and Béranger, 12, 189n12
friendship network, *99*, *101*, 102
and July Monarchy, 189n12
and love affairs, effect of politics on, 48
police surveillance of, 51
politics of, *101*
La Ferronnays, comte de, 119
Laffitte, Jacques
and Béranger, 12, 164
friendship network, 102, *106*, *107*
La Fontaine, Jean de, 62
Lamartine, Alphonse de
and Béranger, friendship with, 12, 107
friendship network of, *106*, *107*
Lamennais, abbé de
and Béranger, friendship with, 12, 107
foreign relations, 106–7
friendship network, 105, *106*, *107*
politics of, 108

Lamourette, Antoine Adrien, 32
land nationalizations, and post-Revolution tensions, 42
language of friendship
 implication of political equality in, 130–31
 as marker of political loyalty, 10–11, 16, 21, 22–25, 111–19, 121–22, 122–25, 130, 147–48
La Trémoïlle, Mme de, 88, 135–36, 138, 149, 152
Law of 22 Prairial, 33
Law of Suspects, 31–32, 33
Lazare, Bernard, 162
Lebrun, Pierre, 78
Leclercq, Théodore, 75–76
leftists
 gathering places in Paris, 116
 and White Terror, distrust created by, 44–45
Légion d'honneur, 36
Legislative Assembly, and kiss of Lamourette, 32
legitimists
 friendship networks of, 105, *107*
 politics of, 105
Le Moine, Jean Baptiste, 96–97
Lenormant, Amélie (née Cyvoct)
 friendship network of, *106*, *107*
 political activity of, 146–49, 150–51
 Récamier and, 100
Leroux, Pierre, 39–40
Le Roy Ladurie, Emmanuel, 24
Le Tellier, Michel, 23
L'Honnête homme à la cour et dans le monde (1816), 68
liberal opposition in Restoration
 as product of Hundred Days, 45, 46
 fragmentation of in July Monarchy, 54
liberals
 friendship networks of, 100, *101*, 102
 gathering places for, 116
 ideology, 100
 on individualism after Revolution, 39
 in July Monarchy, 104
 police surveillance of, in Restoration, 51
Lieven, Dorothea von (née Benckendorff)
 biography of, 169
 friendship network, 105, *106*, *107*; as limited to elites, 158; sources on, 92
 and Guizot, 55, 109–10, 157
 and male friendship networks, maintenance of, 88–89
 political activity of, 143
 politics of, 109
 as salonnière, 116, 158, 189n23
Liszt, Franz, 106
Louis-Philippe (king of France), 54, 56–57, 124
Louis XIV (king of France), 24
Louis XV (king of France), 24–25, 26–27
Louis XVI (king of France), 24–25, 31
Louis XVIII (king of France), 43, 100, 167
love. *See also fraternité*; romantic love
 centralization of, under *étatiste* model, 31–32
 expressions of in Old Regime, as political tool, 21, 22–25
 vs. friendship, Balzac on, 62
 in Napoleonic era, as basis of cohesion in military, 38, 76
 sentimentalist view of: as challenge to Old Regime views, 21, 25–26, 27–28; as horizontally-operating, freely-chosen bond, 21, 25–26
loyal opposition
 French inability to imagine, 45, 127
 political uses of friendship as precursor to envisioning of, 127
loyalty
 as expectation of male-to-male friendship, 66, 77–80, 121
 political, language of friendship as marker of, 10–11, 16, 21, 22–25, 111–19, 121–22, 122–25, 130, 147–48
Loynes, Mme de, 162
Luynes, duchesse de, 96

Maistre, Joseph de, 39, 41
male affection, celebration of, 2
Manuel, Jacques Antoine
 and Béranger, friendship with, 1, 94; closeness of, 97; as political act, 1, 2, 102, 118; possible erotic component of, 1, 75
 biography of, 165
 and Dupont, friendship with, 118–19
 friendship network, *99*, *101*, 102
 police surveillance of, 51
 political career of, 118

politics of, 1, *101*
tomb of, 1
Marguerite de Navarre, 23–24
marriage
19th century conception of, 9
as political force in 19th century, 3
sentimentalist views on, 26
"La Marseillaise" (Rouget de Lisle), 78
Martel de Janville, comtesse de ("Gyp"), 161–62
Martignac, vicomte de, 119–20
Masons. *See* Freemasonry
mass politics, rise of, reshaping of political terrain by, 159–60
Mazarin, Cardinal, 23
Mélanges biographiques et littéraires (Guizot), 96
memoirs, reliability of, 94
men's clubs, as gathering places for liberals, 116
Mignet, François, 142
moderates
friendship network, 100, *101*
gathering places in Paris, 116
political platform of, 100
Molé, Mathieu, comte
and Barante, correspondence, 76–77
friendship network, *99*, *101*, 109
Guizot and, 55–56
and love affairs, effect of politics on, 48
political career, 128
politics of, *101*
and Talleyrand, political alliance with, 127–31, 132
women's political role and, 139
Mollien, Juliette Dutilleul, comtesse, 83
Le Moniteur secret (Couchery), 38
Montagnards
on *fraternité*, as duty, 31
on friendship, as suspicious activity, 33
friendship networks among, 32
Montaigne, Michel de, 74–75
Montalembert, comte de, 96, 146, 147–48
Montbel, comte de, 119–20
Montcalm-Gozon, Armande Marie Antoinette de Vignerot du Plessis de Richelieu, marquise de
biography of, 167
and Chateaubriand, friendship with, 167
and factionalism of Restoration, 48
on friendship, elusiveness of, 17, 48
friendship network, 98, *99*, *101*, 103; sources on, 92
health of, 144
and Hyde de Neuville: correspondence, 87, 88; friendship with, 143–46, 151–53, 166, 167
on ideological divisions of Restoration, 46–47
personal life, documentation of, 12
political activity of, 134, 139–40, 141, 143–46, 149, 150, 151–52
politics of, 11, *101*, 103–4, 149
on women's role, 134
Montmorency, Mathieu de, 99, 131, 138–39, 150, 167
Les Mystères de Paris (Sue), 10, 68

Napoleon. *See also* Hundred Days
on atomization of French society, 36
and homosexuality, 75–76
return to France in 1815, and political factionalism, 4
Napoleonic era
court life in, 37, 38
culture of fear in, 22, 35, 37–38
and ideological passions, cooling of, 35–36, 38, 179n62
military of, love-based cohesion in, 38, 76
new elite, creation of, 36–37, 38
police surveillance in, and distrust among elites, 22, 35, 36–37
and social cohesion, efforts to restore, 35–38, 42
social model, failure of, 40
Le National (periodical), 151
National Assembly, arrival of First and Second Estate members, as emotional event, 28
National Convention, and abolishment of clubs and societies, 31
National Guard, and *fraternité*, 30
new groups, entry into parliamentary life, political culture of friendship and, 157
Ney, Marshal, 43
Noailles, duc de
friendship network, *106*, *107*, 109

Noailles, duc de (*continued*)
Guizot and, 146
women's political activity and, 147
Nord, Philip, 159–60
notables, 12, 159–60, 195n6
Nouveau guide de la politesse (Éméric), 81–82
novels
of 18th century, 26–27
of July Monarchy, homosexual and bisexual themes in, 76
of 19th century (*see also Illusions perdues* [Balzac]): celebration of male affection in, 2; on friendship, 17, 81

"Of Friendship" (Montaigne), 74–75
Old Regime
collapse of, and social order, efforts to replace, 28
emotional self control as value in, 25, 26
personal ties as political tool in, 21, 22–25, 113, 117
political practices, reuse of in early transition to parliamentary government, 4, 6, 22, 113–14, 134, 156
sentimentalism as challenge to order of, 21, 25–26, 27–28
women's role in, 4, 113, 134
Orglandes, Mme d', 48

pacification, as term, 179n62
Pamela (Richardson), 26
"Parisian Sketches" (James), 160
parliamentary government. *See also* political parties
and alliances, importance of, 142
British model and, 115, 117
and political uses of friendship, as unhealthy, 156–58
political uses of friendship in early transition to, 113–14, 115, 154
Restoration as apprenticeship in, 6, 114–15, 154
and trust, necessity of, 115, 116, 142
women's role in functioning of, 133, 142, 153, 156
patronage
expression of friendship through, in post-Revolution period, 77–80 62–63
in Old Regime, and personal ties as political tool, 22–25
Péguy, Charles, 162
Penal Code, Article 291 of, 36–37, 52, 54
Périer, Casimir, 51, 65
Périsse (deputy), 29–30
Peyrat, Alphonse, 161
Picquart, Colonel, 162
Piscatory, Théobald, 88
Pisieux, Mme de, 138
Pissarro, Camille, 162
police
Rémusat on, 54
in Restoration: anomie generated by, 155; inheritance of from Napoleon era, 37, 42, 51; tactics of, 50–52
surveillance, and distrust among citizens, 22, 35, 37–38
Polignac, prince de, 142, 157, 166, 191n4
political campaigns, male friends as proxies in, 118–19
political parties
absence of, and alliances, necessity of, 142
creation of in Third Republic, 159, 161
factions/friendship networks as substitute for, 102, 113, 115–17
French rejection of British model for, 115
of Third Republic, political legacy of July Monarchy and, 116
politics
and friendship networks, influence on, 100–102, *101*, 104, 105, *107*, 108–10
in July Monarchy: alliances in, 56; as brutal arena, 4, 55–56, 58–59; and factional hostilities, 4; organization of around patronage networks, 54; poisoning of by self-interest in, 53, 56–59; scholarly interest in, 5; uses of friendship in, 115
perception of as brutal arena, 4, 48, 50, 53, 55–56, 58–59 (*See also* denunciations)
post-Revolution, lack of necessary institutions for, 3–5
in Restoration: as apprenticeship in parliamentary government, 6, 114–15, 154; electorate, size of, 116; ideological divide in, 3–4, 42, 44–48, 181n20; influence on latter half of 19th century,

162–63; Old Regime political practices, use of, 4, 6, 22, 113–14, 134, 156; political instability, causes of, 156–58

post-structuralism, social history and, 92

Protestantism, and self-exploration, 84

psychology, early 19th century, and feminization of emotions, 89–90

public-private separation
- breeching of in common practice, 7, 8
- emergence in 19th century, 3, 6–7
- and personal ties, political importance of, 3
- and women as bridge to private inner life, 72–73, 81, 90
- and women in friendship networks, 100
- women's political role and, 103, 109, 134, 148, 153, 154

Putnam, Robert, 9

Ramel, General, 44

Récamier, Juliette (née Bernard)
- biography of, 167
- and Broglie, Mme de, 97
- as Chateaubriand's mistress, 51, 87, 166, 167
- daughter of, 146
- friendship network, 98, 99, *99*, *101*, 102, 104, 105, 106, *106*, *107*; Guizot on, 96; sources on, 92, 95
- political activity by, 138–39, 150
- politics of, 100–101, *101*, 103
- as salonnière, 98

The Red and the Black (Stendhal), 78

Reddy, William, 14

Régis de Cambacérès, Jean Jacques, 37, 75

Régusse, Charles de Grimaldi, marquis of, 23

Reinach, Joseph, 162

Rémond, René, 46, 193n15

Rémusat, Charles de
- and Barante, homoerotic overtones of correspondence, 76–77
- biography of, 169
- and Broglie, political support of, 121, 140
- friendship network, *99*, *101*, 102, *106*, *107*, 109
- and Guizot: correspondence, 71, 73; friendship with, 16–17, 55, 71–72, 73, 109, 120–21, 132, 169
- and Guizot's wife, friendship with, 73
- memoirs of, 71–72
- on police surveillance in July Monarchy, 54
- political career, 120–21, 132
- politics of, *101*
- as source, 105
- women's political activity and, 140–41, 149

Rémusat, Claire de, 37

Renneville, Mme de, 161

Republican France, political uses of friendship in, 159–63

Restoration
- anomie during, 41 (*See also* anomie, post-Revolution)
- as apprenticeship in parliamentary government, 6, 114–15, 154
- and associational life, efforts to control, 49, 52–53
- crisis of trust in, 3–4
- electorate, size of, 116
- friendships destroyed by ideology in, 47–48
- ideological divide in, 3–4, 42, 44–48, 181n20
- influence of political culture on latter half of 19th century, 162–63
- leftist opposition to, 45
- and men's personal ties, effect of politics on, 91
- and Old Regime political practices, use of, 4, 6, 22, 113–14, 134, 156
- and police state: anomie generated by, 155; inheritance of from Napoleon era, 37, 42, 51; tactics of, 50–52
- political instability, causes of, 156–58
- scholarly interest in, 5

Revolution of 1789. *See also* anomie, post-Revolution
- August 4 events, 29
- culture of sentimentalism and, 21
- damaged social fabric due to, 3
- early years of, positive emotions in, 28–29
- fear engendered by, 29; and failure of *fraternité*, 28, 30–31
- and friendship, reshaping of, 29–30
- influence on French history, 160, 161
- and love as element of social order, destruction of, 21–22
- political polarization created by, hopes for *fraternité* and, 33–34

Revolution of 1789 (*continued*)
recovery from, as subject of scholarly interest, 5–6
and sexual attitudes, 76
Revolution of 1830, causes of, 157
Revolution of 1848, causes of, 157
Richardson, Samuel, 26
Richelieu, duc de
and Decazes, 123–24
friendship network, 103
political career, 136, 191n4
and women's political activity, 134, 138, 139–40, 141, 143–46, 150, 151
on women's role, 134
Robespierre, Maximilien, 32, 33, 34
Roger, Madame, 49–50
Roland, Jean Marie, 32
Romanticism
French, Chateaubriand and, 165
and willingness to discuss emotions, 81
romantic love, and friendship (platonic affection), blurred boundary between, 2, 9–10, 65, 76, 86, 87–88, 94
Rosanvallon, Pierre, 6, 31
Rouget de Lisle, Claude Joseph, 78
Rousseau, Jean Jacques, 26, 27
Royer-Collard, Pierre Paul, 39, 71, 88, 109

Sainte-Barbe, Edward, 76
Sainte-Beuve, Charles Augustin
and Allart, 82–83, 87, 93
friendship network of, *106*, *107*
Saint-Just, Louis Antoine de, 31, 32
salons
attendance at, as marker of political allegiance, 115–17
bridging of political factions by, 98–99
and democratic sensibility, rise of, 27
and elite social reproduction, 158
and friendship, reshaping of, 29
in Napoleonic era: surveillance of, 38; use of to create new elite, 37
in second half of 19th century, 159, 160–61
and women's impulse toward reconciliation, 149
and women's role as social facilitators, 89
Salvandy, Narcisse Achille de, 46, 50, 52
Sand, George, 76, 106
Scènes de la vie politique (Balzac), 57–59
Scheffer, Ary, *106*, 107, *107*
Scheurer-Kestner family, salon of, 161
Sébastiani, Horace, *106*, 107, *107*
Second Empire, institutions of sociability in, 159
secrets, revelation of. *See* self-revelation (*épanchement*)
self, as permeable, and conception of friendship, 65–66, 68, 73, 75, 77, 86
self-exploration
as function of friendship, 65, 66, 68
Protestantism and, 84
women's role in facilitating, 84, 90
self-interest. *See also* individualism
destructive influence of, post-Revolution, 4, 9, 18, 34
friendship as solution to destructive influence of, 60, 63–64, 67, 73, 77, 79–80
in July Monarchy, poisoning of politics by, 41, 53, 56–59
in Old Regime, 25
self-revelation (*épanchement*)
as expectation in friendship, 17, 67–69, 77
in male-female friendships, 13, 17, 81–87, 137, 141, 146–48, 155; and political role of women, 5, 7, 88–90, 137, 141, 146, 148, 152
Sennett, Richard, 27
sentimentalism
democratic current in, 26–27
efforts to unite post-revolutionary France through, 28, 30–35, 40
fraternité as product of, 30
and friendship, rise of as paradigm, 27
love in: as challenge to Old Regime views, 21, 25–26, 27–28; as horizontally-operating, freely-chosen bond, 21, 25–26
Napoleonic era and, 38
and the Terror, 34–35
Serre, Hercule de, 116
sexual attitudes, upheaval of Revolution and, 76
sisters, as confidantes, 84
Smith, Adam, 26
Smith, Jay, 23
Smith-Rosenberg, Carroll, 76

social cohesion. *See also* anomie, post-Revolution
friendship's role in restoration of, 3–5, 7
Napoleon's efforts to restore, 35–38
and the Terror, 34–35
women's role in restoration of, 3, 7, 91
social history, post-structuralism and, 92
social organization, post-Revolution, lack of credible model for, 40
social ties, importance of, in Old Regime politics, 23–25
Société des Amis de la presse, 52
Soult, Marshal, 124–25
sources, 11
correspondence as, 67, 94–95
on friendship networks, 92–98; and definition of friendship, 93–94, 95–98; as incomplete record, 92–93, 94–95; reliability of, 94–95
and sincerity of affection, as issue, 11, 15, 16, 67
Southey, Robert, 29
Souza, Mme de, 68
Spuller, Eugène, 161
Staël, Auguste de
and Broglie, Mme de, 94
friendship network, *99*, *101*
politics of, *101*
on Restoration, factionalism in, 181n20
Staël, Mme de, 99, 167, 168
Stendhal, 2, 78
Sue, Eugène, 2, 10, 68

Tackett, Timothy, 29
Talleyrand-Périgord, Charles Maurice de
death of, 109
and Dino, Mme de, 97, 168–69
friendship network, *99*, *101*, 102, 103; maintenance of by female friends, 88
and Molé, political alliance with, 127–31, 132
political career of, 128
politics of, *101*, 102
Tallien, Jean Lambert, 34
tensions, political, relief of through language of friendship, 125–27
the Terror
origins of, 31
and sentimentalism, 34
and social cohesion, destruction of, 34–35
spread of distrust during, 33–34
Teste, Jean Baptiste, 158
Teste-Cubières affair, 158
Theory of Moral Sentiments (Smith), 26
Thermidorian period, 34
Thiers, Adolphe
Béranger and, 55
biography of, 165
cabinet of, negotiations surrounding, 120–22, 123, 140
friendship network, 98, *99*, *101*, 102, *106*, 107, *107*
gathering places of followers, 116
and Guizot: correspondence, 111–13; political alliance with, 121–22, 143, 152, 169; rivalry with, 54, 55–56
and *Le National*, 151
opposition to, 143
political education of, 115
politics of, *101*, 102, 104, 107
Rémusat and, 55
supporters of, 106, 109
women's political activity and, 140–41, 142
Third Republic
institutions of sociability in, 159–60
legacy of Old Regime and, 6
political landscape in, 159–61
political parallels with post-Revolutionary era, 161–62
political uses of friendship in, 156
Thompson, Victoria, 76
Tocqueville, Alexis de, 39
Touchard, Jean, 95
trust. *See also* distrust among citizens
as basis of friendship, 74, 80; Balzac on, 60, 62, 64; Guizot on, 65; in male-female relationships, 81; and male loyalty, expectations for, 66; normative expectations on, 66, 67–68, 69, 80; normative texts on, 66
crisis of, in Bourbon Restoration, 3–4
definition of, 8–9
emotions as means of creating, 144
in parliamentary system, necessity of, 115, 116, 142
political importance of, 9

trust (*continued*)
- among politicians, women's role in creating, 133, 135, 138–41, 147, 148, 153
- in politics of July Monarchy, self-interest and, 53, 56–59
- post-Revolution anomie and, 3–4, 9, 22, 33–34, 154
- as subject of scholarly interest, 9

two Frances
- origins of, 42
- and politics in Republican France, 159, 161, 162–63

The Two Friends (La Fontaine), 62

ultras
- friendship networks of, 100, *101*
- gathering places in Paris, 116
- and Hundred Days, disgust created by, 43
- in July Monarchy, 54, 104
- platform of, 46
- police surveillance of, in Restoration, 51
- political platform of, 100
- as product of Hundred Days, 45–46
- tone of politics of, 193n15

utopian generality, 31

Vaudémont, Mme de, 128

Versailles, personal ties as political tool at, 22–25

Veuillot, Louis, 146

Villèle, Joseph de
- and cabinet negotiations, 119–20
- Chateaubriand and, 165
- and friendship in politics, 117
- political career, 139
- women's political role and, 138, 151

Virieu, comte de, 29–30

Vitet, Ludovic, 74, 75, 79

Vitrolles, baron de
- friendship network, *99*, *101*, 102, 103
- politics of, *101*, 102

Vues politiques (Salvandy), 46, 50

White Terror
- excesses of, 44
- fear created by, 43–44, 143
- and ideological divide, widening of, 44–46

Woloch, Isser, 36

women
- in Anglo-American politics, 5
- as connection between families, 24
- correspondence of, as less often preserved, 14
- friendships with men, 80–88; as bridge to private inner life, 72–73, 81, 90; confidences and secrets in, 83–84; erotic overtones in, 86–88; expressions of affection in, 85–86; and friendship networks, maintenance of, 88–90, 98–100; normative expectations for, 66; normative texts on, 81–82; play of formality and intimacy in, 82–83; psychological relief as function of, 69, 81, 82, 84–85; self-exploration as function of, 84, 90; self-revelation (*épanchement*) as expectation in, 13, 81–87, 137, 141, 146, 148, 155; unreciprocated love in, 87–88
- official exclusion from public sphere, 3, 6–7; and bridging of political factions, 103, 109, 134, 148, 153, 154
- political role: access to men's emotions and, 5, 7, 88–90, 137, 141, 146, 148, 152; alliance formation as, 142–49, 157; as behind-the-scenes political brokers, 7; calming of male emotions as, 139–41; cooperation among politicians, facilitation of, 133, 135, 138–4; and culture of political friendship, unhealthiness of, 157–58; effectiveness of, as result of apolitical stance, 134–35; for ends of others, 136, 138; for ends of their own, 137, 138; as entirely through men, 133, 135, 153; factional unity, ensuring of, 135–38; and female politics, evidence for, 149–50; and functioning of parliamentary government, 133, 142, 153, 156; inability to reach beyond elite class, 158–59; information circulation as, 135–36; limited political power of, 149, 151–53, 158; male views on, 134, 135; manipulation of by men, 141;

manipulation of men in, 144; motives for, 144, 149–52; in Napoleonic era, 37; in Old Regime, 23–24, 113; political factions, bridging of, 4, 5, 91, 98–100, *101*, 102–4, 105, 109–10, 133, 149; public-private separation and, 103, 109, 134, 148, 153, 154; roots in Old Regime role, 134, 156; scholarly interest in, 7; in second half of 19th century, 162; significance of, 153; and social cohesion, rebuilding of, 3, 7, 91; tools employed in, 137, 144

role of, early-19th century opinions on, 7, 134, 152

social role of: as bridge to private inner life, 72–73, 81, 90; as facilitator of male relationships, 88–90

"Z. Marcas" (Balzac), 57–59

CPSIA information can be obtained
at www.ICGtesting.com
Printed in the USA
FFOW02n0126080118
44323560-43975FF